WRITERS AND READERS IN
MEDIEVAL ITALY

WRITERS AND READERS
IN MEDIEVAL ITALY
Studies in the History of
Written Culture

ARMANDO PETRUCCI

EDITED AND TRANSLATED BY
Charles M. Radding

~ YALE UNIVERSITY PRESS ~ NEW HAVEN AND LONDON ~

DESIGNED BY JILL BREITBARTH AND SET IN ADOBE CASLON
TYPE BY RAINSFORD TYPE, DANBURY, CONNECTICUT.
PRINTED IN THE UNITED STATES OF AMERICA BY BOOKCRAFT-
ERS, INC., CHELSEA, MICHIGAN.

Library of Congress Cataloging-in-Publication Data

Petrucci, Armando.
    Writers and readers in medieval Italy : studies in the
history of written culture / Armando Petrucci; edited and
translated by Charles M. Radding.
        p.   cm.
    Includes bibliographical references and index.
    ISBN 0-300-06089-0
    1. Books and reading—Italy—History.   2. Written
communication—Italy—History.   3. Books—Italy—
History—400-1400.
    4. Manuscripts, Medieval—Italy—History.   I. Radding,
Charles.
    II. Title.
    Z1003.5.I8P48   1995
    302.2'244—dc20   94-41633
                                                          CIP

A CATALOGUE RECORD FOR THIS BOOK IS AVAILABLE FROM THE
BRITISH LIBRARY.

THE PAPER IN THIS BOOK MEETS THE GUIDELINES FOR PER-
MANENCE AND DURABILITY OF THE COMMITTEE ON PRODUC-
TION GUIDELINES FOR BOOK LONGEVITY OF THE COUNCIL ON
LIBRARY RESOURCES.

10   9   8   7   6   5   4   3   2   1

Contents

INTRODUCTION

THE EXTENT OF ARMANDO PETRUCCI'S European reputation is suggested by an occurrence when he gave one of his first seminars in a major European capital. Already recognized as a distinguished paleographer, he naturally drew an audience of the paleographers and diplomatists of his host country. Also attending the seminar were numerous historians, who were drawn by Petrucci's unique contributions to the study of literacy in medieval Europe. And for an interesting moment before the seminar, many members of the audience—who, despite residing in the same city and being professional medievalists, had not met before—took the opportunity to introduce themselves to each other.

It is worth considering the aspects of Petrucci's work that make it important to such a wide range of scholars. Being a paleographer means, first of all, having an exceptional visual memory; in this respect, paleography resembles no field more than art history, and it may not be a coincidence that Petrucci's father was an art historian and curator in Rome. But a visual memory must be nourished by experience, and it is therefore significant that Petrucci has, as one of his colleagues told me, "seen everything." In particular, Petrucci knows Italian sources. In articles and monographs not translated here but providing the foundation for many of his broadest conclusions, Petrucci has written on subjects ranging from the books and documents produced at Lucca or Salerno in the early Middle Ages, to Roman uncial script, to the handwriting of Petrarca and Salutati. Readers of this book will note the careful paleographical analysis in the discussion of various types of capital letters in the essay on symbolism and writing, or the analysis of signatures in the essay on literacy and schools.

INTRODUCTION

But Petrucci has also, together with many of his coworkers in Italy and elsewhere, contributed to expanding the competence of paleography from the technical analysis of handwriting to a broader focus on what he calls "written culture." As Petrucci uses the term, written culture comprises virtually all human activities where writing is used: documents and books, of course, but also seals, coins, epigraphy, wax writing tablets, texts that discuss reading or writing, artistic representations of writing and books, and even graffiti.[1] In part, this long list reflects the unique character of Italy and Italian culture. Ancient writing on stone, for example, was far more common in Italy than in the rest of Europe; moreover, Italy and especially Rome functioned as a treasure house of books for several centuries after the Germanic invasions, providing the rest of Europe not only access to specific texts but also models of what books themselves should look like. To this wealth of antique codices, which for the most part survive now only as fragments, there came to be added after the eighth century a wealth of documents—charters at first, and later also notarial registers and even private letters; as a practical matter, therefore, Italian paleographers must also have an extensive training in the diplomatic skills used in studying such evidence. Finally, it was in fourteenth- and fifteenth-century Italy that humanists began the process of reconstructing not only the definition of learning and reading but even the graphic characteristics of books themselves.

What is involved in the study of written culture, however, is not only an expansion of the base of data to be studied. In Petrucci's hands, paleographical analysis itself becomes a tool for studying people—writers and readers, the producers and consumers of writing in its various forms. Indeed, although the essays translated here were written over a span of nearly two decades, they show a remarkable consistency in the methods applied to very different kinds of evidence.

In studying writers, Petrucci looks for a variety of evidence that formerly did not attract the interest of paleographers: the quality of the parchment, for example, or the lining of the page, or whether the scribe was capable even of writing letters that followed the lining and conformed to a consistent letter size. His objective is not simply to note inferior manufacture but to identify the circumstances of book production: the loss of basic skills that occurred after the arrival of the Lombards, for example, or the existence of nonofficial or nonstandard environments in which individuals or communities produced books for their own use. In dealing with individual writers,

1. See, for example, the programmatic statement "Per una storia della cultura scritta nell'alto medioevo," in Petrucci and C. Romeo, *"Scriptores in urbibus": Alfabetismo e cultura scritta nell'Italia altomedioevale* (Bologna, 1992), pp. 237–45.

similarly, Petrucci consistently asks what kind of graphic education those writers had. Applying this criterion to copyists of books in Chapter 5, he teaches us to notice the difference between professional or trained copyists, experienced in using book hands and able to execute them correctly, and untrained or partially trained individuals who copied books. Applying it to nonprofessionals, moreover, he can provide glimpses of schools normally hidden from our view, as the schools where laymen continued to learn new cursive script into the seventh and eighth centuries (Chapter 4), or those for the artisans and merchants who copied vernacular books for their own pleasure in the fourteenth and fifteenth centuries (Chapter 9).

Petrucci also notes how books were used or meant to be used. The physical clues involved are various. Were codices square or rectangular? How large were they? Could they be carried easily, read comfortably while sitting in a chair? Did they require a desk and reading stand, or (like some of the great Bibles of the early Middle Ages) were they even so large that they could not really be read at all—books as symbols rather than instruments for reading? Was space left in the margins for notes? Were the books stored in closed chests or armoires, kept loose in a bedchamber, or chained to a shelf in a library? What repertory of books did libraries own—not just in terms of subject or titles, but of language? As Petrucci arrays his evidence, we are led to consider not only the codex or document but also readers in their cells, offices, studies, or libraries. There were, it becomes clear, multiple kinds of reading, just as there were multiple kinds of writing.

In making sense out of the evidence produced by such inquiries, Petrucci employs a number of analytical concepts. One is that of the model. At the simplest level, model can mean an actual physical prototype that was used as the basis for imitation, as Roman uncial provided a model for scribes across Europe. But Petrucci also suggests that written culture is essentially conservative. Only rarely are new forms created, with innovation more often proceeding (as in the Carolingian "graphic renaissance" and later with Petrarca and his successors) by reviving models that had fallen into disuse; even the canon of books regarded as being worthy of preservation grew only slowly, with many readers and writers of vernacular texts—most strikingly Petrarca and Boccaccio—disposing of their books in Italian separately from those in Latin, the official language of culture. Encountering such evidence of how written culture resists change, one can easily be reminded of the predictions made a decade ago for the "paperless office," in which electronic texts would make obsolete traditional forms of communication. What has happened since then, of course, is quite the reverse: not only has the spread of computers multiplied the quantity of paper consumed and the number of documents circulated by making the whole process of producing "documents" simpler; but computers themselves have sought to imitate the models provided by traditional written culture, including letter styles from the period covered by this book. Indeed, the process of imitation is often quite conscious (again as in the fifteenth century), as witnessed by the fact that one desktop printing program is named after the early Italian typographer Aldus Manutius.

A more complex concept involves the juxtaposition of and contrast between documentary and book cultures. The study of early medieval subscriptions in Chapter 4, for example, reveals a category of writers whom Petrucci describes as "semiliterate": able to write in a "rustic" language that conformed to neither written nor spoken norms, but probably with little or no experience of books. Chapter 8, similarly, is a beautifully argued juxtaposition of documentary and book-writing habits in which Petrucci is able to trace the origins of authorial practices that survive into our own time. Petrucci not only traces back to twelfth- and thirteenth-century notaries, who had to produce multiple drafts of documents, such still-familiar practices as using oblique or cross-hatched lines to cancel passages that had been changed or were no longer needed; but he can show that it was Petrarca, the son of a notary, who brought those techniques into book production, resulting in a process of writing that carried texts through multiple autograph drafts elaborated over a comparatively long period of time. Elsewhere, especially in Chapters 8 and 9, he invokes the distinction between documents and books to indicate other contrasts that operate within the world of written culture:

1. character of text preserved, in that books are "complex texts." Implicit in this distinction is a potential approach to analyzing different kinds of reading; thus, Petrucci notes that Cassiodorus recognized that simple brethren could not and did not read in the way that he did himself. One could ask, by extension, what happens when documentary texts or book texts are read using reading strategies for which the texts themselves were not originally intended.
2. graphic types, especially (but not only) the difference between cursive and book hands.
3. transmission, specifically whether a text is meant to be preserved as a unique copy or reproduced. Thus, Petrucci describes texts preserved in codices not intended for reproduction as having "documentary" transmission; examples include histories or document collection preserved only where they were written, and Italian texts copied into the empty spaces of Latin codices.

In effect, instead of looking only at the external form of the container (and indeed the codex could be adapted to documentary purposes such as registers), Petrucci suggests a conception of "book culture" that includes the complexity of the text contained, the formality of the internal graphic presentation, and the extent to which, by being copied and distributed, a specific text becomes the property of a wide reading audience.

What Armando Petrucci has done, in short, goes beyond increasing our store of knowledge about specific material examples of writing. His work, as represented in these essays and in his many other studies, also reframes many longstanding questions in medieval cultural history and permits more subtle and interesting solutions. As one example, one can observe that the evidence presented here demonstrates that the categories of "literacy" and "orality," although much discussed for the last twenty years, do not do justice to the full range of medieval written culture. There clearly also existed a class of "semiliterates": people who were able to read but were unaccustomed to books, and whose habits of reading were far different from those of people with more formal educational training.

Petrucci's distinction between document and book—or between simple and complex texts—also raises a number of other questions worthy of study. For example, the rare student notebooks that survive from the tenth and eleventh centuries reveal that beginning students in that period (although not only in that period!) seemingly read books as sources of information, such as definitions that could be copied and memorized: in effect, they were applying documentary techniques to reading their texts, rather than treating them as complex texts requiring meditation and study. Also deserving consideration is the process by which emerged the scholarly strategies of the central Middle Ages—strategies that eventually produced those essential tools of medieval universities, the glossed book and the library of consultation. Finally, and in a different sphere, the distinction between documentary and book transmission implies new questions that might illuminate the role of vernacular poetry in medieval culture, and especially the changing relationship of audience and text that resulted as romances and epics came to be read rather than heard.

These observations are offered in the spirit of suggesting how the history of books and their use has become an essential component of cultural history generally; intellectual history, traditionally conceived of as the study of texts that are known exclusively through their printed editions, must learn to consider as well the manuscripts that physically contained and embodied those texts. But such methodological questions apart, the essays in this volume have the merit of focusing our attention both on important aspects of very well known materials and on materials that previously have received little attention at all. We see early medieval charters not for their text but for their subscriptions; we encounter notaries' manuals not for information serving the purposes of social and economic history but for the techniques of the notaries themselves; we learn of texts stored in books (the early medieval miscellanies that became libraries in themselves), books stored in chests, in monastic cells, and finally in the reference libraries of the mendicant orders and state libraries of the Renaissance. In short, Petrucci guides us through the world of medieval writing as Virgil guided Dante, gracefully and always insightfully calling our attention to phenomena ranging from seventh-century semiliterates painfully learning to copy their own names to the joyous, free readers of the fourteenth and fifteenth centuries who copied enthusiastically for their own pleasure; from "inexpert" scribes painfully trying to imitate book-forms to the assuredly expert scribes who produced the books symbolizing the majesty of Charles the Bald; from the polymath Frederick II with his multilingual library to the great *volgare* poets Petrarca and Boccaccio, who excluded from their own library legacies any texts written in vernacular. The world of scholarship is very much in his debt.

CHARLES M. RADDING
Michigan State University

TRANSLATOR'S NOTE

In making this translation, I have attempted to render Petrucci's complex and elegant Italian into an English that, if not especially elegant, is at least idiomatic and clear. Any success I have had in this regard, however, owes a debt of thanks to Armando Petrucci himself, not only for clarifying his technical paleographical vocabulary for me, but for encouraging me, through his interest in and attention to the translation, to restructure certain sentences and even paragraphs where necessary in order to conform to English usage. Thanks are also due to Prof. John MacManamon, who read the entire translation and suggested many improvements. Responsibility for errors or infelicities that may remain is, of course, mine.

ACKNOWLEDGMENTS

The author and translator would like to express our appreciation to the original publishers of these articles for granting permission for them to be translated in this volume: Laterza Editore for Chapter 1; *Studi medievali* for Chapters 2 and 3; the Centro Italiano di Studi sull'Alto Medioevo for Chapters 4 and 6; Brepols Publishers for Chapter 5; the Ecole Française de Rome for Chapter 7; Editore Quattroventi for Chapter 8; Einaudi Editore for

Chapter 9; and the Società degli Storici Italiani for Chapter 10. We also wish to express our appreciation to Dean John Eadie of the College of Arts and Letters, Michigan State University, who provided funding for the illustrations for the book.

ABBREVIATIONS

API   *Archivio paleografico italiano*

BEC   *Bibliothèque de l'Ecole des Chartes*

CDL   Luigi Schiaparelli, *Codice diplomatico longobardo*

CLA   Elias Avery Lowe, *Codices latini antiquiores,* vols. I–II and
        Supplement (Oxford, 1934–71); 2² (Oxford, 1972). Addenda by B.
        Bischoff and V. Brown, *Medieval Studies* 47 (1985): 317–66,
        with 18 plates

ChLA   *Chartae latinae antiquiores,* ed. A Bruckner and R. Marichal
        (Zurich, 1954–)

MGH   *Monumenta Germaniae historica*

PL   J.-P. Migne, *Patrologia cursus completus, series latina* (Paris,
        1841–64)

1

FROM THE
UNITARY BOOK TO
THE MISCELLANY

THIS ARTICLE CONSTITUTES A preliminary and still provisional overview of research that began from the observation
that late antique written culture saw a structural modification of
great import for the nature of the book as a container of texts: the birth of
the miscellaneous book. The classical Greco-Latin world knew and used
unitary books—a book made up of only one work (or only one book) of a
single author; alternatively, especially after the codex became common, a
unitary book might contain several works of the same author gathered into
an organic "corpus." The early medieval world, in contrast, is characterized
by the widespread use of a different and opposed model of the book, the
miscellany in which several texts of different authors are more or less co-
herently juxtaposed in a single container.

The present inquiry proposes to clarify when, where, how, and why this
new model of book appeared, and its typology, functions, and extent of
diffusion (both geographical and social) in the period before it became generally popular in the early Middle Ages. Before setting out the results to
which, in this multiple perspective, this research has led, it seems to me
desirable to clarify the methodological presuppositions that have guided it,
the extent of the investigations undertaken, and the research instruments
being employed in the course of the work (which is still far from complete).

First of all, I must explain that I have excluded from research those books

Originally published as "Dal libro unitario al libro miscellaneo," in *Società romana e impero
tardoantico*, vol. 4: *Tradizioni dei classici trasformazioni della cultura*, ed. A. Giardina (Bari,
1986), pp. 173–87, 271–74 and pls. 40–48.

that do not strictly conform to the definition of miscellanies that I gave at the beginning. These include anthologies of excerpts or of citations of different authorities, liturgical books, and so-called composite books, in rolls or in codices, in which different texts share a common container because of being written separately in successive phases over time. I also decided to base my conclusions solely on material evidence, paleographical and codicological, thus excluding from my examination (except for occasional references) those examples of collections of different texts witnessed not by late antique exemplars surviving in whole or in part but only by later, especially Carolingian, copies. These last, although they form a line of inquiry that has been intensely pursued by philologists and art historians, do not provide any certainty about the actual existence or date of the presumed archetypes that from time to time have been ingeniously hypothesized, and thus they are useless or even detrimental to our ends.

As these remarks suggest, my research at the beginning was limited to book production in Latin script and was based entirely on the scrutiny of the *CLA* of Elias Avery Lowe, from which some results of notable importance were obtained for a period from the fourth to the eighth centuries. But it turned out that the least documented chronological subperiod was precisely the oldest, encompassing the third, fourth, and fifth centuries; and this was also the most interesting period, both for "uncovering the mystery" of the origins of the new model of book and because it is consonant with the overall purpose of our research sample. In numerical terms, documentation of Latin books for the period under examination is notoriously and irremediably scanty. In contrast, thanks to the sands of Egypt, Greek evidence is relatively abundant, so that it seemed to me at a certain point opportune to extend the research to the Greek book and eventually, for reasons of completeness, even to the Coptic book.

The research instruments adopted vary, therefore, not only in the linguistic and graphical materials covered but also in their own organization. After the scrutiny of the *CLA* proved insufficient, I also examined Pack's inventory in the second edition of 1967 for Greek materials,[1] Van Haelst's inventory of 1976 for Christian and Coptic materials,[2] and the edition of the Nag Hammadi Coptic codices.[3] The resulting census of late antique miscellaneous books, whose data I will briefly report here, is certainly incomplete. It is also surely defective because of some insuperable objective conditions: the absence

1. R. A. Pack, *The Greek and Latin Literary Texts from Greco-Roman Egypt*, 2d ed. (Ann Arbor, 1967).

2. J. Van Haelst, *Catalogue des papyrus littéraires juifs et chrétiens* (Paris, 1976).

3. *The Facsimile Edition of the Nag Hammadi Codices* (Leiden, 1977–79).

of an inventory of surviving manuscripts comparable to Lowe's for either the Greek or the Coptic worlds; the excessively high percentage of surviving Greek books as compared to Latin books; and the fragmentation of papyrological material, which doubtless means that a certain number of existing miscellaneous books cannot be recognized as such from the surviving pieces. On the other hand, the extension of the research to Greek and Coptic books has permitted a more appropriate chronological focus. As a result, this presentation is concerned with the rise in production and use of the miscellaneous book in the Mediterranean world from the third and fourth centuries to the sixth and seventh centuries, with the period of the early Middle Ages being deliberately neglected.

As already mentioned, the antique book was a unitary book. This is entirely natural, given that it was a book that took the form of a papyrus roll.[4] The first question to pose, therefore, is this: Do there exist miscellaneous papyrus rolls? The answer, based upon the present state of the documentation I have gathered, is surely negative. Some examples can clarify this inference.

Certainly to be excluded is Pap. Didot of the Louvre of the second century B.C. (inv. 7171 + 7172 = Pack[2] nos. 31, 401, 1319–20, 1435), where different texts of Aeschylus, Euripides, Menander, and Posidippus of Pella were written on recto and verso at different times and with such lack of skill as to make one suppose that school exercises are involved. Similarly to be excluded is the well-known papyrus Lond. 130 + 133 + 134 of the first century B.C. containing Heperides and Demosthenes (Pack[2] nos. 337 and 1234),[5] because the latter's Third Epistle was added after some time by a different hand in the space left open by the first writer. And also certainly to be excluded is the famous roll containing the *Res publica Atheniensium* of Aristotle and some other texts of a scholastic nature (P. Lond. inv. 131, 2 = Pack[2] nos. 163, 197, 307), because, as Eric G. Turner has lucidly explained, this is a reused roll in which the various literary texts were transcribed in different times, manners, and spaces by more than one hand.[6]

Of a different nature, but equally outside the typology that interests us, is the well-known *Livre d'écolier* of Cairo studied and edited by O. Guérard and P. Jouguet;[7] this is a papyrus roll attributable to the last quarter of the

---

4. As Giorgio Pasquali asserted: "There was . . . a point in the history of ancient tradition when displacements of this kind were natural: the passage from the roll, which contained a single 'book,' to the codex, to the *corpus*." *Storia della tradizione e critica del testo* (Florence, 1952), p. 377.

5. See also E. G. Turner, *The Typology of the Early Codex* (Philadelphia, 1977), p. 82.

6. Ibid., p. 82.

7. O. Guérard and P. Jouget, *Un livre d'écolier du IIIe siècle av. J.-Ch.*, 2 vols. (Cairo, 1938).

third century B.C. that contains, in addition to models for reading exercises, excerpts from different authors reproduced for didactic purposes. This was a common practice in ancient schools, as can be seen from several polyptychs of waxed tablets containing dense, numerous, and sometimes casual sequences of excerpts or brief texts of varied origin—one thinks of the seven tablets of Leiden containing Babrius and Hesiod (Pack² nos. 174 and 491) and dating to the third century A.D., or of the Paris polyptych of five tablets joining profane classical texts (for example, Menander), exercises, and a psalm that belonged to a fourth-century A.D. Egyptian scholar named Aurelios Pafnution.⁸ Other instances of the same kind include some papyrus notebooks belonging to scholars, such as that in the Rainer collection of Vienna (Van Haelst no. 136), which contains Greek and Coptic texts of the fourth to fifth century A.D., or that from the second half of the fifth century A.D. in the Chester Beatty collection of Dublin (Van Haelst no. 511; *CLA Suppl.* no. 1683), which contains Greek and Latin texts.

Between the second and fourth centuries A.D., books in codex form, often initially made from *quaterniones* of papyrus leaves, existed at first alongside books in the form of papyrus rolls, only later overtaking this form and replacing it in use; the process by which this occurred is well known, its development and causes having been investigated first by Roberts and then by Cavallo.⁹ And it is precisely among the papyrus codices of Egyptian provenance of the third/fourth and of the fourth centuries that one encounters the oldest examples of a book originally produced as a miscellany, as a container of a series of different texts by different authors. The first two examples, similar in place and time, both being from between the third and the fourth centuries, present a model of a rich, articulated, and only apparently disorganized miscellany such as will reappear frequently in the evidence of the mid-fourth century. The first of these is cod. 1 Crosby of the University of Mississippi, consisting of a single large fascicle of fifty-two folios containing five Coptic texts, all except the last on Christian subjects, laid out in double columns by a single hand.¹⁰ The other is Pap. lib. 1 of the Staats- und Universitätsbibliothek of Hamburg, containing alternate Greek

8. See B. Boyaval, "Le cahier scolaire d'Aurelios Paphnouthion," *Zeitschrift für Papyrologie und Epigrafik* 17 (1975): 225–35.

9. C. H. Roberts, "The Codex," *Proceedings of the British Academy* 40 (1954): 169–204; C. H. Roberts and T. C. Skeat, *The Birth of the Codex* (London, 1983); G. Cavallo, "Libro e pubblico alla fine del mondo antico," in Cavallo, ed., *Libri, editori e pubblico nel mondo antico. Guida storica e critica* (Rome and Bari, 1975), pp. 81–132; and Cavallo, "La nascita del codice," *SIFC* 112 (1984): 118–21.

10. See W. H. Willis, "The New Collection of Papyri at the University of Mississippi," in *Proceedings of the IX International Congress of Papyrology* (Oslo, 1961), pp. 383–89; Turner, *Typology*, pp. 79ff.

and Coptic texts written by the same two hands.[11] And if the common de-
nominator of the Crosby codex is the subject treated—Easter—that of the
Hamburg codex is scriptural texts, including the *Acta Pauli,* very popular in
Egypt, a Greek version of which opens the collection.

With these being the earliest examples, it comes as no surprise to find
that the overwhelming majority of fourth-century examples originally
stemmed from Christian environments and constitute typologically relatively
homogeneous pieces, even if they are written in different languages. Apart
from a Paris papyrus on magic (Van Haelst nos. 580 and 1074) and a small
codex containing some biblical extracts and a homily by Melito of Sardi
(Van Haelst nos. 578, 579, 677), the most important and imposing block of
miscellaneous books attributable to the fourth century is formed by the thirteen Coptic codices found in 1945 at Nag Hammadi, the village in Upper
Egypt corresponding to the ancient Khenoboskion. These are papyrus codices of small to medium format,[12] all except one consisting of a single fascicle, with writing disposed across the whole page. Nine different hands have
been distinguished, which only in one case alternate in the same codex;[13] the
sequence of texts seems at time casual, dictated more by the exigencies of
free space than by the coherence of subject matter; in any case, each codex
is host to from two to six different treatises, with divisions between them
marked by lines of simple, vaguely geometrical ornamental motives as well
as by titles. Together they formed a "library" of gnostic texts assembled over
a brief span of time (the codices seem practically all from the same period),
probably within an orthodox religious community that intended to provide
itself with documentation sufficient for polemical and apologetic purposes.
Especially interesting from this point of view are the comments of some of
the scribes, inserted at the end of one text or another, that directly address
the community of readers, here and there explaining the reasons for the
choices made. Thus, for example, the scribe/collector of codex VI justifies
his work: "I transcribed this *logos.* But many have come to hand that I have
not transcribed, thinking that they were also known to you. Indeed, I am
always unsure if I should transcribe these works, because it is possible that
they have already come to your hands and disturbed you. Many indeed are
the *logoi* that have come to my hand."

In the codices of Nag Hammadi there appears an extremely simple system

11. Turner, *Typology,* pp. 80–81; Van Haelst nos. 263, 605.

12. See J. M. Robinson, "On the Codicology of the Nag Hammadi Codices," in *Les textes
de Nag Hammadi: Colloque du Centre d'Histoire des Religions, Strasbourg, 23–25 oct. 1974* (Leiden,
1975), pp. 15–31.

13. Robinson, "On the Codicology," pp. 17ff. But a satisfactory paleographical study of the
Nag Hammadi codices is still lacking.

of distinguishing and separating texts, based on the principle of a succession of texts on the same page: the texts are divided from each other by recourse to lines of ornamental signs and identified by explicit titles in larger-sized letters. Only exceptionally is recourse also made to white spaces (codices I and III), and in only one instance does the new text begin at the top of the page (codex VI), but even then it is not done consistently.

Very different in nature but of great importance, especially for the multilingual character that sets it apart, is a witness from a little later than the Nag Hammadi codices. This is the papyrus codex P. Barc. Fond. S. Luca Evangel. 149–157 + Duke University P. Robinson inv. 201, a small-sized book of twenty-eight folios containing a notably heterogeneous miscellany of Greek and Latin texts laid out in full-page format in a thick semicursive script.[14] This miscellany contains rather extensive parts of the First and Second Catilinarians of Cicero and the so-called *Psalmus responsorius* in Latin, an anafora, a prayer for the eucharist, and other Christian texts in Greek, a brief Latin poem on Alcestis, and probably other matter as well. The two Catilinarians and the *Psalmus* are written in the same hand; the editor attributes the writing of the whole book to one writer, a young Copt knowledgeable in Greek who was doing exercises for his Latin studies.[15] This is, therefore, a miscellany for study that, however, is made unique by the bilingualism and the integrity of the texts copied. These two peculiarities make the little Barcelona book in some measure a precursor of the disorganized miscellanies born in the church schools of the Western early Middle Ages.

Lowe attributed the Barcelona codex to the turn of the fourth and fifth centuries, and this does seem to be the best dating for the Latin parts thus far reproduced, which are the only ones I have been able to evaluate.[16] Alongside it one can set the Bodmer codex "of visions," made up of a single papyrus fascicle of twenty-two folios, written in Upper Egypt by six different Greek

---

14. *CLA* 1650 and 1782; Van Haelst nos. 862, 863, 1210; R. Roca Puig, *Himne a la Vierge Maria. Psalmus responsorius. Papir llatí del segle IV* (Barcelona, 1962); W. H. Willis, "A Papyrus Fragment of Cicero," *TAPhA* 94 (1963): 321–27; R. Roca Puig, "Sui papyri di Barcellona. Anafora greca secondo la liturgia di san Marco," *Aegyptus* 46 (1966): 91ff.; idem, "New Literary Latin texts in the Papyri Barcelonenses Collection: Hexameters on Alcestis," in *Proceedings of the XIV International Congress of Papyrologists, Oxford, 24–31 July 1974* (London, 1975), pp. 111ff.; idem, *Ciceró. Catilinàries (I e II in Cat.)* (Barcelona, 1977); R. Seider, *Paläeographie der lateinischen Papyri*, vol. 2, pt. 2 (Stuttgart, 1981), no. 49, pp. 126–28, pl. XXIII; W. D. Lebek, "Das neu Alcestis-Gedicht der Papyri Barcinonenses," *ZPE* 52 (1983): 1–30; P. J. Parsons, R. G. M. Nisbet, and G. O. Hutchinson, "Alcestis in Barcelona," *ZPE* 52 (1983): 31–36.

15. Roca Puig, *Ciceró*, p. XXII.

16. Although Roca Puig proposed an attribution to the first half of the fourth century, Lowe dated *CLA* 1782 to the second half of the century and *CLA* 1650 to the turn of the two centuries; this dating, which seems correct to me, is accepted also by Seider ("um 400").

hands, probably at the beginning of the fifth century.[17] This codex contains a series of ten different poetic texts on Christian subject matter. Some of them, such as the visions of Dorothy and the three visions of Erma which open and close the collection, have common themes; others, however, such as the two poems about Cain and Abel, the poem about Abraham, and the poem on the Just, are entirely heterogeneous. The six hands, which differ among themselves in their graphic types and in the quality of execution, wrote the various texts in strict succession without any hands returning or making second appearances. Like the preceding example, therefore, this little codex gives the impression of being a prototype of the container book, filled by successive additions written by different writers.

Also attributable to the turn of the fourth and fifth centuries is a papyrus codex originally from the archive of Flavius Dioscoro, the poetaster of Aphroditus, that contains a corpus of comedies of Menander (*Eros, Epitrepontes, Perikeiromene, Samia*) and at least one comedy of another author, the *Demoi* of Eupolus.[18] This codex is a book written, apparently, by a single hand in a fluid but orderly cursive majuscule, with the text laid out at full page with fairly ample margins. It is, in short, a typical codex for private use and study rather than for school, belonging to a socially and culturally elevated environment. This conclusion is not contradicted by the organic and internally coherent nature of this miscellany, which is devoted to a well-defined literary genre.

The substance of the picture thus far sketched is to some extent confirmed even by the cases of apparent miscellanies attributable to the fourth century that had to be excluded from my census for one reason or another. Since at least some of this evidence is already quite familiar, it will be worthwhile to note briefly why these cases have been omitted. One instance is the well-known Bodmer fragment XXVII (whose intricacies are still not well understood)[19] containing a passage of Thucydides as well as scriptural passages and moral exhortations; but the texts were written by different hands, and the various texts are divided by white spaces and in all probability were executed at different times. Of the same character are: the Ulpian of Manchester (*CLA*

17. See the description in *Papyrus Bodmer XXIX. Vision de Dorothéos*, ed. A. Hurst, O. Reverdin, and J. Rudhart, with description by R. Kasser and G. Cavallo (Cologne and Geneva, 1984), pp. 99–120.

18. Pack² nos. 375 and 1301; repr.: G. Lefebvre, *Papyrus de Ménadre, Catalogue général des antiquités égyptiennes du Musée du Caire* (Cairo, 1911), no. 43227; R. Seider, *Paläographie der griechischen Papyri*, vol. 2 (Stuttgart, 1970), no. 50, pp. 153–55, pl. XXXI; *The Cairo Codex of Menander (P. Cair. J. 43227)* (London, 1978).

19. See A. Carlini, "Il papiro di Tucidide della Biblioteca Bodmeriana (P. Bodmer XXVIII)," *MH* 32 (1975): 33–40; Turner, *Typology*, p. 81.

1722) that also contains other juridical texts, probably representing what remains of an anthology of excerpts collected for study; the analogous grammar miscellany contained in a small Berlin codex recently studied by M. Maehler;[20] and, finally, the large miscellany identified by M. Testuz in some Greek Christian codices now in the Bodmer Library, although in all probability this was physically assembled only after the individual pieces that make it up had been written separately.[21]

From the typological point of view, almost all of the oldest examples of miscellaneous books belong to a rather low level of production. Medium to small in format, written at full page for the most part in hurried, informal scripts and without ornamentation, they very often were structured in a single notebook formed by leaves obtained from rolls cut for the purpose: the most "popular" codex form in Egypt at the time. One has the impression of dealing with products of a private or autarkic nature, destined not for sale but for circulation in restricted groups of users. But a thorough codicological and paleographical investigation of the whole range of evidence thus far considered is almost entirely still to be done.

In effect, this conception of the book in codex form—as a container of texts with varied authorship and subject matter laid out in a free-form sequence with simple divisions consisting of some ornamental lines and crude titles—represents a true and authentic revolution that cuts deeply into a number of historical issues: the evolution of book-forms, of modes of reading and thus of the mentality of readers, of the mechanisms of text transmission, and of the manner by which texts were preserved. The few examples examined thus far are sufficiently characteristic to reveal at least some of the motivations that must have induced those particular milieus of Mediterranean culture to elaborate the new model of the book between the end of the third and the beginning of the fourth centuries A.D. Both practical and ideological reasons are involved that, when considered together, permit us to single out the very milieu that promoted the silent revolution that is our subject.

At the practical level, the miscellaneous book of medium/small format permitted the preservation of a large number of texts in a restricted and poorly equipped space: in essence, it constituted a library without a library. Further, it rendered individual reading more comfortable and feasible despite uncomfortable circumstances and places or during more or less unforeseen

20. M. Maehler, "P. Berol. 21.163: Philologische Miszellen?" in *Miscellanea papirologica*, ed. R. Pintaudi (Florence, 1980), pp. 149–62.

21. See *Papyrus Bodmer VII–IX*, ed. M. Testuz (Cologne and Geneva, 1959), pp. 8ff.; Turner, *Typology*, pp. 79ff.; and *Papyrus Bodmer XX*, ed. V. Martin (Cologne and Geneva, 1964), pp. 8ff.

displacements. At the cultural and ideological level, the miscellaneous book repeated the scholastic model of concentrating diverse texts ordered for didactic purposes into a continuous series, except that the texts were reproduced in their entirety rather than in excerpts; with the use of one or very few containers, it permitted the eventual reader to obtain a fairly articulated culture. On the other hand, it was influenced by the liturgical model, characterized by a succession of different passages handsomely laid out in sequence for uses extraneous to their origins (homilaries, Gospels, etc.). In short, the miscellaneous book corresponded to a conception of texts that was both global and hierarchical, in whose circle the individual textual segments, rather than being considered autonomous, were seen as parts of a whole, belonging to a textual stream neither interrupted nor interruptible: a conception quite typical of Christian written culture.

All the facts, elements and characteristics thus far discussed were certainly well adapted to the Copto-Christian communities of the Egyptian church between the third and fourth centuries, and especially to the smaller ones confined to peripheral localities such as Khenoboskion. More generally, they correspond well to the level of culture and of links with books that characterizes, exactly in this period, the newly literate and newly Christian strata of Egyptian society and, by extension, of Mediterranean society. As a result, one describes the decision to create the miscellaneous book in much the same terms as Guglielmo Cavallo used in 1975 when discussing the practically contemporaneous substitution of the codex for the roll: "The technological renewal of the book was therefore determined by a push from below."[22] In our case, this push was accompanied by a profound renewal of the links between reader and text and of the very conception of reading as technology and as function.

Following the examples from the period from the fourth to the turn of the fourth and fifth centuries comes a quite complete documentary void regarding the miscellaneous book (with the single exception of the already mentioned "Bodmer Visions" codex) that includes nearly all of the fifth century. At present I cannot suggest any explanation for this gap in the evidence. With the sixth century, however, the situation changes almost completely and for numerous reasons. In the first place, documents recovered through excavation lose importance with respect to those, now predominating, from libraries; by extension, documentation in Greek or Coptic of Egyptian origin is replaced by predominately Latin documentation of Italian or Gallic origin; finally, papyrus codices of careless manufacture are replaced by parchment

22. Cavallo, "Libro e pubblico," p. 85.

codices of good-to-excellent execution. Is this diversity due only to the chances of preservation, or does it also reflect more substantial and significant differences of production, use, and public? Probably a bit of both. For if it is true that preservation through libraries tends naturally to privilege deluxe books, it is also true that with time and the definitive affirmation of Christianity, the structure of book production received the imprint of the Christian model of the book, while the great religious communities began to provide themselves with their own means of producing books.[23]

My provisional census counts a total of fourteen examples of the miscellaneous book for the sixth century, with another ten for the period at the turn of the sixth and seventh century. Twenty-two of these are Latin, with one instance each in Greek and Coptic, both belonging to the later period. Although the Coptic example (Leiden, MS D'Anastasy no. 9),[24] consisting of a small paper codex with a collection of prayer and apocryphal Christian texts, does not diverge from the typology already noted of two centuries earlier, the Greek example merits greater consideration. This is, indeed, the well-known *Codex Thebanus* of the Papyrussammlung of the Museum of Berlin:[25] a membrane codex palimpsest containing as *scriptio inferior* fragments of two Greek romances—that of Cherea and Calliroe by Carito, and an anonymous romance about Chion. Through the Berlin fragment, therefore, we meet a special typology of miscellaneous book, tied no longer to a religious environment but to a lay one; no longer a community production but rather "popular"; no longer on papyrus but on parchment. In short, it is an indication that the model of miscellaneous book had now reached beyond its original environment and had conquered new strata of the public.

In fact, this conclusion seems to be confirmed by the examination of Latin evidence attributable to the sixth century, and in particular by a group defined by its obviously lay characteristics. These are four Latin codices, differing in their external typology and textual program, but substantially homogenous in their area of diffusion and potential public: all are attributable to the turn of the fifth and sixth centuries or the first decades of the sixth century, and all, it seems certain, originated in Gothic Italy—the Italy of Theodoric, Symmachus, Boethius, and Cassiodorus. One of these codices, today reduced to only two leaves (*CLA* 30), contained an organic "corpus" of satirical poets, Juvenal and then Persius, and was written in artful rustic capitals. It is an

23. For the circumstances of book production in the Latin world during the sixth century, see my comments in "Scrittura e libro nell'Italia altomedievale. Il sesto secolo," *Studi medievali* 3d ser. 10 (1969): 157–212.

24. Turner, *Typology*, pp. 82, 139.

25. Pack² no. 244; U. Wilcken, "Eine neue Roman-Handschrift," *Archiv für Papyrusforschung* 1 (1901): 227–72.

organic miscellany, literary in nature, transmitted in an ancient graphic formula made to live again by imitation. Also literary, at least in appearance, is the miscellany preserved in fragments in two codices, at the Vatican and the Ambrosian libraries (*CLA* 29). But the texts contained in it, the *Orationes* of Quintus Aurelius Symmachus and the *Panegyricus* of Pliny the Younger, retained a rather marked ideological value in the circles of the traditionalist Italian senatorial nobility. Contrary to what we might have expected, however, the writing is a rigid, heavy, semiuncial, not at all elegant, attributable in my opinion to the first three decades of the sixth century.

Extremely elegant, in contrast, are the two codices containing the "corpus" of the Roman Agrimensores, both preserved at Wolfenbüttel (*CLA* 1374). One of them, the older, is attributable to the period at the turn of the two centuries, and the other, richly illustrated, is from the heart of the sixth century. In this case we are dealing with two deluxe productions, written in a monumental uncial that in all probability is roman,[26] and an organic collection of technical texts, in places only partially transcribed. It is the residue, admired by Cassiodorus himself,[27] of an ancient science now become the object of the cult of the antique. These two codices document unmistakably a system of marking the boundaries between texts that seems to derive directly from a classical antique tradition; thus, it also appears in late antique Latin codices containing multiple works or multiple books of the same author, such as the Bembino Terence, the Vatican Virgil (fig. 1), and especially the Medicean Virgil (fig. 2).[28] So far as I can determine from a summary investigation of the published facsimiles, this system has a number of features: the use of a double and complex formula of explicit-incipit; the functional presence of lines of ornamental signs; the recourse to inks of different colors (alternately red and black) and (from the sixth century) to differing scripts for titles and text; and—above all—the presence of spaces left empty of writing for the purpose of marking boundaries, from time to time post-

26. See *Corpus Agrimensorum Romanorum. Codex Arcerianus A der Herzog-August-Bibliothek zu Wolfenbüttel*, ed. H. Butzmann, Lugduni Batavorum 1970 (and also the review of G. Cavallo, *Rivista di Filologia e di Istruzione Classica* 100 [1972]: 511–18). For the attribution to Rome, A. Petrucci, "L'onciale romana. Origini, sviluppo e diffusione di una stilizzazione grafica altomedievale (sec. VI–IX)," *Studi medievali*, 3d ser. 12 (1971): 107–09.

27. See *Cassiodori Senatoris Variae*, ed. Th. Mommsen (Berlin, 1894), *MGH, AA*, 12, pp. 107ff.

28. Examine the available complete facsimiles of these famous codices: for the Bembino Terence, S. Prete, *Il codice di Terenzio Vaticano Latino 3226*, Studi e Testi, 262 (Città del Vaticano, 1970); for the Vatican Virgil, the recent important complete facsimile *Vergilius Vaticanus. Vollständige Faksimile-Ausgabe im Originalformat des Codex Vaticanus Latinus 3225 der Biblioteca Apostolica Vaticana*, ed. D. H. Wright (Graz, 1984); for the Medicean Virgil (Florence, Biblioteca Medicea Laurenziana, MS 39, 1), *Il Codice Mediceo di Virgilio*, ed. E. Rostagno (Rome, 1931).

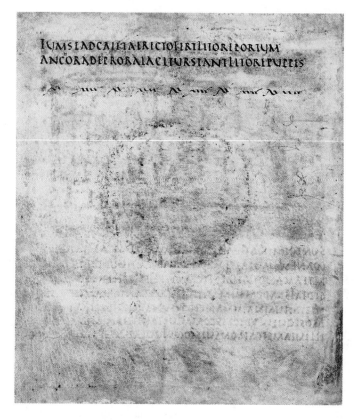

1. Biblioteca Apostolica Vaticana, Vat. lat. 3225, fol. 57v

poning new text to the top of the following page. It is, therefore, a system
that is not only complex and articulated but also based on a vision of the
space on the page rather different from that generally occurring in the codices
of Nag Hammadi; instead, it seems to be appropriate only to organic *corpora*.
We cannot here deepen the analysis just now sketched, which asserts a precise and complex relationship between the text or texts on one hand and the
book as container and product on the other. Indeed, this would deserve a
study of its own devoted either to the origins of the system whose essential
features were just defined, or to its developments and then its gradual disappearance from use.

To these four products written in Gothic Italy can be added a medical
miscellany that is also Italian, attributable to the second half of the century
(*CLA* 1582), written in a rather irregular uncial and containing various texts

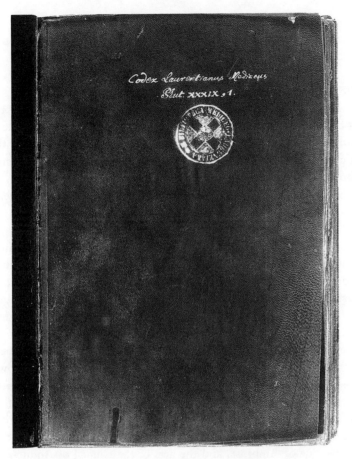

2. Florence, Bib. Medicea Laurenziana, Plut. 39.1, fol. 1

(an Antidotarium, an Antonius Musa, a pseudo-Apuleius) of herbalist subject matter. It should also be remembered (in partial correction of the principle stated at the beginning) that two other lay *corpora*, transmitted not directly but in early medieval copies, have been attributed to Gothic Ravenna. A well-known instance consists of historical and geographical texts put together by Flavius Rusticus Elpidius Domnulus, *vir spectabilis* and *comes consistorialis*, the other, of medical nature, contains works of Oribasius, Alexander of Tralle, and Dioscurides.[29] According to the well-founded argu-

29. On these two miscellanies, see G. Cavallo, "La cultura a Ravenna tra Corte e Chiesa," in *Le sedi della cultura nell'Emilia Romagna. L'alto medioevo* (Milan, 1983), pp. 30ff.

ments of Maddalena Spallone,[30] the collection of poetic texts and various prose, including the *Anthologia Latina,* witnessed by the well-known Paris, B.N. lat. 10318 of the eighth to ninth centuries (Salmasiano = *CLA* 593), comes instead from south-central Italy of the same period; this collection is characterized by a certain encyclopedic-didactic internal coherence. All in all, the Latin miscellaneous books of nonreligious content and directed toward a lay readership share two characteristics: a very high or even decorous standard of production that at least in some cases—as where we see the use of rustic capitals and monumental uncial—suggests origins in still active lay workshops; and the absolutely organic quality of the texts contained, always tightly connected to each other by subject matter, so that they formed genuinely coherent *corpora.*

The miscellaneous Latin books of religious nature from the sixth century are significantly more numerous. There are seventeen examples in all, which can be divided into three groups based on the epoch when they were produced. The first, rather meager group belongs to the beginning of the century; the second to the middle or to the second half; and the third to the Gregorian age at the turn of the sixth and seventh century.

Three rather diverse witnesses belong to the first decades of the sixth century. The palimpsest fragments of the collection of sermons followed by a fragment of Psalm 14 written in a handsome "new style" Italian uncial (*CLA* 31) should be assigned to an Arian environment. In contrast, the very beautiful and well-known codex Paris, B.N. lat. 8907 (*CLA* 572), written in a splendid Italian "new style" uncial and containing three apologetic works of Hilarius, one of Ambrose, and the acts of the council of Aquileia of 381, should be assigned to an anti-Arian environment.[31] To the cathedral of Verona should be assigned the famous Veronese XXXVIII (36) (*CLA* 494), dated to 517 by the highly erroneous subscription of the scribe and lector Ursicino; written in a rather rough semiuncial, it contains hagiographical works of Sulpicius Severus and Jerome's Life of Saint Paul of Jerusalem.

The religious miscellanies of the mid- to late sixth century are predominately patristic, with a strong preference for the three great names—especially Augustine and Jerome, and then Ambrose. There is nothing surprising about this. I will mention here the best-known codices of the group (of which there are seven in all).[32] Paris, B.N. lat. 12205 (*CLA* 633) contains, in

---

30. M. Spallone, "Il Par. lat. 10318 (Salmasiano): Dal manoscritto altomedievale ad una raccolta enciclopedica tardo-antica," *Italia medioevale e umanistica* 25 (1982): 1–71, esp. 59–71.

31. Erroneously dated to the first half of the fifth century in the recently published facsimile edition: R. Gryson and L. Gilissen, *Les scolies ariennes du Parisinus latinus 8907. Un echantillonage d'écritures latines du Ve siècle* (Turnhout, 1980).

32. In addition to the codices cited in the text, there are also *CLA* 463, 550 (a production

addition to Augustine, the famous *Regula magistri*; it is to be attributed for paleographical reasons to the middle of the century and very probably to the zone around Rome.[33] There are two codices in elegant, formal semiuncial, one (*CLA* 1614) containing Jerome and Augustine,[34] and the other, probably originally from southern Italy, containing the *Confessiones* of Augustine, Cassian, and Ambrose, among others (*CLA* 420a). Finally, Leningrad codex Q v I 6–10 (*CLA* 1614) contains Pelagius, Fulgentius of Ruspe, Origen, and Jerome; at the beginning of this manuscript a hand contemporary with the manuscript has inserted an annotation, orthodox in tone, in which the pelagian character of the first text is denounced and the "pius lector" is invited to eliminate it ("unde hortor caritatem tuam ut hanc blasphemiam de vestro codice abscidatis [whence I urge your charity to excise this blasphemy from your codex]") and to insert in its place an Augustinian text ("ut quantitatem codicis reparetis [so that you repair the size of the codex]"). In my opinion, this invitation goes beyond the purely material preoccupation about the integrity of the desecrated book and was dictated rather by a conception of the miscellaneous codex as a container of texts. Because the codex's value and function result from its completeness and reciprocity, these must be "repaired" every time an accident or intentional intervention occurs to diminish or wound them.

The situation in Italy during the second half of the sixth century, when it was upset by the Gothic wars, was quite different from that of the first half of the century, and the change is decisively reflected even in the quality and models of book production.[35] Certainly it was not by chance that it was precisely then that Cassiodorus, taking refuge in his Calabrian monastery of the Vivarium, elaborated an authentic theory of the miscellaneous book, equipping the monastic library with a great number of collections of texts of different authors. He himself described the plan and program of these collections in his *Institutiones*. These were to be substantially coherent miscellanies, predominantly made up of patristic and scriptural texts but also including medical, historical, rhetorical, and philosophical materials.[36] Cassiodorus in all probability should also be credited (as Ludwig Traube sug-

from the Ravennate for G. Cavallo, "Cultura," p. 42, but attributed by me to the Roman region at the same period; "Onciale romana," p. 127), and 358.

33. In 1971, I suspended judgment on the origin of this codex ("Onciale romana," p. 127, no. 160 *bis*); now, however, I think I can abandon any reservation about its attribution to the Roman region, but I hope in the near future to be able to return to the question after a final autopsy of the codex.

34. For this MS, see M. Palma, "Nonantola e il Sud. Contributo alla storia della scrittura libraria nell'Italia dell'ottavo secolo," *Scrittura e civiltà* 3 (1979): 78 and n. 6.

35. A. Petrucci, *Scrittura e libro*, pp. 203–07.

36. P. Courcelle, *Les lettres grecques en Occident de Macrobe à Cassiodore* (Paris, 1943), pp. 352–63.

gested)[37] with the expression "in uno corpore continentur" (contained in one corpus) that introduces the description of the miscellanies of the Vivarium and that returns in many (too many for Courcelle)[38] early medieval codices. In truth, it is very likely that the example offered by the Vivarium library and canonized by Cassiodorus's *Institutiones* constituted for several centuries a quite important model in the area of early medieval book production, at least until the Carolingian period. But it is also true that when Cassiodorus arranged and publicized his "corpora," the reality of the miscellaneous book already had a long history behind it and was widely diffused in Western Christian culture following models which came from far away.

To the last chronological period that I examine, which I term "Gregorian" for Gregory the Great, belong seven Latin examples of the miscellaneous book.[39] Some of these collections are coherent and organized, such as Jerome and Augustine in *CLA* 405. Others, in contrast, are miscellanies for which it seems to me difficult to find a common denominator at the level of subject matter or interests: thus, for example, in Veronese MS LIX (57) (*CLA* 509), the sequence of texts includes Virgil of Tapse, Athanasius, the acts of the synod of Calcedonia, and others. In reality, however, only a more thorough examination of the textual contents of such codices than I have so far been able to make could measure and document the degree of coherence of every miscellany belonging to this crucial period.

One has the impression, indeed, that it was only toward the end of the Gregorian age or immediately afterwards that the model of miscellaneous book as incoherent, unorganic, and reduced purely and simply to being a container of heterogeneous texts—a model already in use in Egypt's Christian community—was introduced into European written culture. This phenomenon seems of great importance because the unorganic miscellaneous book ends up being one of the greatest and most significant novelties of book production in the eighth century. The most exasperating forms, which incorporated liturgical texts and patristic excerpts together with medical works and historical or grammatical compilations, covered almost the whole spectrum of contemporary monastic (more than ecclesiastical) culture.

Because the greater part of the unorganic miscellanies of the eighth century were produced in continental centers of insular foundation or under insular influence, it is possible to hypothesize that, after a certain point, one

37. L. Traube, "Einleitung in die lateinische Philologie des Mittelalters," in *Vorlesungen und Abhandlungen*, vol. 2 (Munich, 1965), p. 130.

38. Courcelle, *Lettres,* p. 352.

39. In addition to the two cited in the text, these are *CLA* 438, 1612, 789, 589, and 324 (a disorganized private miscellany).

channel of diffusion of the model itself in Western Europe, and possibly the most important, had been exactly that established by the arrival and activities of the *peregrini Scotti*. That would agree to some extent with the conclusions revealed in recent work by Julian Brown,[40] a perceptive student of early medieval insular book production, who found that the Irish seem to have perpetuated and transmitted to early medieval Europe a poor and technically backward model of book—the model we have found to be typical of the minor and peripheral religious communities of Egypt (and the East). In all probability, this model was not particular to the Egyptian Christian church, even if it is only the sands of Egypt that have miraculously preserved it. Rather, it is likely that in late antiquity this model was diffused outside the East, in other regions and in Western Europe itself, wherever the environmental and cultural factors that had generated it were repeated. In this manner one could explain some of the more important and apparently contradictory or obscure phenomena that characterize the long history of the miscellaneous book between hellenism and late antiquity: its distant, apparently entirely Egyptian origin; the birth and later destruction of the great, organic miscellanies of Gothic Italy; and the reappearance of the model of incoherent miscellanies in the insular colonies on the continent in the course of the early Middle Ages.

At the end of this brief presentation of research that could be deepened and extended at several points, it seems to me opportune to indicate some points that can constitute both the provisional conclusions of the current state of this research and the working hypotheses for its eventual further development.

1. It is reasonable to suppose, as a point of departure, that the gradual but irreversible introduction of the miscellaneous book into the written culture of the late antique Mediterranean, wherever it occurred, would have produced very important modifications in both the production and use of books. These would be worth investigating thoroughly.

2. In the process of constituting miscellanies of different texts, several problems, many of them entirely new, had to be resolved, ranging from selecting the texts to deciding the sequence they would follow, and from applying a sufficiently clear system of separating texts to

40. J. Brown, "The Oldest Irish Manuscripts and Their Late Antique Background," in *Irland und Europa. Die Kirche in Frühmittelalter [Ireland and Europe: The Early Church]*, ed. P. Ní Chatláin and M. Richter (Stuttgart, 1984), pp. 311–27.

making indices. These problems were solved in different ways according to the different cultural environments involved.

3. At the level of reproduction and transmission of texts gathered into collections, it may have happened that copyists lost sight of their specific and singular individuality and that the collections to a certain extent came to constitute unitary and solid traditions, with important consequences for the quality of transmission of the texts contained in them.

4. The new type of book must also have exercised a strong influence on the practice of reading and study. This is true above all to the extent that late antique and early medieval readers, in the slow and repetitive reading that was typical of them,[41] must inevitably have ended up considering the individual texts contained in the book that they had in their hands as a single whole; they then used them and memorized them as a whole, that is, in their unitary sequence.

When concluding a work, historians often cannot refrain from casting a glance beyond the original limits of an investigation, so that they can divine (or intuit) the ultimate implications of the phenomenon investigated. Insofar as one can divine of the basis of additional examples examined, the miscellaneous book, whether in its organic or unorganic version, constituted a crucial cultural instrument in the early medieval world. It became less important only with the appearance of the university-scholastic written culture which was rigidly tied to the use, both didactic and scholarly, of individual texts within an articulated division of written culture into different disciplines. But even then it survived in the private practice of individual scholars and especially, in the fourteenth and fifteenth centuries, in the vernacular *zibaldoni* of the urban bourgeoisie. This fact virtually confirms, in sociocultural conditions entirely different from those which saw the origins and first phases of development, the vitality and instrumental functionality of the miscellaneous books, above all for those who find themselves separated from and marginalized in respect to the mainstream of written culture.

41. See below, Chap. 7.

2

THE CHRISTIAN CONCEPTION
OF THE BOOK IN THE
SIXTH AND SEVENTH
CENTURIES

THE DIFFERENCES BETWEEN THE book of late Roman antiquity and the early medieval book—in short, between the Medicean Virgil and the Book of Kells[1]—are so numerous and profound as to leap off the page, even to the eyes of an unskilled reader. This is not a matter only of handwriting, or ornamentation, or the preparation of the parchment, or the way the page is lined, but extends to the very appearance of the book: its format, one might almost say its deepest nature. This radical transformation goes well beyond those changes in specific aspects of script or books that we have seen occurred in the course of the sixth century.[2] Where and how did it occur?

Writing is a tool that people in different periods, environments, and circumstances have employed for widely varying intentions and purposes. Today writing is preeminently an instrument of communication and of the diffusion of ideas. Indeed, for those who write and read, writing essentially carries the meaning of the sounds which it represents visually: it has the merely verbal meaning of a graphical rendering of language. But writing also always contains a figural or visual aspect, produced by the graphic sign and the series of graphic signs, that can and has assumed a meaning that is sometimes

Originally published as "La concezione cristiana del libro," in *Studi medievali* 3d ser. 14, no. 2 (1973): 961–84.

1. Such a juxtaposition has already been made by Hans Jantzen, "Das Wort als Bild in der frühmittelalterlichen Buchmalerei," *Historisches Jahrbuch* 60 (1940): 507.

2. A. Petrucci, "Scrittura e libro nell'Italia altomedievale. Il sesto secolo," *Studi medievali* 3rd ser. 10 (1969): 157–212.

magically evocative, sometimes aesthetic, and sometimes both, depending on the period and cultural environment.

Discovering the different meanings that alternate or coexist in the sphere of the same writing, and studying the processes by which such meanings are formed, displayed, and received, should constitute the main theme (although certainly not the only one) of a "historical semantics of the graphic sign" that is still in its beginning stages.[3] It is not our present purpose either to define or to develop this historical semantics in any detail. But because we are convinced that the profound transformation that European Latin writing and books underwent between antiquity and the Middle Ages (and in Italy especially during the sixth and seventh centuries) resulted from a radical displacement of function and meaning of which educated society was the agent, it seems necessary to examine the educated class's conceptions of the book and of writing, and how and to what extent those conceptions differed from those of Ennodius and Cassiodorus that have already been studied. In this way, we can reconstruct the *intentio* that, underlying the use to which writing and books were put in the early Middle Ages, consequently shaped their characteristics. Making explicit the process by which meaning was transposed in the sphere of a specific script, moreover, will provide an exemplar of that historical semantics of the graphic sign mentioned above.

3. The premises of such a semantics of the graphic sign are laid out quite lucidly in the fine article of Rosario Assunto, invaluable for the history of writing, "Scrittura come figura, figura come segno," in *Rassegna della istruzione artistica* 2 (1967), 2:5–18; 4:5–15. I am also indebted to Professor Assunto for many references and suggestions used in the preparation of this article. Naturally, a prospective semantic analysis applied to graphic expression can and should embrace all types of writing and graphic production; and possibly the very nature of some writing outside of the limits of Western Greco-Latin paleography, such as Egyptian hieroglyphics or Chinese and Arabic writing, have induced the scholars specializing in those scripts to engage their aesthetic and symbolic aspects more than has so far been done for Latin and Greek writing. With regard to the history of Latin writing, a lively interest in aesthetic and symbolic meaning can be found above all in some German scholarship published between the wars, of which perhaps the best is Hermann Delitsch's *Geschichte der abendländischen Schreibschriftformen* (Leipzig, 1928). In addition, it would be opportune to mention volume II (1928) of *Buch und Schrift. Jahrbuch des deutschen Vereins für Buchwesen und Schriftum*, whose numerous articles are all dedicated to the theme "Schrift als Ornament"; of these, the essay by O. Hurm, "Die Schrift als Ausdrucksform," pp. 9–15, contains some general formulations. Also published in 1928 was the *Ursprung des deutschen Trauerspiels* of Walter Benjamin, a work in which an entirely new problematic of graphic symbols was posed for the first time, including far-reaching historical-critical prospectives; see Assunto, "Scrittura," 2:5–6, and W. Benjamin, *Schriften*, vol. I (Frankfurt am Main, 1965), pp. 141–365 (esp. pp. 283–314). In Italy, Augusto Campana underlined the connections "of method because of object" between art history and paleography, placing in evidence the aesthetic meaning present in every graphic manifestation; he affirmed that "the history of writing is primarily the history of visual forms." See A. Campana, "Paleografia oggi. Rapporti, problemi e prospettive di una 'coraggiosa disciplina,'" in *Studi Urbinati di storia, filosofia e letteratura* 41, n.s. B, nos. 1–2 (1967), II, pp. 1027–1028.

CHRISTIAN CONCEPTION OF THE BOOK

Writing has often assumed in the course of its long history—and always can assume in specific circumstances—a finality and magical-evocative meaning beyond any aesthetic significance. In the simplest and most instinctive cases, such meanings are expressed more or less directly, by graphic forms—ideograms—that reproduce aspects of the external world. But alphabetic writing, although not in itself evocative of other visible meanings, can be burdened with magical or, more generically, ideological-religious meanings that come to be attributed to the graphic signs considered purely as visual forms, independent of their verbal meaning. Such a phenomenon can occur fortuitously (not intended by the first users of the writing), as, for example, when illiterate individuals belonging to a "primitive" cultural area attribute magical value to the alphabetic writing which they happen to see but which had originally been elaborated and used for other purposes and without any intention that it should be transposed into a magical sense.[4] It can also occur consciously, as when certain categories of writers assign particular ideological values to writing, considered from a purely figural point of view, and deliberately invoke complex formal techniques to express them. This latter process, which usually means emphasizing the decorative or monumental aspects of the writing itself, often with the result of modifying its iconography or structure, can be either immediate or mediated. It is immediate when the magico-religious meanings are attributed directly to individual alphabetic elements, each of which in itself expresses a determined "value"; for example, the case of the Jewish Kabbala, whose system of graphic allegories is one of the most perfect and complex known.[5] Alternatively, the process can be, and often is, mediated. In such cases, the magico-religious "value" is not attributed to individual graphic signs in the framework of a rigorous system of symbols but rather to the writing as a whole: to the written page, to the ornamental elements, to the book itself. When this happens, the writing receives, in addition to the magico-religious meaning, an aesthetic meaning

---

4. Lucien Lévy-Bruhl, *Primitive Mentality*, trans. Lilian A. Clare (1923; repr. Boston, 1966), pp. 368–69, has an interesting series of observations about the significance writing assumes to the eyes of the illiterate "primitive." To his eyes, Lévy-Bruhl observes, "reading is a magical process designed to secure for the white man all that negroes ask of their dreams, their visions, and their astragali. . . . How can these printed characters reveal so much to the one who deciphers them? The primitive no more tries to explain this than he does to find out why the rifle and cannon carry death so great a distance. Books are mirrors" (p. 369). And further: "Since reading is a purely magical process which consists in seeing or hearing, it ought not to have to be learnt, but should be acquired, and that not in a series of laborious efforts, but all at once" (370). Also very important are the observations on the limited utility of writing as a means of communication in a society accustomed to oral communication (373) and on the sacred character attributed to written messages (373–75).

5. See Assunto, "Scrittura," 2:18, and G. G. Scholem, *On the Kabbala and its Symbolism* (London, 1965), esp. pp. 166–73.

expressed through the elements already listed; it can work autonomously from the magico-religious meaning and can even supplant it when the ideological reasons that had used writing/figures to give visual expression to specific magico-religious values themselves weaken or disappear.

Phenomena of this type have characterized the transmission of the "sacred books" of the most important historical religions.[6] In cases of this sort, the intensity of signification inherent in the sacred text for which the script is used results in a total transfer of ideological "value" from the text itself to the script, which now expresses meaning in a manner that is synthetic-figural rather than verbal.[7] And because writing together with other elements, such as ornament and the book itself as an object, can express such meaning even apart from the text transmitted, they end up expressing certain ideological values whenever they retain the particularly solemn and elaborated formal structure that the public is used to associating with those values.

To sum up what has thus far been said: entrusting the tradition of a sacred text to writing/book instruments capable of expressing the ideological value of the text in a "synthetic-figural" as well as an "analytical-discursive" (that is, verbal) manner[8] often results in the elaboration of particular types of scripts and books in which monumental and ornamental elements acquire special importance and marked aesthetic prominence. This assumption of meaning, moreover, produces a sacralization of the script and the book that can develop and endure beyond and outside the diffusion of the specific sacred text in which those features first appeared.

The conception of the "sacred book"—that is, of the book as bearer of a specific religious message and thus worthy of devotion in and for itself— was broadly diffused in the ancient world. It was a feature not only of Egyptian and Oriental religions but of pagan Roman religion and, especially, Judaism.[9] Christianity, therefore, found the ground prepared for the elaboration of its own conception of the "sacred book" and for setting in motion an autonomous process of progressive sacralization of writing/book instruments adopted for the diffusion of its own religious message. Two distinct phases can be identified in this process. The first, ideological in character,

6. For the Koran and the Kufic script, it is enough here to refer to the discussion in the *Encyclopédie de l'Islam* 1 (Leiden and Paris, 1913), pp. 391–95; to the observations of Julius Rodenberg, "Die arabische Schrift als Ornament," in *Buch und Schrift* 2 (1928): 63–66; and of Janine Sourdel-Thomine, "L'écriture arabe et son évolution ornamentale," in *L'écriture et la psychologie des peuples* (Paris, 1963), pp. 256–59.

7. As the term *synthetic-figural* is used by Assunto, "Scrittura," 2:13.

8. Ibid.

9. See the ample treatment of Leo Koep, *Das himmlische Buch in Antike und Christentum* (Bonn, 1960), pp. 3–39.

prepared and evolved a complex allegory of the sacred book—or, better, of the "heavenly book" and of its diverse meanings—based especially on Jewish precedents. The second phase, beginning in the sixth century, introduced such conceptions and symbolism into the practice of book production in increasingly accentuated and obvious styles.

The conception of writing as bearer of sacred values was already rather complex in the Christianity and Christian authors of the first centuries.[10] It was not limited to the sacrality of the Bible but also comprised other symbols, including the "book of destiny" written directly in heaven in *divina volumina*, according to Origen,[11] the *cheirographon* of original sins, which appears already in Paul with a long future ahead of it,[12] and that of the *liber viventium*, that is, of the predestined.[13] The symbolism of the *libri caelesti* also provided the basis for a process of sacralization of the function of writing in and for itself, because the angels[14] or even God were considered the authors of many of these books ("Unde constat nostras esse litteras peccati, litteras autem iustitiae Deus scribit" [Thus, it is agreed that ours are the writings of sin, for it is God who writes the letters of justice]," as Origen claimed).[15] Underlying such ideas was the widely diffused conception expressed by Orientius with concise grandiosity: "Est digitus stylus iste: Dei est lex scripta per ipsum" (This finger is the stylus by which the law of God is written).[16]

The sacralization of writing and books is eloquently attested by some singular early Christian liturgical customs and by the iconography of the sacred book that appears in the first centuries of Christian art. The liturgical customs to which I refer concern an authentic cult of the sacred book, the Gospel, that came to be celebrated especially in Eastern, Italian, and Gallic

---

10. See E. R. Curtius, "Schrift- und Buchmetaphorik in der Weltliteratur" in *Deutsche Vierteljahrschrift für Literaturwissenschaft und Geistesgeschichte* 20 (1942): 373–77; and *La littérature européene et la moyen âge latin* (Paris, 1956), pp. 378–82. Other references can be found in J. Leclerq, "Aspects spirituels de la symbolique du livre au XIIe siècle," in *L'homme devant Dieu. Mélanges offerts au père Henri de Lubac*, vol. 2 (Paris, 1964), pp. 63–64; O. Seel, "Antike und frühchristliche Allegorik," in *Festschrift für Peter Metz* (Berlin, 1965), pp. 34–40; and A. Roncaglia, in *Storia della letteratura italiana*, vol. 1: *Le origini e il Duecento* (Milan, 1965), pp. 54–57. On graphic symbolism consciously present in Clement of Alexandria, which bears on the example of Egyptian hieroglyphics, see C. Mondésert, *Clement d'Alexandrie* (Paris, 1944), p. 133.

11. Koep, *Das himmlische Buch*, p. 49, n. 4.

12. Ibid., pp. 55–61.

13. Ibid., pp. 68–69, and esp. pp. 81–85.

14. Ibid., p. 47, n. 3.

15. Ibid., p. 62, n. 10.

16. *Explanatio nominum Domini* in *Poetae Christiani Minores*, vol. 1 (Vienna, 1888) [*CSEL*, 16], p. 249.

churches. Saint Jerome affirmed that "per totas Orientis ecclesias quando legendum est Evangelium accenduntur luminaria iam sole rutilante" (in all the churches of the East, lamps that are reddish like the sun are lighted when the Gospels are read).[17] In the *Peregrinatio aetheriae* the public reading of the Gospels is recorded in these terms: "Thiamatharia inferuntur intro spelunca Anastasis, ut tota basilica Anastasis repleatur odoribus; et tunc ubi stat episcopus intro cancellos, prendet evangelium et accedet ad hostium et leget resurrectionem Domini episcopus ipse" (Thiamatharia are brought into the cave of Anastasis, so that the whole basilica of Anastasis is filled with odors; and then, where the bishop stands within enclosures, he takes the Gospel and approaches the host and the bishop himself reads the resurrection of the Lord.).[18] Saint Germain of Paris made reference to a particular Gallic rite held in honor of the Gospels: "Egreditur processio sancti Evangeli velut potentia Christi triumphantis de morte" (Thus emerges the procession of the holy Gospels or the power of Christ triumphant over death).[19] Finally, a dome mosaic of the orthodox baptistry of Ravenna shows the open Gospels displayed alone on the altar, for the adoration of the faithful.[20]

This last piece of evidence takes us directly into contact with the other important source of information, the iconography of the sacred book in early Christian art. This source is particularly significant because it permits us to gain both an understanding of the intention underlying specific representations and a sense of their changes over time. In Christian mosaics and sarcophagi of the fourth to sixth centuries, one frequently encounters representations of Christ, of the Evangelists, of apostles, and even of saints who all hold in one hand, usually the left, an open book. In most cases, this is a Gospel or liturgical book: it is of small or medium dimensions, rectangular in format, of obvious thickness, and its writing (although obviously not legible) is laid out on the full page. Less frequently, the open book is held straight up, displayed in a manner visible to the faithful, bearing a text in capital letters that refers to the saint who presents it or to the sacred place in which the representation is found. Examples of the first category of representations include: the mosaics of S. Maria Maggiore;[21] the famous sarcophagus of Saint Ambrose in Milan attributable to ca. 380;[22] the repre-

17. *Contra Vigilantium liber*, 7, in *PL* 23:361.

18. *Itinerium Egeriae* in *Itineraria et alia geographia* (Turnhout, 1965 [*CC* 175]), p. 69.

19. *Expositio brevis antiquiae liturgiae gallicanae*, *PL* 72:91.

20. J. Wilpert, *Die römischen Mosaiken und Malerein der kirchlichen Bauten vom IV. bis XIII. Jahrhundert*, vol. 3 (plates) (Freiburg in Breisgau, 1917), pl. 82; G. Galassi, *Roma o Bisanzio. I mosaici di Ravenna e le origini dell'arte italiana* (Rome, 1930), pl. XI.

21. Wilpert, *Die römischen Mosaiken*, vol. 3, pls. 22, 70–72; C. Cecchelli, *I mosaici di S. Maria Maggiore* (Turin, 1956), pls. XXXIX and XLVIII.

22. Reprinted with comment by E. Panofsky in *Tomb Sculpture: Its Changing Aspects from Ancient Egypt to Bernini* (London, 1965), pls. 158–60 and p. 42.

sentation of Saint Lorenzo of the first half of the fifth century in the mausoleum of Galla Placidia in Ravenna, where there is also an open armoire of books alongside the saint;[23] the chapel of S. Vittore in Saint Ambrogio in Milan from the same period;[24] the mosaics of S. Sabina in Rome (ca. 422–432) representing the churches of the Jews and the gentiles;[25] and the Ravennese sarcophagus said to be of Saint Rinaldo, dating from a little after the mid-fifth century.[26]

Examples of the second category include: the mosaic of S. Pudenziana in Rome, from the beginning of the fifth century, in which Christ enthroned carries in his hand an open book in which one reads: "Dominus conservator ecclesiae Pudentianae" (Lord preserver of the church of Pudenziana);[27] the already mentioned chapel of S. Vittore in S. Ambrogio in which, in the open book carried by Saint Vittore himself, the name of the saint can be read;[28] a Ravennese mosaic of ca. 500 representing Christ with a book bearing the inscription: "Ego sum via veritas et vita" (I am the way, truth, and life);[29] and in the S. Luca miniature contained in the so-called Gospels of Saint Augustine of Canterbury.[30] One can add to these two categories the well-known fresco belonging to the ancient library of the Lateran, attributable to the end of the sixth century, in which Saint Augustine is seen intent on reading a book of rather large format placed before him on a reading desk.[31] Finally, nearly everyone knows some medieval example of the widely diffused representation showing the Evangelists engaged in writing with the book open on a desk. According to a recent hypothesis, even this iconographic model is traceable to a late antique model, specifically to a series of the Evangelists represented in the mosaics of S. Vitale of Ravenna and then carried over into a Ravennese miniature of the sixth century that served as an exemplar across several intermediate stages to the medieval iconographic tradition (fig. 3).[32]

From the fourth to sixth centuries, the prevalent representation of the

23. Wilpert, *Römischen Mosaiken*, vol. 3, pl. 49.

24. Ibid., pl. 83.

25. Ibid., pl. 47.

26. G. Bovini, *Sacrofagi paleocristiani di Ravenna. Tentativo di classificazione cronologica*, Amici delle Catacombe, 20 (Città del Vaticano, 1964), fig. 34.

27. Wilpert, *Römischen Mosaiken*, vol. 3, pls. 42–44; G. Matthiae, *Pittura romana del medioevo*, vol. 1: *Secoli IV–X* (Rome, 1965), pl. 29.

28. Wilpert, *Römischen Mosaiken*, vol. 3, pl. 83.

29. Ibid., pl. 89; Galassi, *Roma o Bisanzio*, pls. LXVI–LXVII.

30. See F. Wormald, *The Miniatures in the Gospels of St. Augustine. Corpus Christi College MS. 286* (Cambridge, 1954), pls. II and XVIa.

31. Wilpert, *Römischen Mosaiken*, vol. 4, pl. 140, 2.

32. See E. Rosenbaum, "The Evangelist Portraits of the Ada School and Their Models," *Art Bulletin* 38 (1956): 81–90. For the Evangelists of S. Vitale, see Galassi, *Roma o Bisanzio*, pls. LXXVII and LXXXII.

3. Mosaic of Saint Luke, church of San
Vitale, Ravenna (photo: Alinari)

holy book of Christians is thus of an open book, in which one reads, writes, or can write and read. But in the sixth century, alongside this iconographic model there appears another that presents the book always as closed with a rich binding reproduced in minute detail, and always rigidly held close to the breast of the personage portrayed, as an object of particular respect and veneration. Sporadic earlier examples of this configuration do exist;[33] and it is likely that a survey more exhaustive than ours would discover others. Nevertheless, I believe that one could argue that the iconography of the closed Gospel became widely diffused only in the second half of the sixth century and that only with the seventh century does it definitively replace that of the open book.

The first more than occasional evidence of this new type of figure comes in the imposing series of prophets of S. Apollinare Nuovo of the first decades of the sixth century (fig. 4).[34] Here, the compositional structure of the configuration, in the limited number of cases where it appears, is still not rigidly fixed. Most of the personages portrayed bear not a book but a roll, sometimes closed, sometimes open or half-open. Some who carry a codex, moreover, strike poses different from the rigid and solemn posture of the canonized iconography that alone will survive into the following century. In two other examples of the middle or second half of the sixth century—one at S. Apollinare in Classe, the other in Parenzo[35]—the book is closed; but instead of being positioned straight on, it rests in the personage's hands as permitted by its format, which, in accord with antique models, is still almost square. The last example, still of small format, is the codex held firmly in Christ's

33. See, for example, Gundorf's funerary stele in the Bonn Museum (Panofsky, *Tomb Sculpture*, fig. 186 and p. 49); the symbols of the Evangelists in the vault mosaics of the Ravennese chapel of Peter II of the beginning of the sixth century (Galassi, *Roma o Bisanzio*, pl. LXIV); the representations of the Evangelists on the well-known cathedral of Maximian, also Ravennese but of uncertain origin and date (A. Venturi, *Storia dell'arte italiana*, vol. 1: *Dai primordi dell'arte cristiana al tempo di Giustiniano* (Milan, 1901), figs. 284–85 on pp. 302–03 and text, pp. 466–68; and, finally, the Berlin Museum's fifth- or sixth-century Byzantine sacred diptych portraying an enthroned bearded Christ (ibid., fig. 383 and p. 418 and text on pp. 506–08; reproduced also in *Lexicon der christlichen Ikonographie*, vol. 1 (1968), cols. 361–62, fig. 6). Not to be numbered among the oldest examples of the representation of the closed book is that which appears in the well-known universal chronical of Pap. Goleniscev of the Moscow Museum of Fine Arts (repr. in K. Weitzmann, *Illustration in Roll and Codex: A Study of the Origin and Method of Text Illustration*, Studies in Manuscript Illustration, 2 [Princeton, 1947], fig. 101 and p. 114; and also *DACL* III, 1, fig. 2720, col. 1194); Cavallo now correctly reports that it is to be dated to the end of the sixth or the beginning of the seventh century. G. Cavallo, *Ricerche sulla maiuscola biblica*, Studi e testi di papirologia editi dall'Istituto Papirologico V. Vitelli, 11 (Florence, 1967), p. 116 and pl. 106.

34. Galassi, *Roma o Bisanzio*, pls. XXII–XXXV and pp. 71–78.

35. Ibid., pls. XCVIII–C, CIII.

4. Nave mosaic, church of Sant'Appolinare Nuovo, Ravenna (photo: Alinari)

fist in one of the bas reliefs of the anterior columns of the *ciborium* of San Marco in Venice; these are attributed to the first half of the sixth century.[36]

More frequent and significant evidence of the new iconography in its definitive configuration comes from the seventh century. At Rome, for example, in a mosaic of 640–42 situated in the oratory of S. Venanzio in Laterano, Saints Mauro and Septimo, seen standing frontally, each raises a closed, rather richly bound book in both hands.[37] The same motif figures in the frescos of the tomb of Pope Cornelius in the catacombs of S. Callistus that have been definitively dated to the period 630–60.[38] Three more Roman

36. Venturi, *Storia*, vol. 1, figs. 268 and 271 at pp. 282, 285, and text at p. 446. One could also add the child Jesus in the arms of the Madonna "Regina" of S. Maria Antiqua, which Matthiae attributed to the second half of the sixth century: *Pittura romana*, pl. 63 and pp. 117–23.

37. Wilpert, *Römischen Mosaiken*, vol. 3, pl. 110; Matthiai, *Pittura romanesca*, pl. 57.

38. See L. Reekmans, *La tombe du pape Corneille et sa region cémétériale*, Roma sotterranea cristiana, 4 (Città del Vaticano, 1964), pp. 174–84 and figs. 67–68.

examples can be found in the apse of S. Agnese from 625–638,[39] in the depiction of Christ in the cemetery of Ponziano,[40] and in a representation from 668–85 in the catacombs of Commodilla, where Christ enthroned props a large book on his left knee that instead of being open, as earlier portrayals had been, is closed and studded with gems.[41] Two other Roman examples, finally, come from the first years of the eighth century: one is in the apse of S. Maria Antiqua portraying four popes in procession, with large and precious books closed in their hands;[42] the other is in S. Lorenzo, in which Saint Saba bears exposed on his breast a large closed book decorated with gems of various colors.[43] With the eighth century, the portrayal of the Gospel as a large, closed book displayed to the faithful becomes customary; indeed, it is the only one found in early medieval iconography. Excluded altogether are portrayals of the Evangelists writing, which remain rigidly tied to the model of late antique origin into the Carolingian period and beyond.[44]

At this point it is almost superfluous to ask what was the meaning of the substitution of one iconographic model for another: the answer springs directly from the description that we have furnished of individual representations and, further, from what has already been said about the ideological process of sacralization of the book initiated by Christianity. Following the logic of this process, indeed, the book itself had gradually been transformed from an instrument of writing and reading, to be used and thus open, into an object of adoration and a jewel-box of mysteries, not to be used directly and thus closed. As Gregory the Great explained with great clarity when commenting on verse 2:9 of Ezekiel ("Et vidi et ecce manus missa ad me, in qua involutus liber" [And I looked and behold a hand stretched out to me in which a rolled-up book]): "Liber autem involutus est Scripturae sacrae eloquium obscurum, quod profunditate scientiarum involvitur, ut non facile sensu omnium penetretur" (The rolled-up book is the obscure eloquence of sacred Scripture, which is rolled around the deepest knowledge, and not easily penetrated by the sense of everyone.)[45] The conception of the "liber

---

39. Venturi, *Storia*, vol. 1, fig. 110 at p. 122; Matthiae, *Pittura romana*, pls. 56 and 58.

40. S. Bettini, *Pittura delle origini cristiane* (Novara, 1942), pl. 97.

41. Wilpert, *Römischen Mosaiken*, vol. 4, pls. 148–49.

42. Ibid., pl. 154.

43. Ibid., pl. 169.

44. The only example of the survival of the iconography of the "open book" from the period ca. 700 is in a representation of Christ in the mosaic of the Confession of Saint Peter reproduced in Bettini, *Pittura*, pl. 100. It may be noted, however, that both "open book" and "closed book" iconographic models continue to coexist in Byzantine art for centuries, even after the iconoclastic parenthesis.

45. *Homiliae in Ezechielem* 1.10.30, in *PL* 76:882–83; on this passage, see also R. Manselli, "Gregorio Magno e la Bibbia," in *La Bibbia nell'alto medioevo*, Settimane di studio, 10 (Spoleto, 1963), pp. 67–101.

involutus," itself fruit of the allegorical exegesis of Scripture, in combination with the conception of the Gospel as a sacred object worthy of adoration in and for itself and with liturgical practices of which only fragmentary evidence survives, found expression in new iconographic models: instead of the open and readable codex of the Lateran S. Augustine, there came to be adopted instead the image of the closed reliquary, glowing with gems, rigidly presented for the veneration but not the comprehension of the faithful.

The progressive extension of Christian graphic symbolism beyond its original themes in the fourth century is demonstrated by two instances of the displacement of meaning accomplished by Christians in regard to two expressions—one graphic, the other verbal—already elaborated by official culture. The first case concerns the fate of the so-called monogram of Constantine, originally a magical symbol, then an imperial symbol, and finally, in the first decades of the fourth century, transformed into a Christian symbol.[46] The monogram itself, moreover, already conformed rather well to conceptions of mysteriousness and of the visual-synthetic apprehension of writing rather than to the discursive-analytic manner that was already typical of the Christian conception of the sacred book. A letter by Symmachus lucidly expressed the conception of visual rather than verbal apprehension of meaning apropos the monogram itself: "Non minore sane cura, cupio cognoscere an omnes obsignatas epistulas meas sumpseris eo anulo, *quo nomen meum magis intelligi quam legi promptum est*" (And it is surely not with little concern that I desire to know whether you will take up all my letters sealed by that ring, by which my name is made manifest rather by understanding than reading).[47]

The second case concerns the word *apex,* whose meaning underwent a marked mutation in late antiquity. Originally a synonym for *culmen* or *cacumen,* meaning an extreme endpoint, apex came to indicate the distinguishing signs placed over a single letter, then to designate the letters themselves, and eventually to designate imperial rescripts. The word *apices* thus acquired a sacral significance that it had not had before; this significance, moreover, was accentuated by the word's being joined with adjectives such as *sacri* or *augusti.* By this natural process of displacement from symbols of imperial power into Christian symbols, which is well known in early medieval Christian iconography,[48] the expression "sacri apices" was transferred by the

46. V. Gardhausen, *Das alte Monogramm* (Leipzig, 1924), p. 97.

47. Cited ibid., p. 46.

48. For the treatment of such processes of assimilation, see the magisterial work of André Grabar *L'empéreur dans l'art byzantine. Recherches sur l'art officiel de l'Empire d'Orient,* Publications de la Faculté des Lettres de l'Université de Strasbourg, 75 (Paris, 1936), pp. 189-95.

Church Fathers from imperial edicts to the *liber* containing the Christian message, and came to mean Holy Scripture.[49]

Symmachus's remark "magis intelligi quam legi" (rather by understanding than by reading) dates from the sixth century, a period when the process of the sacralization of writing and books, begun on the ideological level by Christian authors, proceeded to invest environments of lay extraction beyond those directly tied to the Church, eventually shaping the very culture in which it originated. It will perhaps be sufficient in this context to illustrate this process by comparing two definitions of the letter, that basic element of writing and language. The first definition is that codified in the *Instituta grammatica* attributed to Probus the Grammarian, an heir of the classical tradition; the second is that enunciated in the work of the obscure grammarian Virgil of Toulouse. For Probus, "littera est elementum vocis articulatae" (the letter is an element of articulated speech). According to his purely verbal conception of the phonic-graphical element: "Accidit unicuique litterae nomen, figura, potestas. Nomen litterae est quo appellatur. . . . Figura litterae est qua notatur, et qua scribitur. *Potestas litterae est, qua valet, hoc est qua sonat*" (There belongs to every letter a name, appearance, and power. The name of a letter is that by which it is called. . . . The appearance of a letter is that by which it is marked or written. The power of a letter is that of the effect it has, that is, how it sounds.)[50] In contrast, for the Toulousan the letter seems to possess a soul beyond its physical shape, a hidden meaning of its own, thereby resembling a human being. "Litera mihi videtur humanae condicionis esse similis: sicut enim homo plasto et affla et quodam caelesti igne consistit, ita et litera suo corpore hoc est figura, arte, ac dicione, velut quisdam compaginibus arctubusque suffuncta est animam habens in sensu, spiridionem in superiore contemplatione" (The letter seems to me like the human condition: for as man consists of form and breath and some celestial fire, so this letter in its body is figure, art, and power, just as if someone serves combinations and arts having a soul to the senses and a spirit to higher contemplation).[51]

The influence of Christian symbolism, evident in this allegorical vision of the letter, goes well beyond the verbal meanings inherent in every graphic sign. But it is entirely absent from the probably contemporary treatment of

49. See *Thesaurus linguae latinae* 3:226–228, and also an example from S. Augustine in W. Wattenbach, *Das Schriftwesen im Mittelalter* (Leipzig, 1896), p. 423.

50. Probus, *Instituta artium*, in *Grammatici latini*, ed. H. Keilh, vol. 4 (Leipzig, 1864), pp. 48–49.

51. *Virgilii Maronis Grammatici Opera*, ed. J. Hlumer (Leipzig, 1886), p. 8; D. Tardi, *Les epitomae de Virgile de Toulouse* (Paris, 1928), pp. 23, 41. See also Curtius, *Schrift- und Buchmetaphorik*, p. 378, n. 2, and Assunto, "Scrittura," 2:17–18.

the grammarian Priscian, for whom the graphic value of the element "litera" is clearly distinguished from the phonic value, and it is individualized with certainty by its full expressive autonomy: "Litera igitur est nota elementi et velut imago quaedam vocis literatae, quae cognoscitur ex qualitate et quantitate figurae linearum" (A letter is a sign of an element or the image of a certain lettered speech that is recognized from the quality and quantity of shapes of lines). Further, following the classical grammatical conception and a strange but fortunate etymology,[52] Priscian attributes to the written "litera" a primary function of legibility: "Dicitur autem litera vel quasi legitera, quod legendi iter praebeat" (A letter is said to be almost *legitera*, because it offers the path of reading).[53] With Priscian we are still thus in the tracks of a written culture in which the functionality of graphic instruments is valued only in relation to the "legendi iter." This traditional vision is recalled even in the dry definition that Cassiodorus furnished: "Litera est pars minima vocis articulatae" (A letter is the smallest part of articulated speech).[54] But, as we have seen elsewhere, Cassiodorus's learning was so entirely immersed in the ancient tradition of rhetoric that it did not admit any foreign intrusions at the level of instruments, techniques, or instruction.

The contrast between the definitions of *littera* furnished by Virgil of Toulouse and those of Priscian and Cassiodorus can be illuminating, even in their reductive extremism. From one point of view, it helps us understand the extent to which schools and rhetoric in the sixth century were subject to various contradictory ideological pressures and consequently found themselves in a state of uncertainty and confusion. From another, it confirms the impression of isolation and backwardness of the didactic and cultural concepts of Cassiodorus, heir of a vision of things that was now moribund.

The sacral conception of writing and the book is thus of great significance as the representation at the ideological level of the crisis that troubled the world of culture in general in the sixth century. Christianity had elaborated this conception over a long period in a manner autonomous from and even in contrast to the scholarly tradition. It was only after this process was complete, moreover, that the mediation of the ecclesiastical hierarchy gradually led some sectors of traditional lay culture to adopt this conception. But until

---

52. Echoed by Petrarca: see A. Petrucci, *La scrittura di Francesco Petrarca*, Studi e testi, 248 (Città del Vaticano, 1967), p. 66.

53. Priscianus Caesariensis, *Institutionum grammaticarum libri XVIII*, ed. M Hertzii, vol. 1 (Leipzig, 1855), pp. 6–7.

54. Cassiodorus Senator, *Institutiones* 2.1.2, ed. R. A. B. Mynors (Oxford, 1963), p. 95. The Cassiodorian definition repeats verbatim that of Donatus: *Ars grammatica*, in *Grammatici latini*, vol. 4, p. 367.

then—indeed, until well into the sixth century—although the ideological processes here sketched had collided with and profoundly modified the idea of writing and books, as well as the sentiments and opinions held of both instruments by the public who made use of them, the production of books and the type of writing used in Italy were not in the least affected. Nor were there changes in the fundamental characteristics of the "ancient" book, which remained a "legible" book in the sense that it was not yet transformed into an object or monument. Nevertheless, the stylistic revolution of uncial script and the external appearance of Gothic religious books give us the first inkling of the profound transformation that would finish in replacing the Medicean Virgil with the Book of Kells.

In the first part of this chapter we analyzed the forces that, in the course of the sixth century, successfully kept alive the ancient book and the ancient conception of writing: these included both lay workshops of book production, including many religious centers that also imitated traditional products, and a sizable percentage of the lay and ecclesiastical public. But the fall of the kingdom of the Goths and the long war that devastated Italy shattered the unstable equilibrium that against all odds had kept such a fragile social and cultural structure standing. By physically destroying the social categories that had preserved and defended traditional culture, the crisis that led to the fall of the Gothic kingdom gave a free hand to those groups that were forging a different culture in which the sacral conception of the book and writing were organic parts. The result was the final disappearance of the conception of the book and of writing as principally tools for the transmission of culture that had been characteristic of classical paganism.

It has been said that the ancient book—an easily recognizable artisanal product that had developed out of centuries of experience of producing it for the needs of a specific educated society—was tied to rather broad strata of the Italian ecclesiastical hierarchy of the sixth century. But both within and without the hierarchy, new monastic environments were refusing to place the book and writing at the center of society, advancing new measures of value in which learning was replaced by piety and conversation by industrious isolation. In these environments, writing was reduced to a category of manual work and the book was diminished in importance and consequently in prestige: this was, in short, the synthesis—profoundly renewing from a cultural point of view—of the Rule of Saint Benedict.

The extent to which the new religious order, born in the inaccessible places of Latium and Campania, deliberately turned its back on learned traditions can be illustrated by comparing the cultural role of books in the Benedictine Rule and in the later but backward looking *Institutiones* of Cassiodorus. The earliest Benedictine monasticism was not a monasticism of *scriptoria* and books.[55] Too often, the images of Desiderius's eleventh-century Montecassino is superimposed on that of Benedict's rude *cenobia*, which have often been seen as places where the copying labor of monks saved the masterpieces of classical civilization for posterity. This vision of the facts is entirely false. In reality, as Mundò has recently shown[56] and an attentive reading of the Rule can confirm,[57] the *lectio* of the earliest Benedictine monasteries was limited to the *Regula*, liturgical books, the Bible, and a few other religious texts. Further, the relatively few monks present in any cenobium[58] included illiterates[59] and others who could not read well.[60] Finally, the fact that Saint Benedict explicitly stated that monks should personally own "neque codicem neque tabulas neque graphium" (neither book nor tablet nor writing stylus)[61] gives the impression that he wished to impede rather than encourage any independent cultural activity on the part of the handful who could have undertaken it, even if the supplies furnished to every member of the cenobium were to include (in a contradiction that is only apparent) *graphium* and *tabulae*.[62] Taken together, these indications suggest a number of conclusions: that books in sixth-century Benedictine cenobia were few, of exclusively religious content, and at an elementary level; that since there was scarce call for books, the production must also have been limited, with few monks engaging in the labor of copying and only at irregular intervals; and that traditional grammatical and rhetorical learning, already rejected personally by Benedict,[63] was entirely absent.

55. See the balanced account of J. Leclercq, *The Love of Learning and the Desire of God,* trans. Catharine Misrahi (New York, 1961), pp. 14–24.

56. A. Mundò, "'Bibliotheca.' Bible et lecture de carême d'après saint Benoît," in *Revue bénédictine* 60 (1950): 65–92; but see also H. Bloch, "Montecassino's Teachers and Library in the High Middle Ages," in *La scuola nell'Occidente latino nell'alto Medioevo* (Spoleto, 1972), pp. 564–65.

57. The works recommended for the monks' reading, apart from liturgical texts and the Bible (for which see Mundò's article), consist of Cassian (*Regula Benedicti = RB*, cap. 42, 3–4), the Rule itself (*RB*, cap. 66, 8, p. 157), and the rule of St. Basil (*RB*, cap. 73, 3–5), ed. R. Hanslik (Vienna, 1960) = *CSEL* vol. 75:104–05, 157, 164. For the problem of the texts whose reading was usual or recommended in Western monasteries of the period with which we are concerned, see G. Penco, "Lo studio presso i monaci occidentali nel secolo V," in *Los monjes y los estudios* (Poblet, 1963), pp. 50–54, whose views of monastic culture, and specifically of Benedictine culture, are different from those presented here.

58. The number of monks in the earliest monasteries must have totaled at most 20; see Mundò, "Bibliotheca," p. 85.

59. *RB*, cap. 58, 20, p. 136.

60. *RB*, cap. 38, 12, p. 99; cap. 45, 1–3, p. 112; cap. 47, 3, p. 114.

61. *RB*, cap. 33, 3, p. 90.

62. *RB*, cap. 55, 19, p. 130.

63. On the studies and learning of Benedict, see H. S. Brechter, "St. Benedikt und die Antike," in *Benedictus der Vater des Abendlandes, 547–1947* (Munich, 1947), pp. 147–49, 153–62.

The monastery contemplated by the saint of Nursia was a community of men dedicated to work, especially manual labor, and to prayer. It was, in short, as he himself defined it, an *officina* (workshop) and its members were *operarii* (laborers).[64] In the opposing vision of Cassiodorus, however, the monastery was above all a school in which both sacred and profane learning were taught.[65] It was, moreover, a school based on a conception that equated culture with books and philology, as the preface to the *Institutiones* clearly shows: "quocirca, si placet, hunc debemus lectionis ordinem custodire, ut primum tyrones Christi, postquam psalmos didicerint, *auctoritatem divinam in codicibus emendatis iugi exercitatione meditentur* . . . ne vitia librariorum impolitis mentibus inolescant" (by which, if it pleases, we should observe this order of reading, so that novices of Christ, after they have learned the Psalms, may reflect upon divine authority with continual practice in corrected codices . . . lest the faults of copyists become fixed in unpolished minds).[66] It is certainly true that in the text of the *Institutiones* itself, beyond the rich cultural message that was transmitted, one notices the presence of new elements dissonant with the general formulation of the discourse, as when Cassiodorus had to excuse the ignorance of illiterate or unlearned brothers,[67] or when, in the chapter dedicated to the work of the *antiquarii*,[68] he was led to give an allegorical interpretation of Scripture, "quod factum Domini aliquo modo videntur emitari, qui legem suam, licet figuraliter sit dictum, omnipotentis digiti operatione conscripsit" (that they should be seen in some way to imitate the deed of God, who, it may be said figuratively, wrote his law by the operation of his all-powerful finger).[69] But these are isolated instances. Cassiodorus's discourse is directed not to unlearned brothers, whom he pauses to consider only for a moment, but to those few learned brothers who were still able to understand him. And, apart from occasional allegories, he always treats writing purely as an instrument meant to serve the diffusion of the Christian message and traditional culture:[70] an antique interpretation.

This message remained unheard. The work of Cassiodorus was dispersed, "Vivarium" completely disappeared, and the *Institutiones* called forth no echoes in early medieval spirituality. In contrast, the Rule of Saint Benedict passed the test of events and left its impression on all Western monasticism

---

64. *RB*, cap. 4, 78, p. 35; cap. 7, 49, p. 48.

65. For a comprehensive judgment on the cultural program of Abbot Cassiodorus, see Leclerq, *Love of Learning*, pp. 24–30.

66. *Institutiones*, Praef., 2, p. 4.

67. Ibid., 1.12.4, pp. 37–38; 1.26.1–2, p. 69.

68. Ibid., 1.30.1, pp. 75–78.

69. Ibid., 1.30.1, p. 76.

70. See in particular 1.30.2, pp. 76–77, in which philological concerns prevail over the ideological.

for several centuries.[71] These divergent fates are to be explained not only by the success of a Christian ideology that embraced and propagated the simple ideals of the Benedictine message, but also and especially by the impossibility of recreating in altered environments and times the complex didactic and cultural experiences that had not entirely been extinguished from the Rome of 500 and that Cassiodorus anachronistically wished to pervade his cenobitism. The collapse of both elementary and higher education, the growing illiteracy of the religious, the destruction of libraries and the shortage of books, the interruption of links between the greater cultural centers: these are the dramatic circumstances that echoed in the pages of the *Institutiones* and that made its objectives unrealizable even as they made possible the survival and reinforcement of entirely different cultural experiences, including the Benedictine conception of labor "scienter nescia et sapienter indocta" (learnedly ignorant and wisely untaught).[72]

If we did not have the works and especially the register of Gregory the Great, we probably could not give an account of the actual situation in Italy at the end of the sixth and the beginning of the seventh centuries. Indeed, the words, the sufferings, the meditations, and the acts of this great witness to history are our principal evidence for an Italy that, losing its political and cultural unity for the first time in centuries, in this period entered what we are accustomed to call the early Middle Ages. Gregory wrote when the Lombard invasion had swept away the structural framework of the old society and culture in a substantial part of Italy, with such vestiges as remained seeming now dispersed and impoverished, whether at Rome or in other regions still spared Lombard settlement and the importation of their distinctive ways of living, customs, and culture.

Gregory the Great was a convinced exponent and apostle of the allegorical Christian conception of the book and writing, and of the various symbols that expressed it. There is nothing surprising in this, because he was one of the greatest theoreticians of the allegorical exegesis of the Bible.[73] For him, the symbol of *libri caelesti* was alive: "Liber namque vitae est ipsa visio advenientis iudicis. . . . Libri etiam aperti referuntur. . . . Et iudicati sunt mortui

---

71. See again Leclerq, *Love of Learning*, pp. 28. "Cassiodorus did not become part of the monastic tradition . . . ; he remained an isolated figure, never proposed as a model, nor even mentioned by name. No inspiration is sought in his monastic doctrine; he is asked for ideas, but not for directives; *his knowledge is called upon, but not his ideals*" (my emphasis).

72. Leclerq, *Love of Learning*, p. 14, citing a felicitous definition of St. Benedict's culture coined by Gregory the Great, *Dialogi libri IV*, ed. U. Moricca, Fonti per la storia d'Italia, 57 (Rome, 1924), vol. 2, Praef., p. 72.

73. See Manselli, "Gregorio Magno," pp. 67–101.

ex his quae scripta erant in libris" (For the book of life is the very vision of
the judge to come. . . . And open books will produced. . . . And the dead are
judged by what is written in the books).[74] Scripture, similarly, is compared
to heaven: "Quid enim coeli nomine nisi sacra Scriptura signatur? De qua
nobis et sol sapientiae et luna scientiae et ex antiquis patribus stellae exem-
plorum atque virtutum lucent?" (For what is marked with the name of
heaven if not holy Scripture? How else are we illuminated by the sun of
wisdom and the moon of knowledge and the stars of the examples and virtues
of the ancient fathers?)[75] For Gregory the Great, the author's work in writing
Scripture was simply a physical act, even comparable to that of a reed pen,
because the inspiration was entirely divine: "Si magni cuiusdam viri susceptis
epistolis legeremus verba, sed quo calamo fuissent scripta, quaereremus, ri-
diculum profecto esset, epistolarum auctorem scire sensumque cognoscere,
sed quali calamo earum verba impressa fuerint indagare" (If we read the
words of the letters of a certain great man that were written by a pen, it
would really be ridiculous if we sought, rather than to know the author and
understand the sense of the letters, to investigate by which pen their words
were marked).[76] In one justly famous passage[77] from his correspondence, Gregory's symbolism of writing, extended into a comparison between the raw
eloquence of earthly reality and the silent eloquence of books, acquires a
cosmic dimension and poetic inspiration worthy of Prudentius: "Mundi igitur mala, quae dudum ventura audiebamus, aspicimus; quasi paginae nobis
codicum factae sunt ipsae iam plagae terrarum" (We behold, therefore, the
evils of the world of whose coming formerly we heard; these plagues of the
world indeed are made almost as the pages of our books).[78]

The symbolism of the reed pen also returns in a passage from the *Homilies
on Ezechiel* in which Gregory develops his theories about the difference between learning through writing and learning through hearing—in short, between the literate seen now as "reeds" and the illiterate "rushes," following
an image borrowed from Isaiah (35:7): "ut per calamum scriptores, per iun-
cum vero debeant auditores intelligi" (so that writers ought to be understood
by reeds, and hearers by rushes). Illiterates, in particular, "verbum vitae au-
diunt, bonae spei et rectorum operum viriditatem tenent, sed tamen ad scri-

74. *Moralia in Job* 24.8.16 in *PL* 76:295.
75. *Homiliae in Ezechielem* 1.10.30, *PL* 76 883. On this passage, see Manselli, "Gregorio
Magno," p. 81.
76. *Moralia in Job* Praef.1.2, in *PL* 75:517.
77. See Manselli, "Gregorio Magno," p. 99.
78. The passage appears in a letter to the clergy of Milan written to the new bishop
Constantius in April 593; *Gregorii I papae Registrum Epistolarum* 3.29, ed. P. Ewald and L. M.
Hartmann, vol. 1 (Berlin, 1891) (*MGH Epist.* 1:187).

bendum proficere nullatenus possunt" (hear the word of life and hold to the vigor of good hopes and righteous works, but nevertheless they can by no means advance to writing).[79] This passage reveals that for Gregory the allegorical conception of writing and of fourfold exegesis of the Bible itself was not an ideological superstructure lacking contact with reality. On the contrary, it became for him a means of interpreting and transcending the unbridgeable gap between the worlds of literates and illiterates that unmistakably was now serious enough to affect the means used to spread the Christian message and the very success of the effort.

Gregory the Great was fully aware of this predicament. As in the fourth century the Church had assured the diffusion of its message by appropriating the cultural tools elaborated by pagan society, especially writing and the book, so now, in changed conditions, the Church elaborated a differently conceived method of diffusion that took the two levels of culture for granted and devised communication techniques capable of guaranteeing contact with every social stratum. In this painstaking but conscious process of converting the cultural patrimony of the Latin Church, whose traditional structures were no longer adequate for the changed political and social conditions, Gregory the Great occupied a position of great prominence. He was one of his period's most vigorous and coherent advocates of the necessity of a twofold culture and thus of a differentiation of cultural productions into two levels whose contact with each other was mediated by those specialists in communication and diffusion: the preachers.

In an important letter of 602 sent to John, subdeacon of Ravenna, the pope complained that Marianus, bishop of Ravenna, "legi commenta beati Job publice ad vigilias faciat" (had the commentary on the blessed Job read publicly at the vigils), because, he explained, "non est illud opus populare et rudibus auditoribus impedimentum magis quam provectum generat. Sed dic ei, ut commenta psalmorum legi ad vigilias faciat, quae mentes saecularium ad bonos mores praecipue informent" (that is not a popular work, and for uncultured listeners it produces obstacles rather than advances. But tell him that he should have read at vigils a comment on the Psalms that will chiefly mold the minds of the worldly to good morals).[80] Gregory the Great was a cultivated man; like Cassiodorus, he personally was heir to a great rhetorical and scholastic tradition. He had no intention of renouncing this level of culture, as indeed one easily sees in his works of biblical exegesis, which often are difficult and complex, and even in his letters. But this level was reserved to a restricted number of great lords of lay society and the Church.

79. *Homiliae in Ezechielem* 2.1.2 in *PL* 76:943.
80. *Registrum* 12.6, vol. 2 (Berlin, 1899), p. 352.

Below it there must have existed another level consisting of a purely functional culture that was the patrimony of that vast stratum of ecclesiastics
whose task was to guarantee the diffusion of the Christian message among
the *rudes* by oral means, that is, by preaching.[81] It was precisely to provide
preachers with an inventory of *topoi* and as a manual of oratorical technique
that Gregory wrote the *Dialogi.* This was an *opus populare* par excellence, in
which the discourse of staged scenes, often with dialogues in direct speech,
outweighs the analytic and indirect discourse of the scholarly tradition; in
my opinion, the dramatic aspects are a more distinctive characteristic of the
new rhetoric than particular linguistic features that, while they certainly characterize the *Dialogues,* have perhaps attracted an excessive amount of scholarly attention.

Gregory the Great was certainly not unique in recognizing that the patrimony of traditional culture, now almost exclusively administered by the
Church, was in the process of being diversified by necessity into different
levels each with a particular means of diffusion. The *simplicissima plebecula,*
who no longer understood Latin of classical style, made up the overwhelming
majority of faithful. The difficulty of communicating with them was already
apparent at the level of word choice (though not yet at that of graphic
instruments) in most of the Christian Fathers, from Jerome and Augustine
to Caesarius of Arles and Gregory of Tours; Gregory of Tours' remarks in
favor of a style and language that abandoned tradition in favor of ordinary
speech are well known and do not need to be repeated here.[82] But it is
precisely at the moment when Rome saw Pope Gregory's activities that one
finds the idea that culture had to be diversified also appearing, in schematically didactic form, in the work of Isidore of Seville. Taking up a passage
from Jerome, Isidore explicitly proposed an only apparently formal subdivision of all book production, and thus of culture more generally, into three
categories.[83] The first category would comprise *excerpta* or, as Isidore explains,

---

81. There are many pages in the works of Gregory the Great where he insists on the
importance of preaching and the preacher, whom he termed "seminiverbius": *Regulae Pastoralis
Liber* 2.4 in *PL* 77:32; see also *PL* 77:31: "Sacerdos ergo si praedicationis est nescius, quam
clamoris vocem daturus est praeco mutus?" (Is not the priest, therefore, if he is ignorant of
preaching, like a mute herald charged with voicing a summons?) The link between pastor and
faithful is seen in the *Liber* mostly as an oral-auditory function: see pt. 3, Prologus, col. 49,
and pt. 3, cap. 25, cols. 97–99. See also H. Zwick, *Il predicatore nella dottrina di S. Gregorio
Magno* (Rome, 1962).

82. For this we shall only make reference to the classic exposition of E. Auerbach, *Literary
Language and Its Public in Late Latin Antiquity and in the Middle Ages,* trans. Ralph Manheim
(Princeton, 1965), and to the valuable recent pages of Roncaglia in *Storia della letteratura
italiana,* vol. 1, pp. 33–59.

83. For the Hieronymian sources from which it derives and for the meaning of Isidore's
remarks, see J. Fontaine, *Isidore de Seville et la culture classique dans l'Espagne visigothique* (Paris,

extracts, probably together with commentaries explicating a text—in short, a type of grammatical or scholastic production tied to higher instruction; the second, "homiliae . . . quae proferuntur in populis" (homilies that are published to the people), that is, texts intended for preaching; the third, the "tomi, quos nos libros vel volumina nuncupamus" (tomes that we call books or volumes), that is, literary, scientific, and philosophical works prepared apart from immediate practical scholastic or liturgical purposes. The difference in nature and value of the last two categories was profound, for Isidore as for Gregory. The bishop of Seville put it in relief: "Homiliae autem ad vulgus loquuntur, tomi vero, idest libri, maiores sunt disputationes" (For homilies are spoken for the *vulgus,* while true volumes, that is books, are discussions for the better educated).[84]

The existence of this *vulgus,* representing an enormous mass of illiterate Christians, was a constant preoccupation of Gregory the Great. He discussed their condition many times in his letters, indicating the different means to which one might have recourse to assure that the word of the Church reach them. These means were not only oral but visual and figurative as well, following a conception of the communicability of ideas that regarded sustained synthetic discourse employing figural symbols as the instrument best suited for communicating specific ideological content to an audience of illiterates or semiliterates who were incapable of grasping any message, even the simplest, that required a modest ability to read.[85] On this subject, Gregory the Great was more explicit than other Christian authors and frequently expressed his views with great clarity. Thus, in some letters he excused ignorance of writing even in priests, saying that Christ "praedicatores suos, quos in mundum misit, sine litteris elegit" (chooses those without letters to be his preachers, whom he sends into the world),[86] and commended the care of illiterates to bishops (to Agnello, bishop of Fondi: "Tua praedicatione qui litteras nesciunt, quid divinitus praecipiatur, agnoscant" [Let those who do

1959), vol. 2, pp. 751–52. On the literary genre of the extracts, typical of late antique culture and in particular of the sixth century, defined by Fontaine as "une civilisation du *digest* avant la lettre," see p. 765. On the other hand, the enthusiasm for and extensive use of this genre, especially in advanced instruction, is a sympton of the limited capacity of schools of that time and of the public educated in them for elaboration, criticism, and even reception of learning, as can be seen in the explicit admissions of Isidore himself, reported and discussed ibid., p. 768.

84. *Etymologiarum sive originum libri XX,* ed. W. M. Lindsay (Oxford, 1911), 6.8.1–2.

85. For this and earlier comments on the attitude of the Greek Fathers of the Church, see R. Assunto, *La critica d'arte nel pensiero medioevale* (Milan, 1961), pp. 56, 59, n. 5; E. Franceschini, "La Bibbia nell'alto medioevo," in *La Bibbia nell'alto medioevo,* Settimane di studio, 10 (Spoleto, 1963), p. 28 and in general pp. 27–30; and also Seel, *Antike,* p. 35.

86. *Registrum* 11.36, vol. 2, p. 305.

not know letters learn what is divinely ordained from your preaching];[87] to Rufinus, bishop of Ephesus: "Ut qui nescit legere, lingua vestra illi sit codex" [Let your tongue be the codex of those who do not know how to read][88]).

In other letters Gregory proposed explicitly pictures as *lectio* for those who could not read books. Indeed, he used these terms in July 599 when writing Serenus, bishop of Marseilles: "Idcirco enim pictura in ecclesiis adhibetur, ut hi qui litteras nesciunt saltem in parietibus videndo legant, quae legere in codicibus non valent . . . quatenus et litterarum nescii haberent, unde scientiam historiae colligerent" (For thus painting is used in churches, so that those who are ignorant of letters may at least read in seeing the walls what they cannot read in codices . . . whence those ignorant of letters may be able to a knowledge of history).[89] And little more than a year later, in October 600, he explained his thinking on this subject still more precisely in another letter to Serenus: "Aliud est enim picturam adorare, aliud picturae historia, quid sit adorandum, addiscere. Nam quod legentibus scriptura, hoc idiotis praestat pictura cernentibus, quia in ipsa ignorantes vident, quod sequi debeant, in ipsa legunt qui litteras nesciunt; unde praecipue gentibus pro lectione pictura est" (For it is one thing to adore a painting and another to learn the history portrayed in the painting which is being adored. For what writing is to readers, painting offers to uneducated sight, since in it the ignorant see what they should follow, and in it those who know no letters can read; thus especially for the people painting takes the place of reading).[90] Earlier in the same letter he reaffirmed that the function of sacred images was exactly that of permitting "nescientes litteras" to learn "historia" visually, without provoking "illa adoratio, quae picturis fuerat incompetenter exhibita" (that adoration which was unsuitably shown to paintings).[91]

In his theoretical conception and concrete actions, the great pope clearly laid the foundations for a process of cultural diffusion structured around techniques entirely different from those taken for granted by the ruling classes, both lay and clerical, of Theodoric's Italy. Now, at the threshold of the seventh century, the new educated class, made up of clerics and guided by the Church of Rome, took cognizance for the first time of the existence of a huge, substantially illiterate stratum of population. Although it was essential to educate and inform this population, it was impossible to think of rendering it literate because of the collapse of scholastic structures and the drastic reduction of book production. It was at this very moment—when

87. *Registrum* 3.13, vol. 1, p. 172.
88. *Registrum* 7.11, vol. 1, p. 454.
89. *Registrum* 9.208, vol. 2, p. 195.
90. *Registrum* 11.10, vol. 2, p. 270.
91. *Registrum* 11.10, vol. 2, p. 271.

this awareness was being transformed into a cultural program based on a new conception of the diffusion and communication of the Christian message, and when new techniques were being elaborated for this purpose that were founded on figural rather than analytic discourse—that the sacral conception of writing and books, previously latent in Christian ideology, came to prevail even in scriptorial practice. The medieval book, with the particular forms and characteristics examined earlier, replaced the ancient book.

In the Italy of that era, an event of incalculable importance dramatized the mute presence of the *idiotae* and rendered illusory any program of ties with them based on old cultural instruments: the invasion of the Lombards and their establishment over a good part of the penisula. If a date had to be chosen for the beginning of the Middle Ages in Italy, it could only be 569.

3

THE
LOMBARD PROBLEM

ALTHOUGH PRACTICALLY ALL historians agree that the Lombards were illiterate when they arrived in Italy, very few scholars have been interested in the more specific problem of how much they knew of writing in general and of Latin writing in particular.[1] But what do we really mean by the illiteracy of a people? And further, what do we mean when we say in this particular case that the Lombards were illiterate?

When using illiteracy as a concept applicable to an entire autonomous social unit such as a Germanic tribe, which is internally heterogeneous and also in the process of migrating geographically during the period we are considering, one may be referring to situations of total or relative illiteracy. By total illiteracy, I mean a situation in which, within the range of a specific social unit, neither subordinate nor ruling classes employ any kind of writing for a conscious expressive end. Such situations do not, of course, rule out

---

Originally published as "Il problema longobardo," in *Studi medievali* 3d ser. 14, no. 2 (1973): 984–1002.

1. See H. Rosenfeld, "Buch, Schrift und lateinische Sprachkenntis bei den Germanen vor der christlichen Mission," *Rheinisches Museum für Philologie* n.s. 95 (1952): 203–06. See also, in general, G. P. Bognetti, "L'influsso delle istituzioni militari romane sulle istituzioni longobarde del secolo VI e la natura della 'fara,'" in *L'età longobarda*, vol. 3 (Milan, 1967), pp. 1–46 (all citations to Bognetti's writings will be made to this comprehensive collection); and J. Werner, "Die Langobarden in Pannonien. Beiträge zur Kenntnis der langobardischen Bodenfunde vor 568," *Abhandlungen der Bayerischen Akademie der Wissenschaften*, phil.-hist. Klasse, n.s. 55 A (1962). For a balanced consideration of the problem discussed here, with interesting documentation, see the article of P. Delogu, "I longobardi e la scrittura," in *Studi storici in onore de O. Bertolini* (Pisa, 1972), pp. 313–24.

the use of other systems of communicating and diffusing ideas (whether oral or pictographic) that are as functional as the true and distinct systems of writing, alphabetic or otherwise, that are unknown. By relative illiteracy, moreover, I mean the situation in which one finds that a genuine system of writing is used for expressive purposes, but by only a few individuals or by those belonging to restricted social categories within the specific social unit. In this case, the great majority of the population are illiterate and remain so, despite being generally aware of the existence of the instrument of writing within their social unit and able to use writing passively, as a source of intellectual and emotional stimulation. Even these passive uses, however, are indirect and displaced, in the sense that writing is understood not verbally but merely figurally.

The question, then, is: Was the condition of the Lombards in the middle of the sixth century one of total or relative illiteracy?

Responding to such an inquiry is quite difficult. On one hand, we lack practically any direct testimony about the Lombards' knowledge or eventual use of graphic systems before they entered Italy; we cannot even state with certainty that in the sixth century they used the runic writing that other Germanic tribes had known for centuries and used for monumental and sacral purposes.[2] On the other hand, it is known that around 547, in the course of the long march of migration toward the south that took them across the interior of Germany, the Lombards had received Pannonia as *foedus* from Justinian and that their ties with the Roman world, principally through the entrance of sizable armed bands into the ranks of the Byzantine army, were not entirely transitory.[3] Participation in the complex administra-

---

2. With regard to the widely debated question of the origin of the runic alphabet, Mintz ("Die Notae der Germanen bei Tacitus," *Rheinisches Museum* 85 [1937]: 193–203) revives the thesis that the runes derived from a north Etruscan alphabet, which would suggest that they had been formed in the distant past (p. 194). But it seems to me both preferable and better founded to suppose that the runic alphabet derived from the Latin one, having been encountered by the western Germans in the course of trade and other contacts with Roman merchants and soldiers (see R. E. M. Wheeler, *La civiltà romana oltre i confini dell'Impero* [Turin, 1963], pp. 11–101; originally published as *Rome Beyond the Imperial Frontiers* [London, 1954]) and perhaps even with already partially romanized Gauls. This position was argued by H. Pedersen, "L'origine des runes," *Mémoires de la Société Royale des Antiquaires du Nord* n.s. 1920–24: 88–136, where the relevant evidence is cited. For the purely epigraphic nature of runic writing and its highly restricted social diffusion, see Pedersen, p. 118, and R. Derolez, *Runica manuscripta: The English Tradition* (Bruges, 1954), pp. XIVff.; but see also the evidence of private use in J. Werner, "Das Aufkommen von Bild und Schrift in Nordeuropa," *Sitzungberichte des Bayerische Akademie der Wissenschaften*, phil.-hist. Klasse 1966, no. 4: 29–34. With regard to the value of the term *rune*, see F. Albano Leoni, "Runar munt pu finna oc radna stafi," in *Studi germanici* n.s. 10 (1972): 99–120.

3. Bognetti, "Influsso," pp. 29–30. For the cession of Pannonia to the Lombards, see *La guerra gotica di Procopio di Cesarea*, ed. D. Comparetti, Fonti per la storia d'Italia, 24 (Rome,

THE LOMBARD PROBLEM

tive structures of the Roman military, whether direct or indirect, must have brought the Lombards a certain degree of awareness of bureaucratic procedures and the rules and laws that governed them. They would also have gained a rudimentary knowledge of Latin and, at least on the part of the military leaders, of Roman writing and relevant administrative formulas as well.[4] Even so, this very limited and casual acquaintance with an instrument that was one of the principle vehicles of associative life in Roman society must have made cultural contacts between the Lombards and what remained of the Roman ruling class rather difficult, at least at the beginning. Nor did the new rulers, for centuries accustomed to illiteracy, quickly recognize the need to adopt writing systematically for utilitarian and expressive ends.

The true causes of this singularly lacking "acculturation" must be sought in the nature of Lombard society, which because of its very structure remained in a condition of substantial (even if relative) illiteracy until the Lombards' entrance into Italy. Distributed in relatively mobile groups scattered throughout the territory they occupied, and having preserved their social habits and military organization, the Lombards evidently had no more reason to use writing for either documentary or cultural purposes in Italy than they had had in their preceding centuries in Germany. If Roman society was one of dialogue and communication, in which written materials formed the connective tissue of every practical and intellectual activity, German society generally and Lombard society in particular had, in contrast, no real need for communication or dialogue. Or, better, it was a society in which the simplicity of administrative structures and the summary quality of cultural traditions meant that the essential web of social contacts could be formed and governed for the most part by oral means. Nor was any compelling necessity felt to set down dates, news, and legal ties in writing. In part, this was because only a limited circle of individuals was interested in any occasion of community life; in part, too, it was because orality in and of itself guaranteed sufficient clarity and certainty to be used as the dominant means of publicizing, preserving, and transmitting any provision or usage in the administrative and legislative field.

The foregoing considerations lead us to conclude that, at the moment of their arrival in Italy, the Lombards were in a condition of relative illiteracy because there certainly were some among them who could use the runic alphabet and others who could read and write roman writing. That such knowledge and the limited use deriving from it reached strata more strictly

---

1896), 1.3.33, vol. 2, p. 412, and C. Diehl, *Justinien et la civilisation byzantine au VIe siècle* (Paris, 1901), p. 406.

4. Bognetti, "Influsso," p. 42. See also Werner, "Aufkommen," pp. 6–8, 29–34.

illiterate, even if indirectly, is shown by the discovery in the earliest Italian Lombard tombs of numerous objects that, although not of Roman manufacture, bear inscriptions in roman capitals. Often these are interlaced monograms incised by or for the barbarian users and thus conceived or at least understood by them, even if only at a figural level.[5]

What has been said so far, however, is not altered by the fact that the Lombards must also have made some use of Latin writing, in both official and private spheres, from the very beginning of their permanent settlement in Italy. This occurred in at least three different sectors: coinage, epigraphy, and documentation.

With regard to money, it is extremely difficult to locate Lombard coinage precisely in time within the late sixth or first half of the seventh century, or to assign it to specific kings (or dukes); this is, however, the period that is of principal interest to us, for it represents the phase in which the Lombards began to experiment with Latin writing as an instrument of communication, even if in only an indirect and contradictory way. Of this early Lombard coinage we know rather less today than was thought to be known some decades ago, when both Wroth and the *Corpus nummorum* confidently assigned dates to the individual coins that survive.[6] Following Bernareggi's critical reevaluation of the evidence,[7] all that seems certain is that Lombard coinage was based on imitation of Byzantine coinage until the end of the seventh century, and that this process of imitation had the effect of completely obliterating the verbal meaning of the legends inscribed on the money. A typical instance is the famous coin of the Museo Civico di Brescia, signed by the moneyer Marino and bearing a nonsensical inscription on the reverse that used to be incorrectly ascribed to Rothari.[8] The Lombard au-

5. For inscribed materials from Nocera Umbria, see A. Pasqui and R. Paribeni, "Neocropoli barbarica di Nocera Umbria," *Monumenti antichi* 25 (1918), col. 168 and fig. 14; cols. 267–68 and fig. 116; cols. 254–55; the relevant material is now preserved in the Museo dell'Alto Medioevo di Roma. See also Delogu, "I Longobardi," pp. 315–21. For the material of Reggio Emilia, see M. Degani in *Notizie degli scavi di antichità* 74 (1949): 23–27, and, especially, J. Werner and B. Bischoff, "Langobardische Grabfunde aus Reggio Emilia," in *Germania* 30 (1952): 190–94; see also Bognetti, "Influsso," pp. 32–34 and "Le crocette longobarde," in *L'età longobarda*, 3: 145–48. For the inscriptions on crosses, see S. Fuchs, *Die langobardische Goldblattkreuze aus der Zone Südwarts der Alpen* (Berlin, 1938), pp. 42–50.

6. W. Wroth, *Catalogue of the Coins of the Vandals, Ostrogoths and Lombards and of the Empires of Thesalonica, Nicaea and Trebizond in the British Museum* (London, 1911), pp. LV–LVI, 123–32; *Corpus nummorum italicorum*, vol. 4: *Lombardia (zecche minori)* (Rome, 1913), pp. 455–66.

7. E. Bernareggi, "Le monete dei Longobardi nell'Italia padana e nella Tuscia," *Rivista italiana di numismatica e scienze affini* 65 (1963): 35–142.

8. See *Corpus nummorum italicorum*, 4:455; Bernareggi, "Monete," pp. 54–59.

thorities who commissioned this coin, which Bernareggi would assign to some unidentifiable duke, clearly believed that coins should bear some kind of inscription corresponding to the Greek inscriptions of Byzantine examples. But because the meaning of that inscription obviously was not important to them, the moneyer simply portrayed a series of graphic elements that made no sense at all from a verbal perspective. This is not, of course, an isolated case.[9] But in my opinion, it should not be ascribed, as Lopez does for analogous examples,[10] to the illiteracy of the moneyer: the Marino of this particular coin, at least, wanted and knew how to write or have his own name written quite legibly.[11] Rather, one should understand this case as manifesting a total indifference to the verbal meaning of writing that was characteristic of the Lombards and that, in the specific case of early Lombard coinage, certainly would have been reinforced by the desire not to make statements that might compromise the uncertain legal situation of the period and the very fate of that imitative money.

Sketching a hypothesis on the meaning that the coinage of the first dukes and kings acquired in Lombard Italy, as I have done here, is not difficult to the extent that the basic terms defining the problem are clear. Issuing certain types of money was then an aspect of that utilization of certain instruments of Roman society promoted by the highest ranks of the Lombard ruling class (whether kings or dukes): the ease of identifying who was behind the coinage has the effect of clarifying the character and objectives of the effort itself. But the analogous problem of stone carving in the same early period of Lombard occupation is quite different and much more complicated. In this

9. See the examples in Ph. Grierson, "The Silver Coinage of the Lombards," *Archivio storico lombardo* ser. 8, 6 (1956): 131, 133.

10. R. S. Lopez, "Moneta e monetieri nell'Italia barbarica," in *Moneta e scambi nell'alto medioevo* (Spoleto, 1961), p. 77, where he remarks with regard to the illiteracy of a moneyer from Lucca: "If other moneyers can also be said to be illiterate, that helps explain why the inscriptions on coins of the time are illegible."

11. In addition to these considerations, there are other more general ones that would, however, be lengthy to discuss. Let it suffice to observe that in antiquity and in the Middle Ages the illiteracy of specific categories of technicians such as stonecutters, moneyers, or the artists of mosaics and frescoes cannot and should not have any direct effect on the legibility or illegibility of the inscriptions executed by them in the course of their work, because in the majority of cases the artisans would have been entrusted only with the physical execution of the text, the models for which would have been prepared by fully literate persons. One could say, in broader terms, that when writing whose verbal sense is unknown is used on graphic productions that are neither books nor documents but primarily monumental or figural, such as epigraphy or coins, with the result that the inscriptions assume the aspect of a succession of signs deprived of meaning, the explanation for this phenomenon is to be sought not in the cultural level of the artisan who executed the work but in the function assigned to writing in that context by the authors of the product and the public for which it is destined.

case, the very terms of the nexus of production, of the links between author and public—or, alternatively, between sender and recipient—are at first glance obscure. One cannot, in short, assess the exact significance of the numerous engraved stones of Lombard territory without understanding which groups promoted their manufacture, which technicians physically executed the incisions, and to what purpose or public they were directly or indirectly destined.

In an engaging article written in the 1950s, Gian Piero Bognetti highlighted the "poor techniques" of the slab sculpture of the early Lombard period, singling out and describing particularly the practice that decorations were now simply incised or scratched on stone slabs instead of being executed in relief. The slabs themselves usually bore both inscriptions and figural designs,[12] both tasks probably being assigned to the same workers, who were, according to Bognetti's persuasive hypothesis, humble stonecutters. Apparently, they must have introduced into decorative sculpture the same techniques of simple intaglio that they already used for lettering. The adoption of an intaglio technique exclusively based on the "stringcourse" cut (that is, with an incision perpendicular to the groove)[13] had notable consequences not only in the evolution of decorative sculpture of the early Lombard period, which completely lost the sense of relief and color, but also in the appearance and structure of lapidary writing in the same period and region. Since the first century A.D., classical Roman epigraphy had been based on the adoption of a "triangular cut" intaglio technique that permitted every stroke to be given a sense of depth, with consequently strong chiaroscural effects.[14] The stringcourse cut was a simpler and poorer technique that flattened completely the bright reliefs of lapidary writing and eliminated any chiaroscuro, lowering the coefficient of legibility as a result.

Such techniques certainly were not a novelty of Lombard Italy. They had precedents elsewhere and had been typical for centuries of nondeluxe, indigenous, military, and Christian production in every province of the empire; they had, in short, been adopted in every place and every occasion in which the commissioning party was not in a position to go to a lapidary workshop of a high technical level. But from the first century until at least the period we are dealing with, and especially in Italy, the other, more noble tradition had always survived alongside this modest production in the hands of an

12. "Storia, archeologia, e diritto nel problema dei Longobardi," in Bognetti, *L'età longobarda*, vol. 3, pp. 197–266 (orig. pub. 1952); on *graffito* or scratching techniques, see in particular pp. 204–09, 213–15.

13. For this intaglio technique, see G. Susini, *Il lapicida romano*, Archivio di Stato di Bologna, Quaderni della Scuola di Paleografia ed Archivistica, 9–12 (Bologna, 1964), pp. 40–41.

14. Ibid., pp. 40–42.

artisanate capable of using refined tools and a rather complex technique to prepare the slabs and to lay out and incise the epigraphic texts. At Rome, in particular, such techniques had been adopted in the late fourth century for Damasian epigraphy and, still later, for papal epigraphy of the fifth and sixth centuries.[15] At Pavia a small inscription of King Atalaric still reveals in the sixth century an elegant capacity for design of "rustic" capitals, reminiscent of the lettering of the Palatine and Roman Virgil,[16] coupled with a correct incisory technique.

With the Lombard invasion, the use of classical lapidary techniques disappears in the occupied territories, nor does one find there any longer epigraphs with triangularly grooved incisions. One can thus state that for the field of epigraphy, in a process analogous to what has been discovered about book production and to what Bognetti observed for sculpture, the establishment of the Lombard kingdom meant the disappearance of those few lapidary workshops that until then had managed to continue to function within the lay tradition. Their place was taken by simple stonecutters in the provincial or popular tradition—and not many of them—who in the changed social and economic circumstances still found some patrons prepared to seek out their services.

These patrons were now almost exclusively ecclesiastical, as one can see with even a glance at the text of the inscriptions that survive from the early Lombard period. Mostly they belonged to the urban secular clergy organized around the cathedral churches; in practice, this was the only organized order that had maintained some forms of direct familiarity with literary Latin and with the use of writing for religious and cultural purposes. For epigraphy, then, these clerics had the position of commissioning virtually all the inscriptions executed during these decades in the regions occupied by the Lombards. Unlike the situation in book production, however, they could not take the place of the old lay artisanate and perform all the steps in making inscriptions, down to the final carving of the material. In turning to the modest stonecutters then available, these ecclesiastical patrons probably furnished them with the text to be inscribed and perhaps in some cases a graphic rendering of it. This would explain the elegance, more appropriate to books

15. For the use of classical incising technique in Rome of the sixth century, see the comments of N. Gray, "The Filocalian Letter," *Papers of the British School at Rome* 24 (1956): 9–10. Also relevant is A. Silvagni, *Monumenta epigraphica christiana . . .* , vol. 1 (Città del Vaticano, 1943), pl. XI, pp. 7–8.

16. Reproduced in G. Panazza, "Catalogo delle iscrizioni e sculture paleocristiane e preromaniche di Pavia," in *Arte del primo Millennio. Atti del II Convegno per lo studio dell'arte dell'alto medio-evo* (Turin, 1950), n. 10, pl. LXXXIV, and in Silvagni, *Monumenta*, vol. 2, 3: *Papia* (Città del Vaticano, 1943), pls. 1, 3.

than stonework, of the design of some inscriptions, such as that of Agrippinus, bishop of Como,[17] which was probably based on a model designed by
some ecclesiastic with fine calligraphy. But clerics could neither ask of the
stonecutters nor teach them what they themselves did not know: the technique of *ordinatio* (layout) and the carving of triangular grooves, both of
which further required knowing how to use compass and straight-edge and
how to apply the rules of proportion between wide and narrow strokes that
regulated the design of individual letters in high-level epigraphy. Confirmation of the fact that the brusque cessation of the noble epigraphic tradition
in Lombard Italy was due to the new rulers is furnished by the survival of
this tradition in Rome, where at the beginning of the seventh century the
funeral inscriptions of Popes Gregory II and Sabinian still used refined techniques of intaglio and design.[18]

In early Lombard Italy, therefore, ecclesiastics were responsible for commissioning most inscriptions, while those who accomplished their physical
execution were, in all probability, laymen of a rather modest cultural level.
But what was the public for which these inscriptions were destined? Who
would have read them and how would they have received their message?

No one doubts the special solemnity of lapidary writing that, regardless
of epoch or environment, derives from its being on a "monument" and its
being on public display. As a result, an inscription always conveys a sacral
meaning, even when accompanied by an entirely independent aesthetic
meaning, that permits the transmission of specific expressive values beyond
the verbal message contained in the text. For the late antique world, in short,
the medium of epigraphy was a vehicle intrinsically suitable for diffusing
values, subjects, and discourse, mediated by a predominately figural language.
It thus could be used, more than books and almost as directly as pictorial or
sculptural representations, to convey a specific code of values to the illiterate
masses or semiliterate strata of the population. But, naturally, this was not
the only public for whom inscriptions were destined. Also targeted were the
social strata of the patrons themselves, who were capable of receiving both
types of discourse contained in the epigraphic medium: the verbal message,
transmitted by the text, and the figural message, transmitted by the general
appearance, the design of individuals elements, and ornaments. The epigraphy in early Lombard Italy, with a content that generally exalted the merits
of the deceased members of the religious community, thus potentially addressed a public made up of both city dwellers and rural people who peri-

17. Bognetti, "S. Maria," pp. 240–43 and pl. IX; repr. in Silvagni, *Monumenta*, 2, 2; *Comum*
(Città del Vaticano, 1943), pl. VIII, I.
18. See Silvagni, *Monumenta, Roma*, pl. II.3,4.

odically attended church, and especially those who worshipped in the cathedrals, and of the very clergy who wrote and had executed inscriptions as much for themselves as for the wider public. The fact that the clergy of early Lombard Italy did not manage to make frequent and elevated use of this expressive medium, nor of figural ones, thus demonstrates their restricted numbers, modest cultural powers, and general weakness during these hard and difficult decades when the Lombard occupation constrained ecclesiastical organizations to look first to their own survival.

Naturally, not all epigraphic production in early Lombard Italy was ecclesiastic. Eventually, at the beginning of the eighth century, a period markedly different from that we are presently considering, the Lombards did promote and develop a very distinctive epigraphic style that attained elevated aesthetic levels; I will return to it below. But during the long period preceding this epoch it appears that the Lombards had only meagerly contributed to epigraphic production in the regions they controlled. Like all the Germans, the Lombards must have been quite familiar with the value and significance of stones inscribed with relevant ornamentation; as has already been mentioned, runic writing was widely used in Germany for epigraphic purposes. Nevertheless, one finds not the least trace of funerary stone or of commemorative use of writing in their oldest Italian necropolises (Castel Trosino, Nocera Umbria). One must conclude that it was only after a certain period of contact with the populations, cities, clergy, and churches of Italy that some members of the Lombard ruling class finally learned the practice of celebrating the dead through inscriptions on slabs composed in Latin.

Despite their expertise in many arts implying complex and refined techniques, including niello and metal engraving, the Lombards were completely ignorant of Roman lapidary techniques, nor did their number include stonecutters able to cut Latin characters or ornamental techniques on stone or marble slabs. As a result, the rare personages who out of snobbery or simply a taste for imitation wished to have inscriptions made in the first decades of the occupation had to seek out that modest local artisanate that already served the Catholic church, being satisfied with the results that that artisanate could achieve. The inscriptions executed for Aldo in Milan[19] and for Wideramn at Castelseprio[20] thus present formal characteristics analogous to those of similar contemporary ecclesiastical inscriptions. Of the two, moreover, only Aldo's shows any tendency toward an elevated style in the writing,

19. See Bognetti, "S. Maria," pp. 408–09, with edition of the text, and pl. XI; repr. in Silvagni, *Monumenta*, II, 1: *Mediolanum* (Città del Vaticano, 1943), pl. XI, n. 3 (with attribution to the ninth century) and in *Storia di Milano*, vol. 2 (Milan, 1954), p. 139 fig.

20. See Bognetti, "S. Maria," pl. X; repr. also in Silvagni, *Monumenta*, 2, 2: *Comum*, pl. IX, 3 (with attribution to the sixth century), and *Storia di Milano*, vol. 2, p. 183 fig.

impagination, ornament, and even the design of the letters, thus anticipating (and it is entirely appropriate that it should come from seventh-century Milan) the new, properly Lombard epigraphic style that would dominate in the following century.

The finds of epigraphic materials related to King Agilulf are a different case. According to a suggestive hypothesis put forward by Bognetti,[21] Agilulf was the first Lombard chief actively to promote the romanization of the kingdom's institutions of government, probably under the influence of Roman ministers such as the famous Paul. This process is eloquently witnessed by two direct examples of inscriptions for royal use: the plate of Bargello with the inscription "Victuria" in capitals[22] and the clay tile with the seal of Agilulf and Adaloald in elegant relief capitals in Milan's Museo d'Arte Antica.[23] In both cases, it is likely that recourse was had to Roman artists still capable of producing figures and inscriptions by imitation of antique models—direct imitation in the case of the tile, indirect in the case of the plate. But beyond what such finds can tell us about the survival of specific techniques (and there were others that have not come down to us),[24] they also reveal that Agilulf proposed to use Roman epigraphic language for the affirmation and diffusion of specific ideological values that the grandeur, elegance, and sacrality of lapidary writing could express better than any other medium. In the Lombard world, this experiment for the moment remained limited to the "summer of the dead" promoted by Theodolinda.[25] But it had a great significance because it shows that the Lombard ruling class, which rallied around Agilulf and especially his Bavarian queen, meant to address the problem (which the church also confronted in these years) of how to convey institutions and public values (whether religious or governmental) to

21. Bognetti, "S. Maria," pp. 181–84 and 208–12.

22. For this famous work it is enough here to refer to Bognetti, "S. Maria," p. 211, who appraised the metal plate as a symbol of the Romanization of Agilulf's monarchy, and to M. Brozzi and A. Tagliaferri, *Arte longobarda*, vol. 1: *La scultura figurativa su marmo*, and vol. 2: *La scultura figurativa su metallo* (Cividale, 1961), pp. 16–17 and 133–35. A valuable addition to the bibliography is the article of A. Guillou, "Demography and Culture in the Exarchate of Ravenna," *Studi medievali* 3d ser. 10, no. 1 (1970): 210–213 and pl. 11. In addition to a suggestive summary of a series of archaeological finds traditionally considered Lombard, Guillou ventures to attribute the plate not to Agilulf but to Justinian II, relying on an interpretation of the inscription contained in the relic that is entirely new and quite different from that accepted until now.

23. Repr. in Silvagni, *Monumenta, Mediolanum,* pl. V, 2, and in Bognetti, "S. Maria," pl. VII.

24. One can recall, for example, the lost inscription on a crown offered to Agilulf. Formerly at the Cathedral of Monza, it was taken to France on order of Napoleon, where it was melted down. On this, see Bognetti, *Milano longobarda,* in *Storia di Milano* 2:121 (with drawing).

25. For this phenomenon see, in addition to Bognetti, P. Riché, *Education et culture dans l'Occident barbare. VIe–VIIe siècles* (Paris, 1962), pp. 385–87.

the illiterate masses and knew how to employ similarly graphico-figural means of communication to resolve it. Agilulf, in short, tried through the medium of epigraphy to recapture the ability to express sacred lay values, which previously had been the monopoly of imperial ideology. For this effort to succeed, however, he and his Roman councilors would have required a level of cultural adaptation to Roman tradition beyond what the Lombards had yet achieved or the Italian *rustici* still possessed. The failure of the "summer of the dead," which flourished only briefly in early Lombard Italy, should not, therefore, surprise anyone.

"Igitur Alboin cum ad fluvium Plabem venisset, ibi ei Felix episcopus Tarvisianae ecclesiae occurrit. Cui rex, ut erat largissimus, omnes suae ecclesiae facultates postulanti concessit et *per suum pracmaticum postulata firmavit*" (Thus when Alboin came to the Piave river, he was met there by Felix, bishop of Treviso. To whom the king, since he was generous, conceded all the property of his church, and confirmed the requests by a document).[26] This notice of Paul the Deacon, whose veracity there seems no reason to doubt, reveals a fact of notable importance: that since the first dramatic moments of the invasion the king, and thus the ruling group of Lombards, admitted at least publicly the possibility and practice of written documentation. Although no actual documents survive from the early period of occupation,[27] these practices are confirmed by the indirect evidence I shall discuss. Before doing so, however, it will be valuable to consider the extent to which it is possible to distinguish accurately one period from another, one environment from another, and public documents from private.

Learning to use written documents doubtless represents the most significant episode of the assimilation by the first Lombard kings of some of the tools of Roman civilization; Theodolinda's "summer of the dead" marked the culmination of the first phase of this process. But the fact that Alboin issued a *pracmaticum*, or that Agilulf and Adoloald had royal notaries in their entourage,[28] certainly does not permit us to conclude that the Lombard kings possessed a functioning chancery or that they commonly employed a coherent system of public written documentation in the administration of their kingdom. This is especially true since, as is well known, no original royal

26. *Historiae Langobardorum*, 2.12, in *MGH, Scriptores rerum langobardorum*, ed. G. Waitz (Hanover, 1878), p. 79.

27. The earliest genuine document to survive from Lombard-ruled territories is from around 650: L. Schiaparelli, *Codice diplomatico longobardo*, vol. 1, Fonti per la storia d'Italia dell'Istituto Storico Italiano, 62 (Rome, 1909), no. 4, pp. 8–11.

28. See L. Schiaparelli, "Note diplomatiche sulle carte longobarde, 1: I notai nell'età longobarda," in *Archivio storico italiano* ser. 7, no. 17 (1932): 18–19.

Lombard document comes down to us, even for the seventh and eighth centuries.[29] Lacking direct evidence, but by analogy with practices in coinage and epigraphy, one could perhaps advance the hypothesis that in the early Lombard period, until the middle of the seventh century, the kings had resorted to written documentation not because administrative exigencies actually demanded it, but only when issuing privileges that had been requested by (and conceded to) those subjects who remained actively and passively tied to written culture: the Catholic clergy. In short, it may well be that authentically royal documentation really existed only for this purpose: for motives and recipients that remained substantially apart from the culture and customs of the German ruling class.

But beyond the evidence relative to royal documents, there are also references to the existence of private documentation in the *Edictus* of Rothari. Despite the fact that the *Edictus* itself is obvious proof that before its issuance the Lombards lived and governed in ignorance of the practice of writing at least in certain aspects of social life,[30] it does confirm that within the territories of the Lombard kingdom the use of written documents was expected for some types of legal relations between private individuals. Indeed, not only does the *Edictus* include a chapter (chap. 243) entitled "De cartola falsa" (Of false charters), which provided for a forger to lose a hand—the same penalty as for a counterfeiter;[31] but the written document, variously described as a *cartola* or *libellus*, is mentioned with regard to *thingatio* and sale,[32] even if it was not accorded a value that excluded other oral or symbolic forms of documentation. On the other hand, Rothari says not a word in the *Edictus* that would indicate the existence of a category of public scribes responsible for drafting written documents for private use.

29. The essential elements relating to the documentation and related bibliography may be found in G. Cencetti, "Dall'unità al particolarismo grafico. Le scritture cancelleresche romane e quelle dell'alto medioevo," in *Il passaggio dall'antichità al medioevo in Occidente* (Spoleto, 1962), p. 259, and especially in C. Brühl, *Studien zu den langobardischen Königsurkunden*, Bibliothek des Deutschen Historischen Instituts in Rom, 33 (Tübingen, 1970), passim. But it should be kept in mind that for our purposes the presumed original of Astulf of 755 is without question a contemporary copy, because it lacks any external characteristics to solemnize it, as in my opinion certainly would have appeared in an original produced by the eighth-century Lombard royal chancery. See Brühl, *Studien*, pp. 150–52 and pl. 2; and *Codice diplomatico longobardo*, III, 1, ed. C. Brühl, Fonti per la storia d'Italia, 64 (Rome, 1973), pp. 174–76.

30. For the problems posed by the *Edictus* and for its significance from a juristic, political, and cultural point of view, it is enough to refer to Riché, *Education et culture*, pp. 387–88, and especially to G. P. Bognetti, "L'editto di Rotari," in *L'età longobarda*, vol. 4 (Milan, 1968), pp. 113–35.

31. *Edictus Rothari*, ed. F. Bluhme, *MGH*, *Leges*, vol. 4 (Hanover, 1868), n. 243, p. 60; for counterfeiters, ibid., n. 242.

32. Chaps. 224 and 227, pp. 55, 56

In all likelihood this means that, while the ancient tabellionary *scholae* had disappeared from early Lombard Italy, no distinct category of notaries had yet arisen.[33] By extension, it can only have occurred irregularly, in population centers and above all around religious institutions, that there gathered groups of people, lay and ecclesiastic, who possessed the minimal elementary instruction and notion of law needed to draft the written testimony of any legal act or agreement. These people must have shared an embryonic professional culture based principally on a more or less elementary capacity to write in the "new cursive" and to adopt a certain legal formula, known directly or indirectly,[34] following traditional schemes of broadly Roman ancestry.

The principal element of this professional culture must have been above all the written language: the very Latin of Rothari's *Edictus*. This language is often improperly compared at the literary level to other quite different contemporary examples,[35] despite the fact that it represents the fruit of an autonomous elaboration of a practical linguistic instrument for documentary purposes by a semi-educated—for such they were—professional category of jurists and scribes that was still being formed in early Lombard Italy. Comparing this Latin, objectively uncertain, incorrect, and stratified by different influences, with the ecclesiastical language of inscriptions or the curial Latin of letters, is nonsense. Although the inscription of Agrippinus or the letter of Giovanni, patriarch of Aquileia, which Bognetti chose as examples of cultivated Latin, indeed belong to the same regions and period, the cultural environments that produced them were totally different from that associated with Rothari and his army which produced the *Edictus*. Lacking manuscripts contemporary with the text prevents us from taking the next step in the analysis, which would have juxtaposed the linguistic and graphic facts. But in my opinion, two cultures as different *ab origine* as the cultured ecclesiastics and semicultured laymen would have found expression in different writing: the bookhands appropriate to the classical tradition, on the one hand, and on the other the more or less fluid forms of the new documentary cursive. This perhaps could be documented for the later period.

The evidence thus far collected and the inferences we have drawn from them make it clear that for the first decades and perhaps the first century of their rule in Italy, the ruling Lombard groups expressed an uncertain and contradictory political line with respect to the problem of written documents.

33. See Schiaparelli, "Note," pp. 4, 28.
34. See ibid., p. 28.
35. Thus Bognetti, "S. Maria," p. 308, and "I capitoli 144 e 145 di Rotari ed il rapporto tra Como ed i 'Magistri Commacini,'" in *L'età langobarda*, vol. 4, pp. 445–47.

On one hand, the use of writing was unknown and rejected; on the other it was admitted and in a certain sense controlled, although to be sure not officially taken up at the level of the state. This lack of coherence, which although less obviously apparent was also discovered in the analysis of early Lombard coinage and epigraphy, in all likelihood arose from a genuine incapacity to control all aspects of Italian social life on the part of the Lombard governing class: they neither wished nor knew how to use means other than force to impose their own culture and style of life on the subject Italian populations. Within these populations, there either remained or were formed groups of Romans, composed of urban artisans, merchants, and, especially, clergy, who were neither rustici nor illiterate nor personally subject to the Lombards; these groups, by tradition and by the objective demands of the community life—whether civic or within the supernational community of the Church—continued to feel the need for written documents to regulate the legal relationships. The Lombards felt the existence of such exigencies and recognized their legitimacy, even if throughout the early Lombard period they refused to draw the necessary conclusions at the level of legislation. Only in 643 did Rothari, probably for reasons that were purely political,[36] have the royal notary Ansoald assemble a mixture of Germanic law and Roman customs into a written corpus. With this act he also sanctioned the official recognition of written documentation and probably invited Lombards, if only indirectly, to employ it, perhaps for the first time and certainly more widely than they would have done in the past.

The uncertainties and contradictions that characterize the Lombards' various efforts to use some of the instruments of Roman written culture testify to a situation entirely new compared to the late empire or Gothic kingdom. With the installation of the *regnum* of the Lombards, in fact, for the first time in Italy a substantially illiterate ruling class held power itself without delegating it to functionaries possessed of technical qualifications—Romans—and exercised it with practically no use of writing. When they needed writing— for coinage, inscriptions, or documents—they had recourse to technicians, nearly always Romans (the number of Lombards must have been minimal), who had the skills to execute work of artisanal character for a price; the very fact that this work was treated like servile and socially inferior trades must have deprived it of any great dignity. How different this is from the official ideology of the Italy of Cassiodorus and Ennodius, in which the Roman aristocracy survived by transforming itself into the bureaucracy, and thus an indispensable structure of the Gothic state, precisely by virtue of the graphic-cultural functions of which it was the repository.

36. According to Bognetti's hypotheses; see "Editto."

Although this overthrow of values was virtually complete, even if tempered in practice by compromises and contradictions, it did not extend to the world of ecclesiastical culture and thus that of books; toward these, the Lombards themselves maintained an attitude of consideration and admiration, even admitting their utility within the cultural sphere. But the alienation of the Lombard ruling class from the culture of the written, and the fact that this culture at a merely utilitarian and instrumental level was now in the hands of inferior categories of technicians who by both dignity and environment were greatly separated from the ecclesiastical culture dedicated to books, meant more than an overthrow of cultural values without precedent in European history. It constituted as well a formative event with profound consequences for the cultural, linguistic, artistic, and graphic history of Lombard Italy.

Limiting the discussion to the field of graphics, which is my main interest, it is obvious that a situation of the kind that we have traced (in an admittedly summary fashion) must have led to the creation of additional categories of artisans, for the most part lay in origin, who possessed specific writing techniques applicable within the scope of their crafts as stonecutters, moneyers, scribes, and royal notaries. These artisans seem to have lacked any ties with each other at either the practical or intellectual level; but they especially lacked any effective or substantial ties with the contemporary school and book culture. The overthrow of prestige introduced by the Lombards in Italian cultural life had, in short, irreparably lacerated the connective tissue of a single culture, neither lay nor ecclesiastic. Until the second half of the sixth century, this culture had been utilized, at different levels and in different modes, by all those who used writing in any way. But it scarcely seems extreme to affirm that, by the seventh century, the culture of a moneyer and that of a writer of documents in Lombard Italy would have developed according to experiences and paradigms distinct from one another and, still more markedly, totally different from the experiences and paradigms that the monastic scribe of Bobbio or the amanuensis of the Cathedral of Verona would have had. The substantial rejection of the civilization of the written accomplished by the Lombard ruling class thus provoked in Italy a phenomenon of "disassociation of written culture." This favored the separation not only of book culture from that of the document but also of lay culture from that of ecclesiastics. The result was the creation of graphic traditions and cultural independence in every sector in which writing was applied: a particularism, in short, defined not only geographically but vertically, within the social fabric, separating environments, categories, functions, and individuals from each other.

Even the ecclesiastical culture of Lombard Italy could not but feel the effects of this traumatic separation and isolation from other sectors of social life. It was, indeed, in those regions and at that time that schools, activities, and the book production of religious centers show themselves to be wasted, disorganized, and poor. It was not by chance that in 593, writing to Theodolinda in reference to a schismatic cleric of Lombard Italy, Gregory the Great used the expression "qui dum neque legunt neque legentibus credunt" (who, while they neither read nor believe readers),[37] counterposing, with notable polemic force, an Italy in which there still existed a category of educated men, the *legentes,* to an uneducated Italy of non-*legentes.*

---

37. Gregory I, *Registrum epistolarum,* I.IV, 4, ed. P. Erxald and L. M. Hartmann, vol. 1, *MGH, Epist.* I (Berlin, 1891), p. 236; the passage is noted by Bognetti, "S. Maria," p. 226.

4

Book, Handwriting, and School

IN MY OPINION, THERE CAN be no doubt that the Western European book changed both its appearance and its nature between the sixth and eighth centuries. Skeptics, if there were any, could easily be persuaded by placing the Medicean Virgil next to the Amiatina Bible. The juxtaposition of the squarish, modestly proportioned ancient codex, with its sober but elegant writing, and the enormous early medieval volume—so heavy that two people are needed to move it and lettered with a monumental uncial script more drawn than written—would clearly demonstrate how between the end of the fifth century and the end of the seventh, one had passed from a kind of book intended to be an instrument of reading and bearer of culture to a different, opposed kind of book experienced or seen rather as a precious chest of mysteries and at times even itself venerated as a cult object.

But it was not only the external appearance of the book that was modified in these centuries. Equally changed were the internal links between script and book, including the hierarchy of scripts that the Latin world had slowly elaborated. This hierarchy still functioned during the fifth and sixth centuries, assigning a specific function to each graphic style by tying it on one side to a precise repertory of subject matter and on the other to a certain category of public. In the seventh century, however, this delicate series of balances that had linked together literary production, book production, graphic elaboration, and public in a reciprocal relationship of influence was

Originally published as "Libro, scrittura e scuola," in *La scuola nell'Occidente latino dell'alto medioevo*, XIX Settimana di studi sull'alto medioevo (Spoleto, 1972), pp. 313–37 and pls. 1–6.

definitively interrupted, resulting in profound modifications of all the elements. Particularly affected were those that concern us most directly: graphic elaboration and the production of the book. Uncial became clearly prevalent over other scripts, especially in Italy where, calculating on the basis of data offered by the *CLA*, its usage reached a level of 73 percent. One has the impression, too, that no one was concerned to respect the once customary correspondences between text and graphic type, or that these were simply unknown; indeed, some phenomena appear for the first time, including using the same codex to contain texts of varied nature and using different scripts in the same manuscript or even on the same page. It was precisely in this period that new graphic types elaborated from the single ancient model in a process both complex and varying from place to place—the "new common script" or, in short, minuscule—were introduced into book production in a tumultuously experimental manner. It would require a long period before this phase of free experimentation, which at the outset actually seemed to reject the graphic values of the past, could give rise to a new, ordered hierarchy of script types.

By the second half of the sixth century, graphic elaboration and book production were already exclusively the domain of new ecclesiastical writing centers very different from the lay, artisanal, and urban workshops of the ancient world. But even among these new centers there was great variation. Indeed, it is very likely that there was no single model of a "writing center" before the ninth and tenth centuries, with codices being instead produced in circumstances and by processes that varied considerably depending on environment and region. One can recall Giorgio Cencetti's distinction between "writing place" and "scriptorium" that elucidated in an exemplary manner the difference between true scriptoria—where the production of books conformed to a single standard extending to the graphic level, the productive process being overseen by a single directing personality—and places where the scribes were essentially free to write as they wished and in the types of scripts they were used to, without either instruction in calligraphy or the application of precise norms.[1] But my impression is that, apart from monasteries where a certain exterior uniformity had to exist even in the absence of a more organized plan, book production in cathedrals, minor urban churches, and in general among the secular clergy occurred in a variety of ways that often probably precluded any form of common organized center. One cannot even exclude a priori the possibility that some codices were produced for use by an individual or a restricted group. But if it is true that

---

1. "Scriptoria e scritture nel monachesimo benedettino," in *Il monachesimo nell'alto medioevo e la formazione della civiltà occidentale* (Spoleto, 1957), pp. 187–219, esp. 196–97.

no specific script was taught in most scriptoria, at least in Italy and France, and to that extent one cannot speak of true and proper scriptoria, it is nonetheless helpful to clarify where and how the scribes working in these more or less open centers acquired their basic instruction in graphics and where they learned to write the kinds of script that they adopted for their work. This is also a problem that lays bare the tight connections linking the production of the early medieval book to the mechanisms for learning graphics and the organization of the schools.

There were essentially two ways of learning a book hand in the early Middle Ages: teaching and imitation. Actually, these two processes cannot always be clearly distinguished, because imitation was often part of teaching, and teaching, in turn, was based on imitation. But there was a difference between the two procedures that rested precisely on the organization of elementary teaching.

Foundation scripts—that is, those taught with the first rudiments of education in the primary schools of a monastery or cathedral or a notarial *statio*—were taught through the simple process of having a master draw models of letters and then one or more words, according to an ancient system that remained practically unchanged for centuries. These foundation, or elementary, scripts not only became the usual script of semiliterates of the early Middle Ages but often constituted the basis on which were elaborated specific scripts adopted for documents or books. As we will see, in essence they consisted of either simplified kinds of new cursive or simplifications of local book hands themselves. The mediating mechanism by which these scripts were taken up for book production was very simple, because by their very structure they were susceptible to many transformations. Beginning from the elementary script that formed his basic graphic patrimony, any scribe could with little effort elaborate or adopt it for books, either by his personal adaptations or under the directions given him by a calligraphy master. We are used to considering the resulting nontypical early medieval scripts as belonging to sometimes cursive, sometimes semi-uncial, and sometimes uncial graphic matrices; in reality, however, they rest on scripts of elementary instruction and use. Naturally, the scribe applied an even simpler mechanism to the use of local graphic types whose first rudiments he had already acquired at the elementary level. As Bischoff has shown, second-level instruction taught in the "scriptorium" was based in every case on a series of repeated calligraphical tests and exercises in the imitation of models drawn by a calligraphy master.[2] But although imitation occurred here as one of the

2. "Elementarunterricht und Probationes pennae in der ersten Häfte des Mittelalter," in *Classical and Medieval Studies in Honor of E. K. Rand* (New York, 1938); repr. in *Mittelalterliche*

tools of the didactic process, taking up a portion of the time involved given over to formal instruction, it occupied only an occasional and subordinate role. Thus we can make the claim that documentary or book hands born from processes of this kind should all be considered, from a genetic point of view, as "taught scripts."

Contrasting with these scripts are those book hands of entirely different origin that we can term "imitated." These are the scripts such as uncial or semi-uncial that perpetuate without interruption an ancient graphic type that itself was based on stylistic canons formed much earlier. The didactic tradition of these scripts was interrupted toward the middle of the sixth century by the dispersion of the lay artisanal book scribes and the death of the workshops that produced codices "in the ancient style": the two phenomena, in short, that led to the birth of the early medieval codex. With the disappearance of this coherent artisanal tradition, which had kept alive the canons of ancient writing by teaching them, its place had to be taken within the circles of ecclesiastical scribes by the direct imitation of models of various ages—basically, whatever codices were brought in or preserved locally. This kind of imitative work was developed by means of exercises that were repeated many times and, at least in some cases, under the guidance of a master. In this case, however, instruction was intended to support imitation.

The influence on early medieval book production of the codices that served as concrete models of canons to be imitated has not been given the consideration it deserves. The phenomenon suggests, however, two lines of inquiry. The first has to do with the motivations directing the imitative process, that is, the mentality of those who carried it out. The second concerns the deliberate creation and distribution of graphic and book models that were undertaken by some great centers operating mainly in the wake of the ancient tradition.

A concrete example will permit us to illuminate at least partially the issues related to these two classes of phenomena. As a case study, I have chosen the imitation of the uncial of Roman origin that occurred in English uncial

---

Studien (Stuttgart, 1966–81), vol. 1, pp. 74–87. See also the additional documentation of Natale, "Esercizi di calligafia insulare in codici del secolo VIII (Nota paleografica)," in *Archivio storico italiano* 116 (1958): 3–23.

To clarify the fundamental difference between "taught scripts" and "imitated scripts," it perhaps suffices to observe that in the relationship of these scripts to their models (real or ideal, but necessarily existing), the former are characterized by the necessary repetition of the mechanism of tracing (structure) of individual graphic signs, while the repetition of the form (i.e., the design) can be done less; the latter, in contrast, are based on the repetition of the design (i.e., the form) of individual signs, at times achieved by a tracing that may not be (and thus almost never is) the norm of the model.

5. Biblioteca Apostolica Vaticana, Vat. lat. 3835, fol. 39v

of the seventh and eighth centuries,[3] particularly in the Amiatina Bible that I mentioned at the outset as a typical example of early medieval codices. Between the sixth and eighth centuries, Rome not only undertook the necessary work of distributing ancient manuscripts throughout Western Europe but also produced a certain number of new codices in a monumental uncial with calligraphy of a high standard enriched with some characteristic ornamental elements. Testifying to this graphic type are three well-known codices that for some time have been attributed to Rome (fig. 5): the exemplar of

3. For Roman uncial and its imitation, see my article "L'onciale romana. Origini, sviluppo e diffusione di una stilizzazione grafica altomedievale (sec. VI–IX)," in *Studi medievali* 3d ser. 12 (1971): 73–134.

Gregory the Great's *Regula pastoralis,* written in Gregory's own time, preserved in the Bibliothèque Municipale of Troyes (*CLA* 838); the monumental *Homilarium* written by the priest Agimund for the basilica of the Holy Twelve Apostles in Rome at the beginning of the eighth century, now Vat. lat. 3835 and 3836 (*CLA* 18; and finally the rich *Evangelarium* offered by deacon Giovenianus to the Roman Basilica of S. Lorenzo at the beginning of the ninth century, now Vallicelliano B 25² (*CLA* 430). The comparison of these Roman codices—in which the local style, characterized by the forking of the horizontal strokes of some letters and by other minor elements, appears to have survived from Gregorian to Carolingian times—with other uncial manuscripts of Italian origin has permitted me to identify a sizable number of manuscripts with analogous graphic characteristics, presumably produced in various centers and environments in and around Rome. For the most part these are deluxe manuscripts, preferably containing liturgical texts, papal works, and patristic literature.

There are at least three reasons why these luxurious codices were requested everywhere and everywhere received as books—exemplars in the narrow sense. In the first place, Rome used this means to furnish the official rules of liturgy and ecclesiastical chant. Further, because only Rome preserved authentic versions of certain categories of texts, including conciliar acts and papal works, it thus became the sole supplier of books on those subjects. Finally, the very graphical and ornamental excellence of the codices meant that they ended up automatically taking over the function of serving as a model for book production. This process was assisted by the fact that roman uncial—highly artificial in design, large in scale, and rich in ornamental elements—lent itself easily to imitation and copying.

That English uncial derived from Italian models is now certain. In regard to the Amiatina Bible in particular, moreover, Bernhard Bischoff has isolated with great acumen the possible model of its textual uncial in the type of uncial found in an Augustinian fragment of the seventh century, B.N. lat. 1596.[4] This handsome example of monumental uncial reveals exactly the same graphic characteristics as the *Homeliarium* of Agiumundus; in my opinion, it constitutes one of the best examples of roman uncial. Evidently, the seven or eight scribes of the Amiatina Bible, wishing to adopt a script of great dignity and elegance, had looked for and found their model in some of the Roman codices that Benedict Biscop had imported into England some years earlier. The factors that opened the way for a process of imitation are thus

---

4. "Anzeige von E. A. Lowe, English Uncial," in *Gnomon* 34 (1962): 605–15 (repr. in *Mittelalterliche Studien,* 2:328–39) and pls. IX and XI.

multiple: first, the existence of models regarded as exemplary and originating in a prestigious distribution center; second, the desire to adopt a script of ancient tradition; and, last, the presence of scribes capable of adopting a more or less refined technique of graphic imitation.

This last factor must not be overlooked. Any scribe able to copy at sight an "imitated" script had to do so despite his hand's being accustomed *ab origine* to a different basic script: in effect, he had to be able to write at least two scripts. This conclusion brings us back from the processes of graphic imitation and instruction, and from imitated scripts, to those typical of graphic particularism that we have defined as being founded in the elementary writing of the primary schools. We can imagine these scripts, which are still to be defined in paleographical terms, as a graphic substratum common to all those who knew how to write within a vast territorial area, regardless of the cultural level to which they belonged. But how numerous were they? And who were they? And what kinds of foundation scripts were they taught? These are some of the important issues to which we will try to give a preliminary answer after clarifying how graphic instruction worked and what were the fundamental characteristics of the script that was the first product of that instruction.

In an inaugural address given to the Spoleto Settimana di Studi sull'Alto Medio Evo in 1963, Roberto Lopez observed: "In a meeting such as this it is inevitable that attention will be concentrated on phenomena positively dated and documented and thus on the culture of elites. If we are to concern ourself with elites, we must, at least, do our best to count them. Using the few thousand charters that are left to us—not so few, let us note—it would be convenient to make a census of those who could write: an aristocracy of the pen that is certainly more distinct and probably rarer than the aristocracy of the sword. Only in this way can we assign some proportional dimensions (as I borrow Dante's phrase) 'al poco giorno ed al gran cerchio d'ombra.' "[5] In this spirit, necessarily limited to the rather small number of sources that survive and are accessible, I have tried to sketch Lopez's projected census for the seventh and eighth centuries. I base my results on autograph subscriptions to original documents, and on their ratio with the nonautograph subscriptions. Naturally, I can here provide only the results of this work, without other documentation; I thus must rely on the benevolent courtesy of my reader to take my word for what I shall report.

With regard to the seventh century, the scarcity of the evidence means that one cannot speak of a census so much as of a series of generally suggestive data,

---

5. In *Centri e vie di irradiazione della civiltà nell'alto medioevo* (Spoleto, 1964), pp. 21–22. The quotation from Dante translates: "to the little daylight and the great circle of shadow."

more numerous for France than for Italy. For Merovingian France, the examination of eight certainly original documents scattered between the years 654 and about 700 gives a total figure of 138 subscribers; of these, only 37 did not sign for themselves and can be considered illiterate, while 101 executed the whole subscription in their own hand.[6] None of the illiterates are ecclesiastics and two are women. Of the literate, 53 are lay, 37 ecclesiastics, 9 are of uncertain status, and 2 are women. Do these data constitute a partial confirmation of Pirenne's famous thesis about the existence of an extensive and lively lay culture in Merovingian France?[7] Perhaps. But it may be more prudent to say only that they show that no ecclesiastic was illiterate and that a certain graphic instruction was taught even to women. The percentage of lay male literacy—about 60 percent and thus quite high—should be used with great prudence and considered only as indicating that a notable knowledge of writing must have been diffused throughout the Merovingian upper aristocracy.

For seventh-century Italy there are eight papyrus documents, seven from Ravenna and one from Rome, giving a perspective on the diffusion of literacy that is territorially and numerically rather partial.[8] Of the total of 35 sub-

6. The eight original Merovingian documents examined for seventh-century autograph subscriptions are as follows: 1) Diploma of Chlodovech II, 22 June 654. Ph. Lauer and Ch. Samaran, *Les diplomes originaux des rois Mérovingiens* (Paris, 1908), pp. 6–7 and pls. 6–6 *bis*. 2) Foundation act of Chlotilde, 10 March 673. Paris, Archives Nationales (AN), Trésor des Chartes, K 2 n. 10; A. Letronne, *Diplomata et chartae merovingicae aetatis in Archivio Franciae osservata* (Paris, 1851), pl. XIV; J. Tardif, *Monuments historiques. Cartons des rois* (Paris, 1866), n. 19; L. Levillain, "Etudes mérovingiennes. La charte de Chlotilde (10 mars 673)," in *Bibliothèque de l'Ecole des Chartes* 105 (1944): 5–63. 3) Donation of Vandemirus and Ercamberta of 689–90. Paris, AN, Trésor des Chartes, K 3 n. 2²; Tardif, *Monuments*, n. 25 *bis*. 4) Testament of the son of Idda, ca. 690. Paris, AN, Trésor des Chartes, K 3 n. 1; Tardif, *Monuments*, n. 26. 5) Exchange between the abbey of St. Germain-des-Prés and the abbey of Tussouval, ca. 691. Paris, AN, Trésor des Chartes, K 2 n. 9; Letronne, *Diplomata*, n. 23; Tardif, *Monuments*, n. 29. 6) Privilege of Ageradus, bishop of Chartres, of 6 March 696. Paris, AN, Trésor des Chartes, K 3 n. 11; Tardif, *Monuments*, n. 36. 7) Exchange between the abbey of St. Germain-des-Prés and Adalricus, of 25 April 697. Paris, AN, Trésor des Chartes, K 3 n. 12²; Letronne, *Diplomata*, n. 33 *bis*; Tardif, *Monuments*, n. 39; R. Poupardin, *Recueil des chartes de l'abbaye de Saint Germain-des-Prés*, vol. 1 (Paris, 1909), no. XI, pp. 18–19. 8) Testament of Ermintruda ca. 700. Paris, AN, Trésor des Chartes, K 4 n. 1; Tardif, *Monuments*, n. 40.

I have examined all these documents in original in Paris. I have not taken into consideration for this survey the other donation of Vandemirus and Ercamberta attributed to 682–83 (Paris, AN, Trésor des Chartes, K 4 n. 5; Letronne, *Diplomata*, n. 44; Poupardin, *Recueil*, n. IX, pp. 13–14), which is probably a second original or contemporary copy because the subscriptions of the text and of the authors of the acts are in the hand of the *rogatarius* while the document of 689–90 bears autographs.

7. "De l'état de l'instruction des laïques à l'époque mérovingienne," in *Revue bénédictine* 48 (1934): 164–77; see also P. Riché, "L'instruction des laïques en Gaule mérovingienne au VIIe siècle," in *Caratteri del secolo VII in Occidente* (Spoleto, 1958), pp. 873–88.

8. These eight documents are J. O. Tjäder, *Die nichtliterarischen lateinischen Papyri Italiens aus der Zeit 445–770, I & Tafeln* (Lund, 1954–55) (Acta Instituti Romani Regni Sueciae, s. in

scribers, only 3 are illiterate and 2 of these were women. Of the other 32, 3 are ecclesiastics and 28 are lay, almost all of them claiming some official qualifications. Three signed in Latin but using Greek characters. What can be deduced from these figures? Actually, far less that what can be gained from French documents—perhaps only that in the larger centers of non-Lombard Italy graphic instruction was diffused in a way analogous to that encountered for the same period in Merovingian France.

In the eighth century, the size and quality of surviving documentation usable for our purposes change a great deal. For France, the rather few original documents that come down to us cannot in my opinion be taken into consideration, because the high number of nonautograph subscriptions that characterizes them is due more to a diplomatic practice, specifically the frequent intervention of the drafter in the signatures of the witnesses, than to an unexpected decline in the percentage of literates. This interpretation appears confirmed by the fact that, in the French documents of the eighth century that I have been able to consult in the originals, the overwhelming majority even of the *signa crucis* are in the hands of the drafters. For Italy, the panorama is clearly different. Although usable documents are lacking from byzantine regions, Schiaparelli's *CDL* offers us a precious tool for the Lombard ones. As we know, the material included in this tool has precise limits both territorial, since it is limited to the Lombard kingdom, or Regnum, and chronological, since the originals therein span the years 720 to 774. Nevertheless, because of the abundance and reliability of the data included, it permits a genuine census of what Lopez called the "aristocracy of the pen" at least as concerns Tuscia and Lombardia in the mid-eighth century.

In the 180 originals examined, I counted 988 subscriptions in all; of these, 633 belonged to laymen and 355 to religious.[9] Autograph subscriptions totaled 326, while those of the drafter with *signum*, sometimes autograph and sometimes not, came to 662. The percentage of autograph subscriptions is thus 32.7 percent of the total, a figure that is notably high. In this regard, it must be remembered that usually, even if not always or everywhere, the witnesses were chosen from the higher rather than lower or bottom strata of the community; thus, this percentage must be understood not relative to all the adult men of the *regnum* (no literate women appear among the subscribers) but only to those belonging to the higher social levels. Of lay subscribers, the number of autograph subscriptions is 93, making 9 percent of the total and

---

4°, XIX, 1 & 3), nos. 16 (= *ChLA* n. 240), 18–19, 20, 22, 23, 24, 25, 28 (= *ChLA* n. 232).

9. "Scrittura e libro nell'Italia altomedievale," *Studi medievali* 3d ser., 10 (1969): 157–213 and 14 (1973): 961–1002 (= Chaps. 3 and 4 above).

14 percent of the lay subscriptions. The percentage of literacy is much higher among the religious, reaching 23 percent of the total and 65 percent of all religious subscribers (355). Religious able to write make up 71 percent of all literates.

Restricting the investigation to the territory of Lucca, which is adequately documented for the entire period covered by the *CDL*, the percentage of general literacy rises to 36.8, with clerical literacy reaching 63 percent and lay literacy 16 percent. If one separates out the data for the city alone (to the extent that this is possible), the percentage of literacy reaches 43, with the percentage of clerical literacy still about 62. Conversely, the data relative to minor centers of the countryside show an overall level of literacy of 25.5 percent, dropping to 11 percent for the laity, while still at the high level of 66 percent for the clergy. A rather different situation prevailed at Varsi, a small center in Emilia situated near the Ceno between Parma and Bobbio, which seems to have had only one person to draft documents, the *vir clarissimus* Maurace. In fact, he is the only literate laymen in the town, and apart from him only the four clerics who appear as witnesses knew how to write; the other twenty-three subscribers, including three women, were all illiterate.

If the general conclusions that can be drawn from this data, which I have briefly summarized and which ought to be sifted and thoroughly exploited, are fairly obvious and, I would say, not at all surprising, they have at least the value of resting for the first time on something concrete. We can list them in this order:

1. In mid-eighth-century Lombard Italy there existed a certain diffusion of knowledge of writing among the middle and upper groups of society; however, women were completely excluded from it.
2. The clear majority of ecclesiastics, whether from small centers or from cities, were literate.
3. In the countryside and in minor centers, one encounters a clear decline in literacy compared to larger centers.
4. Among laymen, it does not appear that the diffusion of literacy was tied to particular functions or occupations. One finds royal functionaries, moneyers, and goldsmiths among the illiterate, but also among the literate. One must note, however, that the five subscribers described as artisans (a smith, a *magister murorum*, a *magister commacinus*, a shoemaker, a coppersmith) are all illiterate.

That said, we are now in a position to return to the fact that 32.7 percent of 988 subscribers were literate. But what were the kinds of scripts that they had learned and knew how to use? What relation can we establish between these scripts of daily use and the contemporary documentary and book scripts of Lombard Italy? Finally, what can we deduce from these scripts about the nature and characters of those elementary foundation scripts I mentioned above?

At this point, numbers provide little help: we need images. For this occasion, I have chosen six documents out of the embarrassment of riches available. Of these, two were drafted at Chiusi, two at Lucca, one in the area around Pisa, and one from Campione, at the extreme northern limits of Longobardia. All six documents fall between 746 and 771 (fig. 6).

1. The first document is a *charta venditionis* drafted at Chiusi between September 746 and August 747 (*CDL* 92; *ChLA* 734). Seven subscribers appear, of whom three are illiterate and three can sign for themselves: Cuniradu, Gairmundus, and Vuarnicausus, who all used a minuscule with the separated individual elements and rare ligatures of the new cursive: *ra, te, ti*.

2. The second document is a *charta repromissionis* drafted at Lucca between September 749 and June 750 by the priest Gaudentius (*CDL* 99; *ChLA* 931). The subscribers are all clerics. Of them, Tanoaldus, priest, and Magnipertus, priest, use a minuscule with rare ligatures; Sisimundus, priest, and Peredeus, deacon (who would later become bishop of Lucca), adopted an elegant new cursive with chancery elements.

3. The third document is a charta venditionis drafted at Campione d'Italia on 25 October 756 (*CDL* 123; *ChLA* 849) and bearing three autograph subscriptions of laymen in a rough minuscule with some ligatures; Natale argued for some Merovingian elements (*t, e*) in the writing of Arochi and Guatpert.[10]

4. The fourth document is a charta donationis drafted at Lucca on 25 December 765 (*CDL* 193; *ChLA* 988) to which subscribed, in addition to the *rogatarius* and his master (both of whom were lay), three illiterate laymen and four literates—three priests and a layman. Two of these subscribers, Arnicausu and Alvartu, used a dissociated minuscule with some cursive elements; the other two priests, Teuspert and Prandulus, used a minuscule with formal ductus; Teuspert even had recourse to a capital *R*.

5. Constituting the fifth example is a *charta offersionis* drafted at

---

10. A. R. Natale, "Note paleografiche sulle carte private della Svizzera italiana nell'alto medioevo. II. La corvsia di Orso 'scriptor' in Campione nel 756," *Bollettino storico della Svizzera italiana*, ser. 4, 25 (1950): 135–43; the document itself was edited and reproduced by Natale in *Il Museo Diplomatico dell'Archivio di Stato di Milano*, vol. 1 (Milano, [1970]), n. 16.

6. Original signatures from eighth-century Lucca: a) Lucca, 749–750 (= *CDL* 99);
b) Lucca, 25 Dec. 765 (= *CDL* 193); c) Valeriana, August 768 (= *CDL* 222);
d) Chiusi, April 771 (= *CDL* 253).

Valeriana in the territory of Pisa in August 768 (*CDL* 222; *ChLA* 1004), to which four priests, a subdeacon, and a cleric subscribed as witnesses. Among the scripts they adopted one can single out that of the first, Rodpert, which is rough and uncertain, with all the elements separate and a *G* of uncial type, and that of the second, Deusduna, with the elements (note the *g*) typical of new cursive of chancery style as used by some rogatarii of Lucca.

6. The sixth and last example comes from Chiusi and consists of a charta promissionis drafted there in April 771 (*CDL* 253; *ChLA* 746). Subscribing are the author, Ansefrid, marshall, in a rough cursive with some ligatures; Rodcari, deacon, in a new cursive; and a Cuntulus, priest, in dissociated minuscule.

From these subscriptions, as well as the many others that I have been able to examine either in original or through reproductions, we can venture the following conclusions:

1. There were substantially two common scripts used in Lombard Italy in the eighth century:

    a) The new cursive of documentary type, adopted first of all by rogatarii, lay and ecclesiastical, and then by other literates who seem to have learned the same style from the beginning. At times this script, as in examples from Milan, Pavia, and especially Lucca, takes on characteristics of chancery type.

    b) A nonstandardized minuscule based on cursive, of upright orientation, with elements usually well separated from each other and only rarely linked by some elementary ornaments. This was shared by lay and clerics and even some semiliterates, that is, those who appear to have written more tentatively than others.

2. In all probability, this second type of script represents the foundation script that was taught at the first levels of elementary instruction and that remained the only graphic possession of semiliterates, whether lay or ecclesiastic.

3. This elementary graphic type was nothing else but a simplified tracing (sometimes disassociated) of the new cursive, with the various elements executed separately from each other either for didactic reasons or because of the scholastic habit of using lined tablets on which it was difficult to trace curves and ligatures. We are dealing, in short, with an upright new cursive stripped of ligatures: a graphic form, in other words, very close to the common minuscule of antique origin that formed the common substratum of all book minuscule

and documentary types, semicursive and cursive, used in the seventh and eighth centuries.

4. From this foundation graphic type (which we must remember is far from uniform, region to region), one generally passed to instruction in the new documentary cursive, with which many writers have been shown to be acquainted; on the other hand, following a process that Giorgio Cencetti brought to life in a talk given in 1956, one could and did pass more or less easily, without any need for further didactic instruction, to the execution of those many atypical book hands that Pratesi has proposed to call early medieval.[11]

It is appropriate at this point to broaden our perspective to include the seventh-century French documents with subscriptions, mentioned above, that despite the small number of their witnesses offer a panorama of graphics not very different from that found in Italy. In these documents, Merovingian script itself is clearly prevalent; but some cases (the 22 June 654 diploma of Chlodovech II for St.-Denis and the donation of Vandemarius and Ercamberta of 689–90)[12] have subscriptions in fairly rough capitals, while one finds examples here and there of subscriptions in a dissociated minuscule of a type analogous to that of Lombard Italy of the eighth century (private charters of 10 March 673).[13]

For other regions of Europe, the possibility of research analogous to that reported here for Merovingian France and Lombard Italy is compromised by the lack of a sufficient number of ordinary scripts. The reasons for this absence vary from place to place. Although documents are relatively numerous for the eighth-century Great Britain and Rhaetia, they did not use autograph subscriptions; for Spain and southern Italy, the documents are simply lost. The handful of indications that we have, although not always easily interpreted for our purposes, nonetheless permit us to venture some hypotheses. For Spain, for example, most of the forty-six scratched slates, published by Gomez Moréno in 1966 and later studied by Diaz y Diaz, reveal that visigothic cursive forms with some particular characteristics were already in use for documentary and daily purposes in the seventh century. But on one of the pieces (VIII) prepared by a literate, probably traced on the slab for didactic purposes, one finds some individual letters executed with clear separations between them that continue the antique roman cursive minuscule, such as the *t* looped to the left. Some other slates, moreover, probably

11. A. Pratesi, "Note per un contributo alla soluzione del dilemma paleografico: 'Semicorsiva o precarolina?' " *Annali della Facoltà di Lettere e Filosofia dell'Università di Bari* 3 (1957): 3–13.

12. *ChLA* 558, 571.

13. *ChLA* 564, 563, 582.

traced by a not particularly skilled hand, show the use of a dissociated minuscule rather close to that encountered in contemporary Merovingian documents.[14] For southern Italy, three of the oldest surviving original documents
that have been reproduced—dating, respectively, from 792 (Forino), 809 (Ta-
ranto), and 819 (S. Martino al Volturno)[15]—show some laymen using a rough
dissociated minuscule characterized by an *e* shaped like an *8;* other laymen,
numerically greater than the first group, adopted a fluid new cursive identical
with that used by the *rogatarius;* only one, from 792, used capitals. Completely different from any of these, finally, is the situation in Ireland, where
a wooden polyptych of six tablets that has been attributed to the seventh
century, containing Psalms apparently adapted for teaching, was virtually
written in insular capitals;[16] the influence of this type of script seems also
apparent on the oldest insular epigraphy. Yet given that Ireland lacked any
continuity with new roman cursive and that the diffusion of writing there
must have been extremely limited, it clearly constitutes a case apart.

Let us turn now to the schools, to see whether and how these products of
graphic instruction could have belonged to a coherent didactic scheme. In
order to do this, we must be careful not to try to see a rigid scholastic
structure corresponding to every different or successive level of graphic instruction. Scholastic organization in pre-Carolingian Europe varied from
place to place, environment to environment, and was often casually arranged,
as one can easily see from Riché's *Education and Culture in the Barbarian
West.*[17] One can only suppose that different didactic levels were very often
concentrated in a single scholastic institution, while equally often one would
find identical or analogous instruction being imparted in modes and means
that were quite distinct. Within these limits, then, one can speak of a basic
elementary instruction that in the seventh century appears to have followed
the ancient system in including capitals, but that was centered around that
type of dissociated minuscule based on cursive that we have illustrated above.

14. M. Gomez Moreno, *Documentacion goda en pizarra* (Madrid, 1966); M. C. Diaz y Diaz,
"Los documentos hispano-visigòticos sobre pizarra," in *Studi medievali* ser. 3, 7 (1966): 75–107.

15. These documents are reproduced, respectively, in *Codex diplomaticus Cavensis nunc primum in lucem editus,* vol. 1 (Naples, 1873), pl. I (*ChLA,* 701); A. Gallo, "Il più antico documento
originale dell'Archivio di Montecassino" and "Una carta abruzzese del IX secolo con tracce in
volgare," *Bullettino dell'Istituto Storico Italiano* 45 (1929): 163–64 and 167–68.

16. Repr. by E. C. R. Armstrong and R. A. S. MacAlister, "Wooden Book with Leather
Indented and Waxed Found Near Springmost Bog, Co. Antrin," *Journal of the Royal Society
of Antiquaries of Ireland* 100, 1 (1920): 160–66; see *CLA Supplement,* n. 1684.

17. English translation by John Contreni (Columbia, S.C., 1976; orig. pub. Paris, 1962). Also
by Riché is "Les foyers de culture en Gaule française du VIe au IXe siècle," in *Centri e vie di
irradiazione,* pp. 297–321.

Such a first level of instruction took place in ecclesiastical schools associated with cathedrals, monasteries, collegiate churches, and minor rural churches; these schools were open to pupils destined both for a religious life and for lay status. The instruction must also have taken place in schools associated with the *stationes* of lay notaries that were more specifically designed for youths outside religious life. In this last type of school (if we can call it a type), one probably moved directly and without any clear break to being instructed in what is properly called the new cursive, as would seem to be demonstrated by the subscriptions of some laymen who, though apparently semiliterate, had nonetheless learned a certain number of ligatures.

Clearer distinctions between lay and ecclesiastical schools must have existed at the level of reading, even if it is rather difficult for us to evaluate that phenomenon exactly. At least in the larger ecclesiastical schools, in fact, it is known that the fundamental elements of a complete primary education included chant and reading as well as writing. In reading, even before reaching the mastery of expression and rhythm needed to recite, pupils learned simple techniques for understanding that must certainly have extended to the types of script most often used in liturgical, scriptural, and patristic books—uncial and semi-uncial—whose visual elements young readers quickly learned to recognize. In contrast, the study of reading, both as a separate subject and as an element of an incipient book culture, would have been absent from lay schools of notarial and chancery *stationes*, whose graphic repertory must have remained more rigidly limited to new cursives of various types.

One also had higher graphic instruction, which could be in either book or chancery hands. One learned book hands, as appropriate for every institution, in the scriptoria and schools of calligraphy. And one learned chancery hands in chancery schools, which might be royal (in France and perhaps Italy) or ecclesiastical (the papal chancery, or episcopal chanceries as at Ravenna or Lucca); it was in such places that draftsmen of public and semi-public documents were trained, although this is a matter of which little is yet known. In some cases, however, peculiarities of the scholastic structure made for more complex relationships among the different levels of instruction. This was certainly the case at Lucca, where the famous codex 490 shows various levels of technical ability and graphic tendencies among the roughly forty intersecting hands represented. Probably this means that the first level school, the scriptorium, and the chancery school for the *rogatarii* of episcopal documents all maintained close reciprocal relations.

In the second half of the eighth century, the process begun two centuries earlier of separating from the graphic civilization of Rome came to a conclusion in Europe. It had led to the creation of a new kind of book, to the dissolution of an ordered hierarchy of scripts, to the birth of a great number of kinds of scripts differing from place to place. While on one hand the tendency toward graphic imitation kept alive ancient and noble book hands, on the other the teaching of writing continued to rest, at bottom, on models formed from common ancient roman minuscule. This latent and unconscious continuity was maintained above all in France and Italy, the two regions that more than others in Carolingian times would contribute to the formation of a new unity of European scripts.

This unity, which as we know was accomplished by a long, complicated process begun in the second half of the eighth century and lasting until the end of the following century, might be termed the Carolingian graphic renaissance.[18] It certainly contained several different phases and tendencies in writing. But it seems to me beyond doubt that, especially in the first phase that eventuated in the birth of the Carolingian capital, both uncial and semi-uncial, and of the numerous graphic types of minuscule that Cencetti grouped as a "Carolingian class," the method of graphic imitation inherited from early medieval practice and the patrimony of models preserved by didactic practices each played a decisive role. The method of imitation was brought to its highest levels in Carolingian writing centers, especially those of Tours and the court school. I believe its influence can be recognized even apart from its place in the birth of Carolingian capital, uncial, and semi-uncial. But one certainly recognizes that the scholastic minuscule of the early medieval didactic tradition formed the graphic foundation serving as the point of departure for many kinds of "Carolingian class" minuscule that, while rich in cursive elements, are also characterized by a pronounced tendency toward the isolation of individual elements and that lack the uncial *a*. Two eloquent witnesses of these influences, drawn from ordinary circles in Carolingian times, are provided by the signature of Maginarius to a diploma of Carloman from 769, already regarded by Schiaparelli in 1926 as an example of "pure developed caroline," and by the analogous subscriptions of Folradus, abbot of St.-Denis, to the two originals of his will drafted in 777.[19]

18. For the problem of the origins of caroline minuscule and the significance of the Carolingian "graphic renaissance," see A. Gieysztor, "Problem Karolinskiej reformy pisma," in *Archeologii* 5 (1955): 15–80; G. Cencetti, "Postilla nuova a un problema paleografico vecchio: L'origine della minuscola 'carolina,' " *Nova Historia* 3 (1955): 1–24 (with ample bibliography; at pp. 16–24, Cencetti offers the hypothesis that caroline minuscule originated by a conscious process of imitating antique models); B. Bischoff, "La minuscule caroline et le renouveau culturel sous Charlemagne," *Bulletin de l'Institut de Recherche et l'Histoire des Textes* 15 (1967–68): 333–36, and "Panorama des Handschriftenüberlieferung aus der Zeit Karls des Grossen," *Karl der Grosse*, vol. 2: *Das geistige Leben* (Düsseldorf, 1965), pp. 233–54; A. Pratesi, "Le ambizioni di una cultura unitaria: La riforma della scrittura," in *Nascita dell'Europa ed Europa carolingia: Un' equazione da verificare* (Spoleto, 1981), pp. 507–23.

19. "Note paleografiche. A proposito di un recente articolo sull'origine della minuscola carolina," in *Archivio storico italiano* ser. 7, 5.1 (1926): 3–23, esp. 17–19. These signatures are

Certainly, the return to a normal model of minuscule cannot be explained only by an unforeseeable flowering at the level of books of an elementary writing until then relegated to didactic purposes. But two things are certain. This minuscule found new impulse and diffusion precisely at that moment in the renewed and broadened structure of Carolingian schools, in which we found it was the first and principle didactic tool. And it corresponded substantially in the morphology of individual elements to that ancient minuscule whose influence the scribes of Carolingian times still felt, as Giorgio Cencetti boldly argued, and whose graphic style they still imitated.

In short, imitation and teaching are again discovered to be the two fundamental methods of early medieval graphic activity. To them is due the preservation of the ancient patrimony of writing, and in their diffusion we recognize one of the determining factors of the Carolingian graphic renaissance and the recomposition of the writing unity of Western Europe.

---

reproduced in M. Tangl, "Das Testament Fulrads von Saint-Denis," *Neues Archiv* 32 (1906): 167–217.

5

LITERACY AND GRAPHIC CULTURE OF EARLY MEDIEVAL SCRIBES

WISHING TO DISCUSS THE literacy and graphic education of the scribes of any period or society might seem either needlessly obvious or deliberately provocative, for the general view certainly is that ancient or medieval scribes' ability to write, in itself implying an adequate graphic education, was a fact that must be taken for granted without being placed in discussion. Indeed, it does seem natural to assume that whoever writes a text of any substantial length must know how to write, and write well. But it is not a fact of nature—at least, not always and not in its entirety. In practice, the connection between writers and writing is never so absolutely and clearly definable as is usually thought, with clear boundaries between literates and illiterates or between writing technicians and unlearned writers, and it was still less so in the Middle Ages.

Those who study history professionally are well aware, or should be, that it is not easy to reduce reality to rigid schemes, even if in many cases it would be convenient to do so. And historians of writing know (or at least are beginning to learn) the same thing. For some time now, the panorama of early medieval literacy has appeared considerably more complex and varied than one could have supposed fifteen or twenty years ago. We now know that literacy, understood as the ability to write at any level of skill, was relatively well diffused from a social point of view in more developed cities in Europe and especially in Italy: Lucca and Milan in the eighth century,

Originally published as "Alfabetismo e cultura grafica degli scribi altomedievali," in *The Role of the Book in Medieval Culture*, ed. P. Ganz, vol. 1 (Turnhout, 1986), pp. 109–32 (with plates).

Salerno in the ninth, Rome in the tenth and eleventh. It extended to the majority of ecclesiastics and included many lay individuals as full participants, affecting as well a notable number of semiliterate people who were able to write in some elementary or limited way. Moreover, the capacity to write of lay people (notaries, judges, functionaries, counts, royal and imperial missi, and so forth) was quite good.[1]

These considerations lead me to pose the problem of the means and techniques of teaching specifically for those with the responsibility of writing books: to be exact, the problem of the graphic education of scribes or, better, those who copied books. The problem is difficult both to define and to solve, not just because we have only the scarcest information, direct or indirect, but also because the graphic education of scribes itself reflected a complex and diversified situation in which the task of writing books often or occasionally (depending on the case) fell not only to those who knew how to do the work satisfactorily, having received special education for the purpose, but to anyone who in any manner could write.

For the purposes of making my argument clearer and easier to follow, I can anticipate some of the results of my research in a very simple and summary manner by saying that one could basically divide the universe of those who could write or tried to write books in the early medieval West into four categories:

1. True scribes, that is, copyists specifically educated for copying (and sometimes manufacturing) books, who used particular, usually formal, canonized or typified scripts; these make up the majority of the cases.
2. Writers not fully trained in graphics, who nonetheless by imitation or with instruction try to write in canonized scripts and according to the correct norms of their intended models; these generally were apprentices or young scholars.
3. Pure and simple writers, clerical or lay, of moderate or low literacy, who write books in the cursive of daily use or the elementary scripts that are the only ones they know.
4. Learned men, teachers, and prelates who write sections of books or annotations to books, more rarely entire books, in personal scripts

1. For literacy in early medieval Italy generally, see my "Scrittura, alfabetismo e produzione libraria nell'alto medioevo," in G. Cavallo, ed., *La cultura in Italia fra tardo antico e alto medioevo* (Rome, 1981), pp. 539–51; for Rome, the communication of C. Romeo, in *Alfabetismo e cultura scritta. Seminario permanente. Notizie (marzo 1980)*, pp. 5–8; for Salerno, A. Petrucci and C. Romeo, "Scrittura e alfabetismo nella Salerno del IX secolo," *Scrittura e civiltà* 7 (1983): 51–112. Also useful are D. A. Bullogh, "Le scuole cattedrali e la cultura dell'Italia settentrionale prima dei Comuni," *Vescovi e diocesi in Italia nel medioevo*, Italia sacra, 5 (Padua, 1964), pp. 111–43.

they normally use without any particular attention to graphic/book qualities.

That said, before proceeding further I note several caveats: the results presented here, still provisional and open, are based on research experience mostly limited to Italian book production; the chronological period under consideration is that of the early Middle Ages, more exactly, from the seventh to the tenth centuries; the documentation presented here has a purely illustrative value and results from choices based to some extent on chance and in certain instances even on convenience. Finally, I should add that for reasons of brevity, my exposition consists of a general panorama without pretensions to exhaustiveness or completeness.

For all the richness in the tradition of Latin paleography regarding the early Middle Ages, there remains the relatively unstudied problem of what one might call, in generic terms, informal writing. The great English papyrologist Eric G. Turner has recently given this concept a clear formulation by defining it as writing that is not easily reduced to any particular type because it is executed awkwardly and roughly so that it falls outside the norms. One can plausibly attribute these scripts to writers with a fairly low level of graphic education.

This problem is a familiar one to anyone who works with early medieval documents, because a sizable number of those who subscribe at the bottom of documents adopt writing of precisely this kind. It also ought to be familiar to whomever regularly consults—as every good paleographer, codicologist, or philologist must—the great work that everyone agrees is our breviary: E. A. Lowe's *Codices Latini Antiquiores*. For some time now, Lowe's paleographical terminology has been subject to great reservations, and certainly some of the methodological criticisms are quite justified, drawing on a reconceptualization of the discipline of paleography to which Lowe remained substantially an outsider. My interest here, however, is not to the "official" terminology by which Lowe designated, in epigraphic characters at the head of individual descriptions, the type of each handwriting. I refer, rather, to the more discursive remarks that constitute the very substance of paleographical analysis, being inserted into the body of descriptions and often including singular or surprising judgments and definitions. How often do we encounter definitions such as: "Script is ungainly and uncalligraphic" (413); or, "crude and awkward specimen of Celtic minuscule" (648); or "rather careless and debased uncial" (352); or "uncalligraphic, awkward uncial" (482); and adjectives describing scripts as "careless" (518, 676), "crude" (966, 1309, 1552, **604), "untrained" (referring to hand, 448), and so forth?

In these definitions, and in other analogous cases that I omit for reasons of brevity, Lowe expresses negative judgments about individual graphic witnesses based on two fundamental criteria: the transgression of the norms of good writing ("below the standard of calligraphy," 1017) and the roughness of execution. These two criteria coincide only partially, because the first seems to be purely graphic-aesthetic and in some ways external to the process of creation, to which, in contrast, the second seems specifically to introduce into the network of analysis that protagonist to whom Lowe (in common with traditional paleography) paid scant attention: the writer. Indeed, it is only rarely, even in cases of abnormal or informal writing, that Lowe ventured observations or judgments on the person who executed it. When he offers opinions, moreover, he does so at a certain remove: "inexpert scribe" (716); "local amateur work" (483). This restriction of his discussion is especially notable because Lowe himself, through his practice of usually giving precise information on orthography, ornamentation, and the quality and preparation of the writing materials, furnishes us with many of the elements needed to broaden the discussion beyond the purely static graphic phenomenon.

Today an investigation of the level of graphic education of early medieval copyists, and in particular of "inexpert scribes," does not preclude other and more complex elements of judgment. Describing the "scriptorium" of William of Malmesbury, R. M. Thomson recently singled out the following elements as defining "scriptorial inexperience": 1) no graphic ability; 2) lack of the "house style" itself; 3) absence of coordination between the work of different scribes; 4) poor correlation between the problems posed by the text copied and the physical aspect of the book; 5) irregular grouping into fascicles; 6) frequent interruptions in the work of copying. The analysis thus extends beyond the purely graphic facts and purely individual dimensions to deal with the techniques of making the book, the relationship between the book and the text or texts contained, and the cultural level and the overall environment comprising education, the activities of the scribes, and the production of the book. Although Thomson's remarks refer to situations and products of the twelfth century, I believe that they can be taken as valid by anyone who sets about to deal with analogous phenomena of the previous several centuries.[2]

These criteria, then, are in broad terms those that we can adopt to evaluate

---

2. R. M. Thomson, "The 'scriptorium' of William of Malmesbury," *Medieval Scribes, Manuscripts and Libraries: Essays Presented to N. R. Ker* (London, 1978), pp. 117–42, esp. pp. 126 and 128. For the orthographic habits of copyists of early medieval Bible codices, see the useful observations of J. Gribomont, "Conscience philologique chez les scribes du haut moyen âge," *La Bibbia nell'alto medioevo* (Spoleto, 1963), pp. 600–630.

the *imperitia scribendi*, the "scriptorial inexperience," of early medieval copyists. Did their patrons or superiors, or their brothers and the environment in which they worked, have any means of judging someone's graphic and bookmaking ability? Were the workers themselves for their part aware of their greater or lesser technical ability? Although providing comprehensive answers to such an inquiry is difficult, indeed practically impossible, one can obtain some indications in this regard from the subscriptions that early medieval scribes added to their texts. In fact, apart from what seems to be the high opinion of their own work that sets apart some great scribes of the Carolingian age, the subscriptions taken as a whole do not seem to reveal that the scribes had any consciousness of their own role or self-critical attitudes toward their work. Given the mediocre scholastic formalism of the genre, this is not surprising. At most we find ever more frequent references to the physical wear of the work of copying, constrained within customary and mechanically repeated formulas. Rarely do we encounter any references to the scribes' own ability or evaluations of the results of their own work, and the majority of cases where we do (few as these are) are simply *formulae humilitatis*. But it is my impression that for at least one subscription and one codex the scribe's declaration that he is *imperitus* must be taken as self-awareness. I am referring to the well-known and mysterious Gundohinus and his Evangeliarium, written at Vesovio in 754 for an abbess Fausta, at the instance of a monk Falculfus (now Autun, Bibl. Mun. MS n. 3 = *CLA* 716).

Regarding this codex, which at once testifies to and is the protagonist of a decisive turn in the history of medieval art, Jean Porcher has affirmed that "nothing like it had been seen before on the continent north of the Alps: Carolingian art, in fact, begins with Gundohinus, as the so-called Carolingian dynasty begins with Pippin."[3] Porcher underlined the suggestive chronological coincidence between the production of this Evangeliarium and the encounter that occurred at Ponthion in precisely the same year, 754, between Pippin and Stephen II, between the Franks and Rome.

Gundohinus's codex is a book of imitation, from both graphic and iconographic points of view. One can recognize the influence of models from Lombard Italy in its extraordinary miniatures, while in its uncial there is an evident effort to reproduce an uncial, again from Italy, this time from the

---

3. In J. Hubert et al., *L'impero carolingio* (Milan, 1968), pp. 71–74 and figs. 61–63. I wish especially to thank the Institut de Recherche et d'Histoire de Textes of Paris for quickly placing at my disposal the entire reproduction of MS Autun n. 3, thus decisively assisting my work. An exact description of the codex may be found in P. McGurk, *Latin Gospel Books from A.D. 400 to A.D. 800* (1961), pp. 50–52; a page is also reproduced in F. Steffens and R. Coulon, *Paléographie latine* (Trèves and Paris, 1910), pl. 37.

late sixth century. (I think in particular, to illustrate the type, of the Evangeliarium Bibl. Ambrosiana C 39 inf. = *CLA* 313, perhaps of Aquileian origin.) Gundohinus's uncial, which Lowe described as "a broad, bold uncial by an inexpert scribe with a poor sense of spacing," makes an evident contrast with the plan of the book, which has full-page miniatures and great canonical tables, but is quite consistent with the "unusually corrupt" orthography and with the thick, defective, poorly prepared parchment. Apart from the uncial, reserved for the text of the Gospels, Gundohinus here and there in the codex employed a small, tight, cursive-like minuscule, rich in ligatures, with elongated and doubled ascenders; this script he wrote with a certain ability and noteworthy ease. In contrast, he reveals an almost complete "scribal inexperience" precisely in the copying of the Gospels, whose text is executed in an uncial that tries to reproduce the Italian model but that on every page shows obvious signs of dishomogeneity, disorder, and uncertainty (fig. 7).

The defects of *imperitus* Gundohinus's uncial fall into both technical and graphic-aesthetic categories. The first consists of an incorrect *temperatura* of the pen, which usually is cut too broadly for imitating the "coloring" of the model's "new-style" uncial, and his inability uniformly to repeat the design and even the tracing of individual letters. The second category is evident in the dishomogeneity of the letter size, in the various orientations of the strokes, and in the impossibility of maintaining alignment on the line. Indeed, the writing is so dishomogeneous that one would be tempted to posit the intervention of other hands were we not convinced otherwise by the constant recurrence of some characteristic letters or graphic forms such as the *N* with the second stroke nearly horizontal, the *G* with the long tail, the false ligature *li*, and the true ligature *ti*. Rather, the truth is that from about the middle of the codex one sees a progressive amelioration of the uncial's graphic characteristics that can be understood only as the positive result of a constant effort at self-education based on imitation of the model.

One can perhaps try to reconstruct Gundohinus's itinerary of graphic education, from elementary instruction in minuscule to learning a cursive-like precaroline that he executed at a technical level with some ability with a pen cut centrally and slightly sharpened (as would be appropriate for documentary purposes), to the impact of the formal writing in the most elevated tradition of the late-antique model book, which no one had taught him the particular techniques of executing. This last, therefore, he had to learn slowly, during the very work of copying, which he did with much labor while making many errors. He shows himself aware of this fact in the long subscription, written in a "rustic" Latin prose of documentary type. (as if when writing documents to dictation he included the formula of *datatio*) in which twice he calls himself "imperitus."

LIBER GE[N]
RATIO HIS IHU
XPI FILI DAVID
FILI ABRAHAM
ABRAAM GEN
UIT ISAAC ISA
AC AUTE GE
NUIT IACOB IA
COB AUTEM GENU
IT IUDAM ET FRATRES
EIUS IUDAS AUTE
GENUIT FARES ET
ZARA DE THAMAR
FARES AUTE GENUIT

ESROM ESROM AU
TE GENUIT ARA ARA
AUTE GENUIT AMINA
DAB AMINADAB AUT
GENUIT NAASON NAA
ASON AUTE GENUIT
SALMON SALE AUTE
GENUIT BOOZ DE RA
CHAB BOOZ GENUIT
OBED EX RUTH OBED
XPE GENUIT IESSE
IESSE AUTE GENUIT
DAUID REGEM DAUID
AUTEM REX GENUIT
SALOMONE EX EA QUI
FUIT URIAE SALOMON
AUTE GENUIT ROBOX
ROBOA AUTE GE NUIT
ABIA ABIA AUTE GE
NUIT ASA ASA AUTE
GENUIT JOSAFAT JOSA
FAT AUTE GENUIT
IORA IORA AUTE GE
NUIT OZIA OZIAS
AUTEM GENUIT JOTH

7. Autun, 3, × 14r

8. Biblioteca Apostolica Vaticana, Vat. lat. 7809, fol. 14r

The case of Gundohinus is not an isolated one. Parallel in many ways is the situation presented by Vat. lat. 7809 (= *CLA* 55), a *Moralia* of Gregory the Great (ll. XI–XVI) that Lowe attributed to Italy at the end of the eighth century, which is subscribed by an "Anselmus subdiaconus" (fig. 8). Here too are the incorrect orthography, defective parchment, the long and awkward subscription in "rustic" Latin; above all, however, here too is a scribe whose usual script was a cursive-like minuscule and who with great difficulty tries to write an uncial that turns out to be irregular in design, module, and alignment. Inserted into the codex are other hands, two of which were rougher and more irregular than that of Anselmus, while the third seems more able and expert. Also in analogy with Gundohinus, Anselmus improved as he worked through the task of copying, and by the end of the codex had tangibly mitigated some of its coarsest defects, so that for him as well we can hypothesize an educational process that was articulated over several phases and, in regard to uncial, was substantially autodidactic.

A summary examination of the *CLA* and some soundings accomplished beyond the year 800 permit us to group around Gundohinus and Anselmus a series of similar cases, both contemporary and later, that although representing a simple sampling can serve to single out and delimit some particular sectors of early medieval book production that shared some common characteristics. There are, to begin with, four codices, of which three are Italian in origin and one French, all containing texts of religious nature. The Ravennate codex attributed to the eighth century and corresponding to *CLA* 413 is in an extremely rough uncial, perhaps written by several hands that were really semiliterate. The other three, Verona X (8) (= *CLA* 483), from the seventh to eighth centuries, Bibl. Ambrosiana I.101 sup. (= *CLA* 352), and Paris, B.N. 13246 (= *CLA* 653), both of the eighth century, are written in what could be called a "mixed" hand. This is an extremely irregular uncial (Schiaparelli's "rustic uncial") in which are inserted elements of the minuscule system that was apparently the scribes' habitual script and that at times passes from one type to the other, showing that the scribes were not clearly aware of the opposing variants characterizing the new cursive and minuscule on one hand and uncial on the other. The Veronese codex also bears a long subscription in "rustic" Latin prose, in which the scribe (a "local amateur" for Lowe) declares himself to be, in addition to *indignus peccator*, an *ultimus scriptor*. The Ambrosiana codex, probably from Bobbio, among other things is the only one to preserve a liturgical document of great importance and exceptional antiquity, the so-called "Muratorian canon" of the New Testament, transcribed in a notably irregular uncial with an orthography that Lowe termed "ungrammatical and horribly spelled," all in all "barbaric."[4] All four manuscripts are miscellanies, formed of collections that are disorganized

---

4. For the so-called "canone muratoriano" contained in Ambr. I 101 sup., see the complete reproduction and commentary in S. Ritter, "Il frammento muratoriano," *Rivista di archeologia* 3 (1926): 215–63; and also E. A. Lowe, "The Ambrosiana of Milan and the Experiences of a Paleographer," in Lowe, *Paleographical Papers*, vol. 2 (Oxford, 1972), p. 587 and pl. 143.

and perhaps even fortuitous, containing texts differing widely in content. All four, finally, present more or less the same characteristics of orthographical irregularity and poor preparation of the parchment.

These examples might seem to suggest that the phenomenon of "scribal inexperience" between the seventh and tenth centuries substantially consisted of (and was caused by) the fact that some copyists educated to semicursive minuscule or documentary cursive tried to learn to write uncial and did so badly, distorting the fundamental criteria of its execution, which at the time were everywhere forgotten. But this is not the case. Scribal inexperience also appears with regard to other kinds of scripts, thus revealing the breadth and range of issues that had come to be essential parts of a correct technical education for copyists in early medieval Europe, or at least in some cultural centers, regions, and environments.

One need only mention the perhaps overdiscussed case of Winithar, the disconcerting scribe active at San Gall in the third quarter of the eighth century, whose rough, uncertain, large minuscule (which Lowe called "rather gauche," "awkward," and "inimitable") appears in several codices of his monastery and some documents; he addressed his fellow monks, begging parchment to write on and promising to do it "in quantum dederit intellectum Dominus sine ulla contraddiccione" (to the extent that the Lord gives him, without any opposition) (figs. 9, 10). But take the case of Vat. lat. 491 (fols. 1–33 = CLA 5a), containing Augustine's comments on Paul's epistles to the Romans and the Galatians, which was written by multiple hands in insular minuscule in an Italian center and that Lowe attributed to the eighth century (fig. 11). Its first fascicle (fols. 1–8) reveals a rather fluid situation, in which the fairly expert first hand was followed by others that are irregular and uncertain, while the lining, sometimes doubled, does not correspond to the perforations, so that the disposition of the writing is entirely arbitrary. This is evidently a fascicle whose preparation was entrusted to beginners, probably boys, for whom it was part of their technical apprenticeship.

Discussion of a group of five codices or fragments, all attributable to the period between the end of the seventh and the beginning of the ninth centuries, takes us to the different terrain defined by the common subject matter of the texts grouped together. These are, in fact, all codices or fragments containing texts of a medical nature—texts that in the earlier Middle Ages sometimes had distinct and separate channels of transmission and that answered practical interests often foreign to those more specifically literary-scholastic. This is particularly true when, as in four of our five cases, collections of recipes or minor texts were being passed on. In Vat. Pal. lat. 187 (= CLA 80a, 80b, 81), fol. 7r bears recipes written in Italian new cursive, perhaps by a notarial hand of the

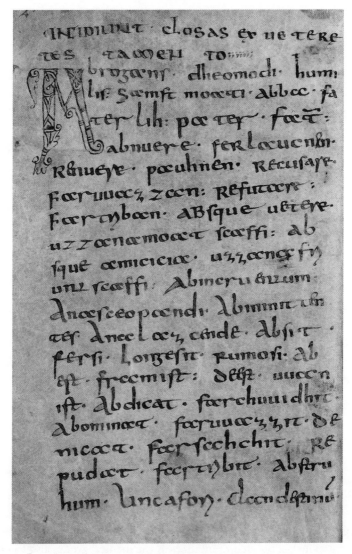

9. San Gall, MS 911, fol. 4

eighth century (fig. 12). But greater interest attaches to the text that follows, Galen's *Alphabetum ad Paternum,* in which there is an alternation between hands markedly different from each other, one of which oscillates between uncial and minuscule, while the other is simply rough. Entirely in uncial, however, are the *Fragmentum medicum* transmitted by a flyleaf of Urb. lat. 293 (= *CLA* 116) and the recipe book, also in a single page, of Paris, B.N. Baluze

10. San Gall, MS 911, fol. 23

270 (= *CLA* 519); in both of these the graphic uncertainty is accompanied by an inability to follow the alignment of the rows and poor preparation of the parchment. The last two representatives of the medical group, also fragments, are a recipe book of the first half of the eighth century (= *CLA* **604, VII, p. 10) written by two unskilled hands in a very poorly executed French precaroline, and the Hippocratic miscellany contained in four folios of Paris, B.N. Nouv. acq. lat. 203 (= *CLA* 676), in which a rough and uncertain uncial is counterposed to a precaroline minuscule of good level.

This phenomenon is also seen in the transmission of another kind of instrumental works: glossaries. The two well-known San Gall glossaries nos. 911 (= *CLA* 966) and 912 (= *CLA* 967a) demonstrate this clearly. No. 912

11. Biblioteca Apostolica Vaticana, Vat. lat. 491, fol. IV

(*Glossarium Aba, Abavus*), from the seventh to eighth centuries, seems to come from a center provided with a good library (perhaps Bobbio?), since this word is placed in particular relief (p. 35: "Bibliothica ubi libri reconduntur"); it is a palimpsest (on fragments of several codices of the fifth and seventh centuries) of small format and is the work of multiple scribes who used a small, irregular, and at times cursive-like uncial, in which was inserted a contemporary Italian cursive (p. 201). As interesting, if not more so, is the

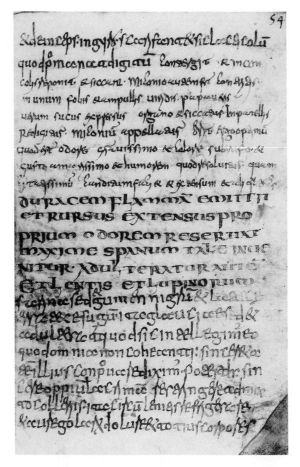

12. Biblioteca Apostolica Vaticana, Pal. lat. 187, fol. 54r

case provided by MS 911 (figs. 9–10), which contains the oldest known Latin-German glossary, the *Abrogans*, followed by the *Liber ecclesiasticorum dogmatum* of Gennadius and the *Pater Noster* and *Credo* in German.[5] This is a small codex written, in Bernhard Bischoff's opinion, in southwest Germany at the end of the eighth century in a center where a substantially similar group of copyists (more than twenty) accustomed to using a "crude precaroline minuscule" worked. Among them one finds for brief stretches at least

5. See the recent complete reproduction *Das älteste deutsche Buch. Die Abrogans-Handschrift der Stiftbibliothek St. Gallen* (San Gall, 1977); Bischoff's description is at pp. 61–82.

five apprentice hands and, surprisingly, even some skilled copyists of different graphic traditions, able to write fluid cursive. Especially notable is the fact that the majority of the copyists shared certain defects owing to inexperience, such as wavy alignment, different-sized lettering, excessively hard strokes, and irregular pagination. Nor do the occasional appearances of skilled hands necessarily indicate that any teaching was involved, given the variety of these and their foreignness to the dominant graphic environment.

To the practical/technical interests revealed by the medical texts and glossaries, one can add the evidence of some codices containing juridical texts. Particularly important for our purposes are: for the second half of the eighth century, the Cresconius *Concordantia canonum* of Berlin (*CLA* 1062), in a cursive-like and disorderly minuscule that clearly recalls some of the later hands of the glossary *Abrogans*; for the beginning of the ninth century, the *Capitulare Theodulf* (*CLA* 1309), in which one encounters two very different hands, the first of which belonged to a beginning scribe, who wrote an oversized and poorly aligned minuscule (fols. 139r–154v, 166v–170r), while the second (fols. 155r–166r), in contrast, executed an elegant caroline with insular traces; for the second half of the tenth century, the *Summa Perusina* (Perugia, Bibl. Capitolare MS no. 32), which we can attribute to central Italy, is written in a heavy minuscule thick with cursive elements and beneventan traces, but characterized by frequent changes in letter size, and irregularity of alignment.[6] In this last case, the scribe's foundation script seemed to have a been a documentary cursive of beneventan type, which he adopted with good effect in the rubrics, a conclusion that also agrees with his entirely "rustic" orthography and with the recurrent uncertainties in reproducing the caroline alphabet (perhaps the exemplar was in roman minuscule?) But even here one can recognize a progressive improvement in technique, evidently achieved in the course of doing the copying.

For a final instance of predominately practical interests, linked to a more general acculturation of local secular clergy, one can turn to Lucca Biblioteca Capitolare codex 490, the famous incoherent miscellany gathered in the cathedral environment there by about forty copyists between 787–796 and 816. This is a manuscript studied at length and partially reproduced by Luigi Schiaparelli in 1924,[7] so I can treat it quickly here, saying that in practice it

6. F. Patetta, *Adnotationes codicum domini Iustiniani (Summa Perusina)* (Rome, 1900), and A. Caleca, *Miniature in Umbria*, vol. 1: *La Biblioteca Capitolare di Perugia* (Florence, 1969), pp. 27–29. My dating to the second half of the tenth century is confirmed by Paola Supino Martini.

7. *Il codice n. 490 della Biblioteca Capitolare di Lucca e la scuola scrittoria lucchese. Contributi allo studio della miniatura precarolina in Italia (sec. VIII–IX)* (Rome, 1924) and *Il codice CCCCXC della Biblioteca Capitolare di Lucca*, vols. 1–3 (Rome, 1924); A. Petrucci, "Il codice n. 490 della

provides an exemplary summary of the most conspicuous characteristics of the codices so far discussed as typical of an informal style of book production, fully deserving Lowe's epithet of a "babel of scripts (*CLA*, VI, p. XII) and the later characterization as a "true and proper antibook." Apart from the extraordinarily high number of copyists and the singular chaos of its contents, it contains a number of other interesting elements:

1. the rather low level of book-graphic capacity of most of the copyists, some of whom adopted what was really a foundation script (as in the case of the *Abrogans* glossary);
2. the fact that some of them have been identified as *notarii* belonging to the Lucca clergy (as in the case of Winithar of San Gall);
3. the participation in the copying of some "outside" copyists of good graphic abilities, one of whom uses visigothic script and the other roman uncial;
4. the presence among the works copied of rare texts, such as the famous *Compositiones ad tingenda musiva.*

To some extent comparable to the Lucca miscellany is Verona, Bibl. Capitolare XC, 85, a codex about a century later, also coming from a cathedral environment, which contains a great number of texts (seventy-four in all!) that varied considerably in subject matter.[8] The codex is written in a more or less disorderly fashion by about thirty different hands belonging, according to the reasonable hypothesis of Meerssman, "to young clerics educated *in canonica matricularis ecclesie* Veronensis" who had varying grammatical, orthographical, and graphic experience. A glimpse of the existence of books destined for the grammatical-graphic education of young clerics even in the post-Carolingian period? Perhaps. But whatever its original function, the Veronese codex also must be seen as symptomatic of the absence in such education of any unifying graphic norm, because the various hands reveal a great diversity of design, tracing, and style.

I will conclude this rapid review, begun with the Evangeliarium of Gundohinus, with one of the older examples of classical texts coming down to us from the Carolingian period and with one of the oldest known codices in "roman minuscule." The first example is the well-known Vat. Pal. lat. 1547 containing Seneca's *De beneficiis* and *De clementia*, attributed to the

---

Biblioteca Capitolare di Lucca: Un problema di storia della cultura medievale ancora da risolvere," *Actum Luce* 2 (1973): 159–74.

8. For this codex, see G. G. Meerssman, "Il codice XC della Capitolare di Verona," *Archivio Veneto* 104 (1975): 11–44.

13. Biblioteca Apostolica Vaticana, Pal. lat. 1547, fol. 115v

region around Milan at the beginning of the ninth century (figs. 13, 14).[9] This is another example of the disorganized practice of alternating among different scribes (about ten in all), some of whom were so unskilled that

9. On this MS, see M. Ferrari, "Libri liturgici e diffusione della scrittura carolina nell'Italia settentrionale," *Culto cristiano e politica imperiale carolingia* (Todi, 1979), p. 227; F. Préhac, ed., Seneca, *De la clemence* (Paris, 1921), pp. VI–XVII; and, most recently, G. Mazzoli, "Ricerche sulla tradizione medievale del *De beneficiis* e del *De clementia* di Seneca. III. Storia della tradizione manoscritta," *Bollettino dei classici* ser. 3, no. 3 (1982): 166–69.

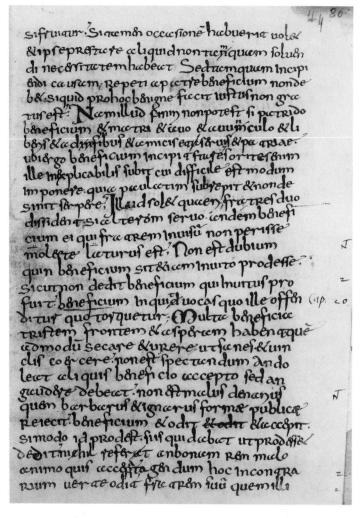

14. Biblioteca Apostolica Vaticana, Pal. lat. 1547, fol. 80r

they may have been young students, others whose levels of execution were more or less degraded, and still others with particular characteristics outside the norm, like using capital *R* and *S* in the context of minuscule. It conveys, in short, the image of a scriptorial environment in which not only did there not exist a single graphic norm but the copying of a text, even one destined for a superior level of rhetorical-literary education, could be delegated off-handedly to inexpert copyists. The other codex (Tours, Bibl. Mun. MS no.

1027), written by a certain John *scriba* and *indignus presbiter* of St. Peter's of Rome at the request of another priest named Benedict of the same basilica, contains the *Vita beati Gregorii* of John Immonides and is attributable to the end of the ninth century. Paola Supino Martini called attention in 1974 to the irregularity of alignment, spacing, tracing, and letter size that is apparent in its minuscule with residues of roman uncial, features that are only partially justifiable by the haste with which the copy was executed.[10] To this list one can add the mediocre condition of the parchment (the codex gives the impression of having been made of discarded leaves), which sometimes contributes to a chaotic impagination.

I believe that the examples listed thus far, even in their randomness, serve to indicate the extent of the phenomenon of informal writing and some of the aspects it assumed between the seventh and tenth centuries. It turns out to have involved or influenced some specific environments of book production and of early medieval written culture that, although perhaps marginal with respect to the whole picture, can to some extent be clearly distinguished: those in which practical medicine and customary law were cultivated (possibly with lay participation); less elevated or advanced expressions of scholastic structures, tied to the use of disorganized miscellanies, glossaries, and manuals; and finally some environments where insular book-graphic culture had emigrated to the continent. But rather than solving our problem, the rapid glance so far given the books has in some cases only marked out its boundaries and especially has added new ones. Thus it now appears necessary to tackle the scribes active in the period from another direction, looking at them both as a general category and as particular individuals, ascertaining as far as possible their social status, the kinds of activities they undertook, and the environment in which they worked. To this end, I believe it will be useful to examine the first results of a census of copyists covering the seventh to tenth centuries that I have sketched out based principally on three sources: the *CLA*, the Benedictines of le Bouveret's *Colophons*,[11] and the fourth volume of the monumental work of Emile Lesne.[12] Because it has not been possible to check most of the data, these results must of course be qualified by the fact that the dating

10. "Carolina romana e minuscola romanesca. Appunti per una storia della scrittura latina in Roma fra IX e XII secolo," *Studi medievali* 3d ser. 15 (1974): 776–78; "Materiali ed ipotesi per una storia della cultura scritta nella Roma del IX secolo," *Scrittura e civiltà* 2 (1978): 56–57; *Roma e l'area grafica romanesca (secoli X–XII)* (Alessandria, 1987).

11. *Colophons de manuscrits occidentaux des origines au XVI* siècle, vols. 1–5, Spicilegii Friburgensis Subsidia, nos. 2–6 (Fribourg, 1965–79)

12. *Les livres. 'Scriptoria' et bibliothèques du commencement du VIII* à la fin du XI* siècle, Mémoires et travaux publiés par des professeurs des facultés catholiques de Lille, 46 (Lille, 1938).

of the codices remains in doubt in several cases and that the geographical distribution of the data seems strongly conditioned by the state of the cataloguing.

In all, 388 names were collected. Seen in isolation, those relating to the first period—comprising the seventh century, eighth century, late eighth and early ninth centuries—seem scanty and not very significant: 67 copyists in all, of whom qualifying details are known only of 24. Fifteen of them are ecclesiastics (4 priests, 3 deacons, 3 subdeacons, 2 clerks, 1 monk, and so forth); 2 are *famuli* directly connected with Charlemagne and his court; and seven are generic *scriptores*. (Among the last is one woman, Dulcia, who appears at the end of the period.) In fact, it is precisely in the chronological slice bridging the two centuries that one seems to find the greatest novelty in the formulation of the texts of the signatures. These include three cases of tironian notations, four texts in verse, one subscription (from Fleury) in Greek letters; in spite of this, the percentage of subscriptions with incorrect orthography is generally high, reaching about 17. As for the zone of origin, known for only 45 cases, 21 come from France, 11 from Italy, 6 from Germany, 5 from San Gall, and 2 from England.

The next period, comprising the ninth century and the years at the turn of the ninth and tenth centuries, offers a picture that is notably richer and more articulated. To begin with, the number of copyists counted is markedly higher, reaching 212. Among the many ecclesiastics represented, there are 13 priests, 10 deacons, 6 subdeacons, and so forth; there is also an abbot and a sacristan (*custos sacrorum*). But the real novelties are the relatively high presence of women (10), the technical designations—including *scriba* (4), *librarius, grafius, magister,* and *didascalus*—and the subscriptions that could be called educated, of which there are clearly more than in the preceding period, with 21 verse compositions, 5 subscriptions in or with Greek letters, 2 with tironian notations, and 2 in runes. It also seems noteworthy that the percentage of subscriptions with spelling errors drops to 7, while the number mentioning specific patrons is high, numbering 37 in all, among whom bishops (18) and abbots (6) predominate, but Charles the Bald, 4 private individuals, a *dominus* and a boy also appear. As for zone of origin, of the 151 cases for which this can be ascertained, 68 are in France, followed by Germany with 50, Switzerland with 17 (but 16 from San Gall), Italy with 11, Spain with 3, and Ireland with 2.

The last period examined comprises the evidence from the tenth century, consisting of only 109 copyists, all of them male. Here, too, those whose social position is ecclesiastical predominate, with 15 priests, 13 deacons, 9 monks, and so forth; also notable are the technical categories used, with 3 "scribes," 2 notaries (these are Spanish ecclesiastics), 1 *magister scholae*, 1 *dis-*

cipulus, and, finally, a copyist who describes himself as *laicus* (Rotbertus, but he worked for the abbot of Fleury). Incorrect subscriptions drop somewhat, to 6 percent. Verse subscriptions are still widely used (10), and those with Greek letters (8). Rather different, however, with respect to the previous period is the geographical distribution of the scribes, of whom 24 worked in Spain, 22 in Germany, 17 in France, 8 in Italy, 2 in England, and 2 in Switzerland.

What can the data extracted from this census tell us about the manner, periods, and characteristic processes of scribes' graphic education? Nothing precise and direct. Nevertheless, they do provide a series of indices tending to single out the century of the Carolingian graphic renaissance (781–875) as the period in which at least some scribes acquired a better grammatical-orthographical culture, a more precise graphic technique, and a more certain awareness of their own role. At the highest levels this is evident in the text of the poetic compositions dedicating some of their deluxe products, in the pride with which technical titles are used, in Ingobertus's encounter with the "Ausonie" calligrapher that he at the end overtook, in the fame of Bertcaudus, royal scribe and creator of the reborn epigraphic capital, and so forth. But even at the middle level this shift seems to be confirmed by the more precise organization of the didactic process, a better individuation of the relationship between *magistri* and *discipuli*, of which a slight reflection can even be gleaned in the context of the subscriptions.

There is little surprising in all this, for it corresponds to what we know about the most closely related aspects of European cultural history between the end of the eighth century and the end of the ninth. But in reality, we continue to know very little about graphic instruction in the early Middle Ages, even after Bernhard Bischoff's famous 1938 article, that of A. R. Natale from twenty years later, that of Bullough, some recent contributions of Julian Brown, and the two general works of Pierre Riché that everyone knows and uses.[13] In substance, it turns out that in the period previous to the affirmation

13. Bernhard Bischoff, "Elementarunterricht und Probationes pennae in der ersten Hälfte des Mittelalter," in *Classical and Medieval Studies in Honor of E. K. Rand* (New York, 1938) (repr. in Bischoff, *Mittelalterliche Studien* [Stuttgart, 1966–81], 1:74–87); A. R. Natale, "Esercizi di calligafia insulare in codici del secolo VIII (nota paleografica)," in *Archivio storico italiano* 116 (1958): 3–23; D. A. Bullough, "Le scuole cattedrali e la cultura dell'Italia settentrionale prima dei Comuni," in *Vescovi e diocesi in Italia nel medioevo [Italia sacra 5]* (Padua, 1964), pp. 111–43; J. Brown, *The Durham Gospels, Together with Fragments of a Gospel Book in Uncial, Durham, Cathedral Library, Ms. A II 17*, ed. C. D. Verey, T. J. Brown, and E. Coatsworth, Early English Manuscripts in Facsimile, 20 (Copenhagen, 1980); P. Riché, *Education and Culture in the Barbarian West*, trans. John Contreni (Columbia, S.C., 1976 [orig. pub. Paris, 1962]); *Les écoles et l'enseignement dans l'Occident chrétien de la fin du Ve siècle au milieu du XIe siècle* (Paris, 1979).

or generalized diffusion of the ideals of the Carolingian graphic renaissance (and in part afterward, at least in some regions), the processes by which the graphic education of scribes was achieved were rather varied and depended on the degree of organization in individual communities and the effort of the local *magistri*. Sometimes there may have been cases of laborious and imperfect efforts at self-education; at others, the process was facilitated by imported models. Where he played a role, the master limited himself to writing a few model lines or tracing some particularly important graphic motive (the "wolf's teeth" for insular scribes). But quite often a guide or model must have been entirely lacking and the work of writing, and everything else involved in the production of books (perforation and lining of the folios), occurred in nearly complete disorder, left to the initiative and ability of writers, sometimes young or very young, who were certainly literate but not technically educated to formal writing for display.

In what manner and to what extent did the Carolingian graphic renaissance, or (better) its promoters, modify this situation?

In the first place, they saw to the strengthening and wider diffusion of schools at various levels that were meant to assure higher literacy and better cultural education of the clergy, the category that provided potential writers and users of books. Adding to this effort, moreover, were precise instructions providing guidance and organization for the production of books containing liturgical and scriptural texts, which were to have been copied by adult men, not boys, and rigorously corrected. Everyone recalls in this regard the words of the *Admonitio generalis* of 23 March 789 and the remarks of the *Epistola de letteris colendis*.[14] These were not empty wishes but initiatives that cut into the reality that existed and to some extent modified it by didactic and technical steps which, after first being employed principally in designated centers such as the palace or St. Martin of Tours, then gradually diffused until they were realized by methods that were substantially uniform throughout the empire even when they differed in details.

Some of Alcuin's letters illuminate the articulation of the Carolingian pedagogic program: letter 114, from 796, sent to Eanbaldus, archbishop of York, foresaw three different levels of teaching, each with it own master: 1) "qui libros legunt" (those who read books); 2) "qui cantilene inserviant" (those who attend to chant); 3) "qui scribendi studio deputentur" (those who are assigned to the study of writing). This distinction recurs in letter 138, which says, "ut sint ibi legentes iuvenes et chorus canentium et librorum exercitatio" (let there be young readers and the chorus of singers and the

14. MGH, *Capitularia regum Francorum*, I:59–60, 78–79.

practice of books).[15] Credit for this precise individuation of the activity and education of scribes, who stand as an *ordo* of their own in the pedagogic and cultural program of the Carolingian renaissance, is probably due to Alcuin and reflects his conscious preoccupation with a specific, graphic, ortho-graphic, and literary acculturation of the scribes. One sees this witnessed both in his treatise *De orthographia*,[16] which is given entirely over to the practice of correct writing, and in his famous letter to Charlemagne on *rus-ticitas scriptorum* (especially that of his scribes at Tours), in which he spe-cifically mentions the emperor's furthering the work of restoring *sapientia* and *eruditio* as a direct cause of the return to a correct use of punctuation.[17] But, we must remember, Alcuin was an intellectual rather than a writing master: in all probability, he never gave up his customary script of Anglo-Saxon minuscule, and the advice to his copyists that Bischoff found in the margins of a codex are those of a scholar, not the head of a scriptorium.[18]

In fact, this was also a level where the Carolingian graphic renaissance functioned as an ideal place for the elaboration of refined techniques of writing and complex graphic models. The examples of this are abundant. Consider the restoration, based on late antique and Byzantine examples, of writing in gold and silver on purple and multicolored backgrounds; the re-activation of a precise hierarchy of graphic types modeled after that used during the fifth and sixth centuries; the reinvention of ancient scripts such as epigraphic capitals, rustic capitals, and semi-uncial.[19] At the highest level, this meant the formation of a group of calligraphic scribes whose role was really to be creators of models (the *famuli* of Charlemagne, Bertcaudus, Charles the Bald's Ingobertus, and so forth). At a middle level, for emulation and imitation, it meant the diffusion of technically expert scribes able to execute several types of script ordered in a system of reciprocal relationships, tied to their work in a regular way, and accustomed to working on a team under the supervision of a master and director. In regard to the precise individuation of the copyist's work as a distinct specialization, I will mention only the practice followed by Ekkehardus, abbot of San Gall, who "quos ad literarum studia tardiores vidisset, ad scribendum occupaverat et lineandum" (employed in writing or lining those whom he saw came later to the study

---

15. *MGH, Epistolae Karolini aevi*, II:169, 190, 284–85.

16. H. Keil, *Grammatici Latini* (Leipzig, 1857–1880), 7:295–342.

17. On Alcuin's educational program, see J. Boussard, "Les influences anglaises sur l'école carolingienne des VIIIe et IXe siècle," *La scuola nell'Occidente latino dell'alto medioevo* (Spoleto, 1972), vol. 1, pp. 417–51.

18. This codex is discussed by Bernhard Bischoff, "Aus Alkuins Erdentagen," *Medievalia et Humanistica* 14 (1962): 31–37; repr. in *Mittelalterliche Studien* 2:12–19.

19. For these deluxe Carolingian books, see below, Chap. 6.

of letters).[20] In regard to the organization of book production in the larger Carolingian scriptoria, Jean Vezin has carefully gathered and discussed the data relative to the work practices of several scribes in a single manuscript, which was divided into *partes* assigned to each scribe by the director of the scriptorium; in this case, however, it does seem to me that the director's oversight often addressed the textual and orthographic work of copying rather than those issues that are specifically graphic, and that the alternation of hands (sometimes, after all, very different from each other) does not correspond precisely to the fascicles assigned to each scribe.[21]

But certainly the most significant and enduring consequence of this successful work—which comprised making educational processes more technical, professionalizing the role and work of copyists, rationally organizing their work—was the clear separation between the writing practices and scripts of elementary teaching, use, and documentation on one side, and the writing practices and scripts used for book production on the other. "Scribere in tabulis" had never corresponded entirely to "scribere in kartis."[22] But now there was born and diffused a precise awareness of this difference, of which we can hear some distant echo in Otlo of St. Emmeran's lively story of his writing apprentice who made his best effort to learn the *ars scribendi*—that is, book-hands—on his own, "furtivo et insolito modo, nec non sine docente" (in a furtive and unaccustomed way, and also without teaching), with the result that he used the pen "ad scribendum inrecto usu" (in a way that was incorrect for writing) so that everyone could tell that he had never learned to write well: naturally, this did not happen, "gratia Dei."[23] I believe that few episodes can better testify to the process of the marked formalization of book scripts, achieved through the work of the Carolingian graphic renaissance, and of the clear differentiation that then arose between the usages of elementary and ordinary scripts on one side and the scripts of books on the other. This situation, as Otlo himself confirms, influenced decisively the processes used in educating copyists, which from now on would be better articulated and more uniform everywhere, at least in programs and intentions.

20. *Casuum S. Galli Continuatio auctore Ekkehardo IV, MGH* Scriptores II:122.

21. "La répartition du travail dans les 'scriptoria' carolingiens," *Journal des savants* (1973): 212–27. My observations of the irregularity of the distribution of work were checked against Vat. Reg. lat. 762.

22. These phrases are reported by Bischoff, "Elementarunterricht," p. 19.

23. *De tentationibus*, PL 146:56–58; on Otlo, see G. Vinay, "Otlone di Sant'Emmeram ovvero l'autobiografia di un nevrotico," *La storiografia altomedievale* (Spoleto, 1969), pp. 15–37.

LITERACY OF EARLY MEDIEVAL SCRIBES

To conclude: what does the data gathered and compared in this summary investigation suggest as the hypotheses for further work and the points worth additional study? I will try to sum up rapidly those that seem to me the most obvious and the most worthy of consideration:

1. It seems incontestable that the traditional vision[24] of book production in the early medieval world as entirely concentrated in the reality of monastic or in any case (Lesne, Battelli) ecclesiastical scriptoria must in some measure be corrected, and moreover the possibility must be granted that, especially for Italy, there existed for different productive methods and environments individual copyists who copied for themselves, *scribae vagantes* who moved from center to center, part-time copyists belonging to the world of documentation, and lay copyists.

2. It seems almost certain that a great deal of room was left in the graphic education of scribes, especially in the seventh and eighth centuries, for self-teaching and direct imitation of models. Moreover, the influence of the head of a scriptorium, where there was one, may have been given over more to checking the orthographical-textual aspects of copying than to graphics. The exception would be the few great centers of calligraphy that were quite different from simple copying centers, where inexpert copyists might still be entrusted with copying all or parts of codices.[25]

3. It would be useful to check whether it is true that specific processes of scribes' graphic education, characterized by didactic autonomy and precise technicalization, generally were formed concomitantly with these factors: increase in book production in numerical terms; formation of a wider group of patrons; and, above all, affirmation of new, more complex, and more uniform techniques of writing and book manufacture. It seems that this may have occurred after the Carolingian period, even as late as the eleventh and twelfth centuries, concomitantly with the diffusion of the technique of writing *a tratto*, with separated strokes.

4. It seems reasonable to suppose that in the early Middle Ages there may have existed distinct sectors of "informal" book production, employed for the conservation or even for the limited propagation of particular texts, generally

24. Lesne, *Livres*, pp. 80–89; G. Battelli, *Lezioni di paleografia*, 2d ed. (Città del Vaticano, 1949), pp. 115–18; but see also the sensible views of M. Morelli and M. Palma, "Indagine su alcuni aspetti materiali della produzione libraria a Nonantola nel secolo IX," *Scrittura e civiltà* 6 (1982): 23–98.

25. On the difference between scriptoria and schools of calligraphy, as well as on the autodidactic efforts of the eighth century, see the fair evaluations of G. Cencetti, "Scriptoria e scritture nel monachesimo benedettino," *Il monachesimo nell'alto medioevo e la formazione della civiltà occidentale* (Spoleto, 1957), pp. 187–219; repr. in G. Cavallo, *Libri e lettori nel medioevo. Guida storica e critica* (Bari, 1977), pp. 73–97.

of technical or practical nature. If so, the symptoms of such production (informal script, irregularity of manufacture, atypical formats) would constitute notably important glimpses for distinguishing cultural environments different from those of official culture. The phenomenon deserves to be better distinguished and studied.

Finally, one cannot ignore, even if only to note the similarities and differences, the situation during the same period in the Greco-Byzantine world. There, as the recent investigations of Browning, Treu, and Cutler have shown, the higher percentage of lay literacy sustained by the diffuse bureaucratization of the state resulted in a more varied articulation of the patronage and production of books, including even the participation of laymen in non-negligible percentages during the ninth and tenth centuries.[26] By extension, for the early medieval West, if only mutatis mutandis, greater attention should be paid to the subjects such as the literacy of the laity, the graphic culture of judges and notaries, and the double activities of religious *notarii* who functioned also as copyists.[27] This last phenomenon, found not only in Italy but also elsewhere in Europe, as at San Gall, in southern Germany, in France, and in Spain, opens again the problem of the relationship between the scripts and culture of documentary production and the scripts and culture of books.[28]

26. R. Browning, "Literacy in the Byzantine World," *Byzantine and Modern Greek Studies* 4 (1978): 39–54; K. Treu, "Die Schreiber der datierten byzantinischer Handschriften des 9. und 10. Jahrhunderts," in V. Vavrinek, ed., *Beiträge zur byzantinischen Geschichte im 9.–11. Jahrhundert* (Prague, 1978), pp. 235–51; and especially the data gathered by A. Cutler, "The Social Status of Byzantine Scribes, 800–1500: A Statistical Analysis Based on Vogel-Gardhausen," *Byzantinische Zeitschrift* 74 (1981): 328–34.

27. On ecclesiastical notaries, see P. Riché, "La formation des scribes dans le monde mérovingien et carolingien," in *Instruction et vie religieuse dans le haut moyen âge* (London, 1981), pp. 75–80.

28. Finally, reference must be made generally to B. Bischoff, "Panorama des Handschriftenüberlieferung aus der Zeit Karls des Grossen," *Karl der Grosse*, vol. 2: *Das geistige Leben* (Düsseldorf, 1965), pp. 233–54 (repr. in *Mittelalterliche Studien* [Stuttgart, 1966–81], 3:5–38); and *Latin Paleography: Antiquity and the Middle Ages* (Cambridge, 1990), which I have obviously used to advantage.

6

Symbolic Aspects
of Written Evidence

THE DELIBERATELY GENERIC title of this paper[1] should not give the impression that I intend to provide a general treatment of graphic symbolism in the early Middle Ages. On the contrary, it introduces a problematic and open attempt to indicate some methodological lines for the study of symbolic aspects of written evidence, using for this purpose the detailed examination of an episode in the history of the book and writing that has been read several times before, although from different angles and in different ways.

I have elsewhere treated the figural-synthetic values that writing/book instruments can assume in certain circumstances, independent of the discursive-analytical values that belong to the text that is transmitted.[2] The

Originally published as "Aspetti simbolici delle testimonianze scritte," in *Simboli e simbologie nell'alto medioevo*, XXIII Settimana di studi sull'alto medioevo (Spoleto, 1976), pp. 813–44 and pls. 1–8.

1. This text corresponds for the most part (except for some formal improvements) to that read in the course of the Spoleto Settimana of 1975. The remaining parts are made up of additions or clarifications resulting from direct consultation of most of the codices cited in Paris, London, and Oxford that was made possible by a generous invitation from the University of London Department of Paleography, which I wish to thank publicly. I express my gratitude to the Direzione dell'Istituto di Patologia del Libro of Rome, which permitted me to study the Bible of S. Paolo; Dr. Johannes Duft, director of the Stiftbibliothek of San Gall, who permitted me to study the Virgil of San Gall; the Direzione dei Servizi Tecnici della Fabbrica of Saint Peter's, which provided every help for studying the epigraph of Hadrian I in the portico of the basilica of Saint Peter in Rome; and Dom Simeone Leone, archivist of the abbey of the SS.ma Trinità di Cava dei Tirreni, who generously helped in the study of the Cavese Bible.

2. "The Christian Conception of the Book," above, Chap. 2.

phenomenon is well known and thus does not require further discussion here. It may, however, be worthwhile to specify at the outset the issues whose investigation in my opinion would be especially interesting:

1. In the period that interests us, can one identify cases in which the figural-symbolic potential inherent in writing/book instruments was consciously and explicitly transformed by those who elaborated graphic models?

2. What was the result that such elaborators proposed to reach at different times?

3. Who formed the public to whom they addressed the figural message? Were they the educated or, at least, reading public to whom the discursive-analytic message contained in the text was addressed, or the semiliterate and illiterate public with whom writing/book instruments could have visual contact only indirectly?

4. How did elaborators at different moments work out the relationship with the likely (and almost always physically present) models to which they referred? This often happened by distorting the sense or attributing a meaning at least partially different from that originally proper to the models themselves.

To initiate a discourse on these many interconnected issues, I have chosen to discuss a case that I believe is exemplary for indicating an approach to them that might be considered both methodologically legitimate and, at the level of concrete conclusions, capable of yielding positive results. At issue are certain graphic aspects of the epigraphy and deluxe books of the period between Charlemagne and Charles the Bald: evidence and events about which, as we all know, Bernhard Bischoff made interpretative contributions of definitive value[3] and to which attention was subsequently called again by a posthumous work of the English historian of writing Stanley Morison.[4] Morison's suggestive comments call for some verification, and provide our point of departure.

3. In addition to other articles cited here and there in the text, one must cite the following, fundamental contributions: "Die Hofbibliothek Karls des Grossen," and "Panorama des Hand-schriftenüberlieferung aus der Zeit Karls des Grossen," both in *Karl der Grosse*, vol. 2: *Das geistige Leben* (Düsseldorf, 1965), pp. 42–62; "La minuscule caroline et le renouveau culturel sous Charlemagne," *Bulletin de l'Institut de Recherche et d'Histoire des Textes* 15 (1967–68): 333–36; and "Die Hofbibliothek unter Ludwig dem Frommen," in *Medieval Learning and Literature: Essays Presented to R. W. Hunt*, ed. J. J. G. Alexander and M. T. Gibson (Oxford, 1976), pp. 3–22.

4. *Politics and Script: Aspects of Freedom and Authority in the Development of Greco-Latin Script from the Sixth-century B.C. to the Twentieth Century*, ed. N. Barker (Oxford, 1972).

According to Morison, one can recognize in some graphic innovations, found both in the inscriptions that can be attributed directly to the environment of Charlemagne's court and in the deluxe books produced in the palace school or at Tours, the expression of a precise political will and a consequent, conscious selection of visual means by which it can be rendered explicit. Morison sees this as happening particularly in two cases: the use of capitals of classical epigraphic type in the epitaph of Hadrian I that Alcuin had made for Charlemagne in 796, today located in the portico of the basilica of Saint Peter; and the introduction of the same capitals of epigraphic type and of so-called rustic capitals in the titles and initial pages of what the English scholar terms the "royal books" of Charlemagne. "The emperor's appropriation of Augustan Roman capitals," writes Morison, "was a political act of the first importance, and as such intended to impress the educated world." He adds that "the notion of a Christian lettering-style appropriate to a Christian Roman emperor was abandoned in favor of an imperial lettering-style appropriate to a pagan Roman emperor." This would have happened through a deliberate decision to break with preceding graphic tradition, whose capitals mixed with uncials would have represented a now inadmissible stylistic dependence on the graphic models of Byzantium. "It may be accepted," concludes Morison, "that Alcuin realized, if he did not design, the later implications of the 'renovatio.' Accordingly, he saw the revived use of Augustan Square capitals as a political act. Did he understand also that the suppression of the mixed Capitals used for titles . . . signified a clean break with a habit of mind having two centuries of precedent? The fact remains that, for a high political reason, the pagan Roman Square Imperial Capitals and the pagan rustic capitals were given a prime place in the displayed Carolingian titling scripts, while the Christian uncials and Half-uncials came second and third."[5]

Some of Morison's assertions, such as his attribution of the irregular minuscule adopted in pre-Carolingian codices to a direct dependence on presumed Byzantine-Greek graphic forms, do not seem valid. But the concept of a direct filiation between monumental Carolingian capitals and classical epigraphic models, more specifically those of the Augustan age, has a long tradition, having been sustained even before Morison by Giovanni Battista De Rossi,[6] Paul Deschamps,[7] and Edward Kenneth Rand.[8] Nicolete Gray

5. Ibid., pp. 143, 145, 171, 172–73.
6. "L'inscription du tombeau d'Hadrien I composée et gravée en France par ordre de Charlemagne," *Mélanges d'archéologie et d'histoire* 8 (1888): 478–501, esp. p. 487: "Dans les lettres des plus beaux manuscrits carloviengiens je remarque une imitation évidemment intentionelle et

even affirmed, in exact agreement with Morison's hypothesis, that "as in paleography, so in epigraphy, the Carolingians introduced a style of writing reflecting the idea of their empire. If the caroline minuscule is classical in its clarity, normality and confidence, the Carolingian inscribed letter is a direct emulation of classical forms."[9] She later gave this opinion a more nuanced and articulated expression by suggesting the doubtlessly correct hypothesis that the earliest Carolingian capitals were "probably copied from late classical manuscripts," but repeating her opinion that the Carolingian majuscule system was "directly based on Roman inscriptional models."[10]

If it were enough to refer to the hypotheses formulated by several scholars at different times, my contribution could stop here: certainly there has already been a clear, adequately documented enunciation of the proposition that writing under Charlemagne assumed the symbolic function of expressing specific ideological values, and the political and intellectual theory of the *renovatio Imperii* in particular. But assertions need to be checked against the sources. And when this is done, by examining and comparing some of the various epigraphic and, especially, book evidence that I have collected, one finds that the reality in which Carolingian book-graphic products were situated is much more complex and richer than appears at first glance. A correct interpretation of the sources—in our case, graphic types, codices, and inscriptions—cannot but take this complexity and richness into account.

The first example to be considered is the famous funerary inscription for Hadrian I that Charlemagne had executed in France on black marble and that today is embedded in the wall of the portico of Saint Peter's Basilica (fig. 15).[11] It is apparent on first glance that the design of the letters of this singular stone is rather similar to those of the capitals used in the inscriptions of the first or second century A.D. Personal study of the stone, moreover, has permitted me to determine that the letters themselves were incised using the ancient "triangular groove" technique, although very lightly and thus without producing particularly noticeable chiaroscural effects. Since this is a tech-

---

étudiées des types classiques de la paléographie monumentale des anciens temps de l'empire, surtout des formes calligraphiques du second siècle et de l'époque des premiers Antonins."

7. *Etude sur la paléographie des inscriptions lapidaires* (Paris, 1929), p. 14 (where he repeats a judgment of L. Delisle).

8. *A Survey of the Manuscripts of Tours*, vol. 1 (Cambridge, Mass., 1929), pp. 40–43.

9. "The Paleography of the Latin Inscriptions of the Eighth, Ninth, and Tenth Centuries in Italy," *Papers of the British School at Rome* 16 (1948): 86–87.

10. *Lettering as Drawing* (London, 1971), pp. 97–98.

11. See, in addition to the article already cited by G. B. De Rossi: L. Wallach, "Alcuin's Epitaph of Hadrian I," in *American Journal of Philology* 72, no. 2 (1951): 128–44; and esp. J. Ramacker, "Die Werkstattheimat der Grabplatte Papst Hadrianus I," in *Römische Quartalschrift* 59 (1964): 36–78.

HIC PA ERECCLESIAE ROMAE DECVS INCLYTVS AVCTOR
HADRIANVS REQVIEM PAPA BEATVS HABET
VIR CVI VITA DS PIETAS LEX GLORIA CHRISTVS
PASTOR APOSTOLICE SPROMPTVS AD OMNE BONVM
NOBILIS EX MAGNA GENITVS IAMGEN TE PARENTVM
SED SACRIS LONGE NOBILIOR MERITIS
EXORNARE STVDENS DEVOTO PECTORE PA STOR
SEMPER VBIQVE SVO TEMPLA SACRATA DO
ECCLESIAS DONIS POPVLO ET DOGMAT ES CO
IMBVIT ET CVNCTIS PANDIT ADASTRA VIAM
PAVPERIBVS LARGVS NVLLI PIETATE SECVNDVS
ET PRO PLEBE SACRIS PERVIGIL IN PRECIBVS
DOCTRINIS OPIBVS MVRIS EREXERAT ARCES
VRBS CAPVT ORBIS HONOR INCLYTA ROMA TVAS
MORS CINIL NO CIT XP QAE MORTE PEREMPTA EST
IANVA SED VITAE MOX MELIORIS ERAT
POST PAREM LACRIMIS KARLVS HAEC CARMINA SCRIBSI
TV MIHI DVLCIS AMOR MODO PLANGO PATER
TV MEMOR ES TO MEI SEQITVR EMENS ME A SEMPER
CV TX POT ENEAS REGNA BEATA POLI
TE CLERVS POPVLVS MAGNO DILEXIT AMO
OMNIBVS VNVS AMOR OPTIME PRAE SVLERAS
NOMINA IVNGO SIM VT TITVLS CLARISSIME NOSTRA
HADRIANVS KAROLVS RE EGO TV Q PATER
QVISQ LEGAS VERSVS DEVOTO PECTORE SVPPLEX
AMBORVM MITIS DIC MISE RERE DS
HAEC TVAN VNC ENEAT REQVIES CRSSIME MEMBRA
CVM SCIS ANIMA GAVDEAT ALMA DI
VLTIMA QVIPPE TVAS DON EC TVBA CLAMET IN AVRES
PRINCIPE CVM PETROS VRGE VIDERED M
AVDITVR SERIS VOCEM SCIOI VDICIS ALMAM
INTRAN VNC DNI GAVDIA MAGNA TVI
TVNC MEMOR ES TO TVI NATI PAE R OPTIME POSCO
CVM PATRE DICN ATVS PERGAT ETIS EMEVS
O P ETE REGNA PATER FELIX CAELES TIA XPI
INDE TVVM PRECIBVS AVXILIA REGE REGEM
DVM SOLIGNICO MOR VTILVS SPLENDES CITA BAX E
LAVS TVAS CE PATER SEMPER IN ORBE MANET
SEDIT BEATAE MEMORIAE HADRIANVS PAPA
ANNOS XXIII MENSES X DIES XVII OBIIT VII KLIAN

15. Funerary stone of Hadrian I, basilica of Saint Peter
(photo: fabbrica of S. Pietro)

nique that was unknown in the early Middle Ages, I do not believe that there can be any doubt that its reappearance derived from the study and imitation of ancient epigraphy.

But some elements of the funerary inscription of Hadrian I, relating not to the techniques of execution but to the design and form of individual letters, suggest other sources and reveal different models. These include: the frequent links joining two letters, sometimes in ways that were not customary; the *T*'s higher than other letters; the occasional *M*'s with a hint of an ornamental, leftward-facing tail added to the meeting point of the central shafts (unfortunately not distinguishable in the photograph); and the *X*'s with the crooked second and third strokes (apparent in the fourth line from the bottom). Although these elements do not appear (or appear only rarely) in classical Roman epigraphy, one does encounter the first two in some of the epigraphs designed by Furius Dionisius Filocalus, using his well-known monumental capital rich with ornamental elements, which Pope Damasus (366–84) had placed in numerous Roman churches during his pontificate.[12] These parallels, especially in regard to the links between letters, were noted by Johannes Ramacker in an important article sustaining the thesis of a direct dependence of the Carolingian monumental capital on that of the *tituli Damasiani.*[13]

Yet there are two essential characteristics of filocalian stylization that do not figure in the epitaph of Hadrian I: the ornamental curls at the ends of the vertical shafts and the strong chiaroscural contrasts of the strokes. That is natural enough, if one considers that in the Gaul of the twilight of the eighth century it would not have been easy for either the *ordinator* or the Carolingian stonecutter to be inspired by the graphic forms of the distant roman model. One can, therefore, postulate the existence of an intermediate model that should be sought, I believe, not in epigraphy but in the world of manuscript books, where (as we shall see) one often encounters those somewhat particular *M*'s and *X*'s already mentioned. But determining this intermediate manuscript model requires a discourse that, while starting from that complex phenomenon which has been aptly called the "Carolingian graphic renaissance," also considers its more or less immediate antecedents. In fact, as is well known, the Carolingian graphic renaissance does not con-

---

12. See texts and reproductions in *Epigrammata damasiana*, ed. A. Ferrua, Sussidi allo studio delle antichità cristiane, 3 (Città del Vaticano, 1942); and, from a paleographical perspective, N. Gray, "The Filocalian Letter," in *Papers of the British School at Rome* 24 (1958): 5–13; as well as some comments in A. Petrucci, "Per la datazione del 'Virgilio Augusteo': Osservazioni e proposte," in *Miscellanea in memoria di Giorgio Cencetti*, P. Supino, ed. (Turin, 1973), pp. 29–45, esp. 38–40.

13. "Werkstattheimat," esp. pp. 66–67, 76.

sist only of a mechanical imitation and artful resurrection of ancient monumental capitals on one side and so-called rustic capitals on the other. It also entailed the rebirth of uncial and semi-uncial, the reconstruction of an authentic hierarchy of script types, and, finally, the creation a new kind of deluxe manuscript, illuminated or only ornamented, based on late antique models.

Carolingian uncial—mainly chosen for deluxe books—is not a stylistically homogeneous script nor, beyond the generic imitation of late antique models of the sixth century shared by practically all exemplars, can it be considered an independent typification with precise characteristics of its own. One can distinguish at least three different strands. Only the first of these, represented by the codices of the court, reveals a direct dependence on the uncial used at Rome during the sixth and seventh centuries. The Viennese "Coronation" Gospels group, although produced by a different school that also belonged to the court environment, drew its direct inspiration instead from models of north Italian uncial attributable to the sixth century. The last strand, represented by the uncial of Tours—and specifically the Tours of Alcuin—has its own characteristics, and only later, toward the middle of the century, did it turn into an autonomous reelaboration of the graphic forms of roman derivation.[14]

Similarly lacking in homogeneity were monumental capitals, which appear in manuscripts of the Carolingian court parallel to and contemporary with the renaissance of late antique uncial. But in the oldest exemplars, they certainly took on forms rather close to those of the epitaph of Hadrian I, especially in Godescalc's Gospels of 781–83 (fig. 16).[15] One sees there, in fact, both some letters higher than others (*T, I*) and the *M* and *N* with the little ornamental tail turned toward the left. The same forms also appear in the Psalter written by Dagulfus for the pope around 783,[16] in the Arsénal 599 Gospels,[17] and in the well-known so-called Ada Gospels conserved at

---

14. A. Petrucci, "L'onciale romana. Origini, sviluppo e diffusione di una stilizzazione grafica altomedievale (sec. VI–IX)," in *Studi medievali*, 3d ser. 12 (1971): 127–31.

15. Paris, B.N. MS nouv. acq. lat. 1203 (= *CLA* 681). See W. Köhler, *Die Karolingische Miniaturen*, vol. 2: *Die Hofschule Karls des Grossen* (Berlin, 1958), pp. 22–28, pl. 1–12; J. Porcher, "I manoscritti dipinti," in J. Hubert, J. Porcher, and W. F. Volbach, *L'impero carolingio* (Milan, 1968), pp. 75–78.

16. Vienna, Nationalbibliothek MS lat. 1861 (= *CLA* 1504); see *Monumenta palaeographica Vindobonensia. Denkmälerder Schreibkunst*, vol. 1, ed. R. Beer (Leipzig, 1910), pls. 17–26; H. J. Hermann, *Die frühmittelalterlichen Handschriften des Abendlandes*, Die illuminierte Handschriften und Inkunabeln der Nationalbibliothek in Wien, 1 (Leipzig, 1923), pp. 57–63, n. 10; Köhler, *Hofschule*, pp. 42–46 and pls. 31, 32; *Charlemagne. Oeuvre, rayonnement et survivances* (Aix-la-Chapelle, 1965), n. 413, pp. 245–46.

17. *CLA* 517; Köhler, *Hofschule*, pp. 29–33 and pls. 13–19; J. Boussard, "L'evangélaire d'or ms.

SYMBOLIC ASPECTS OF WRITTEN EVIDENCE

16. Paris, B.N., MS nouv. acq. lat. 1203, fol. 4a

Trier;[18] in this last, however, the horizontal strokes of individual letters end in obvious ornamental forkings that are sometimes exaggerated and curled. In all these examples, moreover, the tracing of individual letters is rather

---

599," in *Mélanges d'histoire du livre ... Frantz Calot* (Paris, 1960), pp. 3–14; *Charlemagne*, n. 412 and pl. 53.

18. *CLA* 1366; Köhler, *Hofschule*, pp. 34–41 and pls. 20–30; *Charlemagne*, nn. 416, 416a, pp. 247–48.

heavy, the breadth of the strokes is not uniform but tends instead to fatten toward the ends with more or less obvious triangulature, and the round letters are far from being perfect circles.

The capital used for the *initia* in the manuscripts of Saint Martin of Tours attributable to the period before Alcuin has nothing to do with the monumental capital of the court school, except for an evident effort at regularity that recalls insular antecedents (such as the "Codex Bigotianus" of the Gospels)[19] or Mordramnus of Corbie's examples of the Bible.[20] It is characterized by the insertion of letters distant from any ancient model, such as the squared *C* or the *A* with double horizontal bars. According to Rand, credit is due to Alcuin for introducing at Tours between 796 and 804 not only a "genuine renaissance of ancient styles" but also the "ancient form of the squared capital,"[21] a hypothesis for which he finds confirmation in the stone of Hadrian I. In reality, attributions of Touraine manuscripts specifically to the period of Alcuin's rule—which after all was fairly brief—are somewhat dubious; while Ramacker's carefully reasoned remarks make his direct participation in the manufacture of Hadrian I's epitaph also seem improbable. One can thus concur with Porcher that, given the abbey's rich tradition of its own, the stylistic influence of the old, almost blind Anglo-Saxon scholar must have been minimal at the level of graphics and book production.[22] In fact, to the extent one can judge from the limited perspective of our investigation, there is not much that is really epigraphic in a classical sense in capitals such as those in the codex Urbinate lat. 532 of Boethius (fig. 17),[23] which despite their notable elegance lack harmony in the relations between letters and are characterized by the use of thin forkings at the ends of *C*'s and *S*'s; similarly discordant are the capitals of Donatus codex Vat. Reg. lat. 1484, in which Rand rather imprudently wished to see "the dignity of an inscription of the Augustan age."[24] Rather, both manuscripts unmistakably announce the presence of book models. The same can also be said of other early ninth-century codices attributable to Tours, where one finds a precise change of graphic style only at the end of the rule of Fridugisus.

It thus seems beyond doubt that in the first Carolingian period there was a notable stylistic and technical divergence between the books produced at Tours and those of the court school. At Tours, a model based on the late

19. Of the late eighth century: *CLA* 526; E. A. Lowe, *English Uncial* (Oxford, 1960), pl. XXXa.

20. *CLA* 707; repr. in Morison, *Politics and Script*, pl. 121.

21. Rand, *Survey*, pp. 40, 41.

22. *Impero carolingio*, p. 127.

23. Rand, *Survey*, n. 20, pl. XXXII; his evaluation is at p. 101.

24. *Survey*, n. 89, p. 143 and pls. CX–CXI.

SYMBOLIC ASPECTS OF WRITTEN EVIDENCE

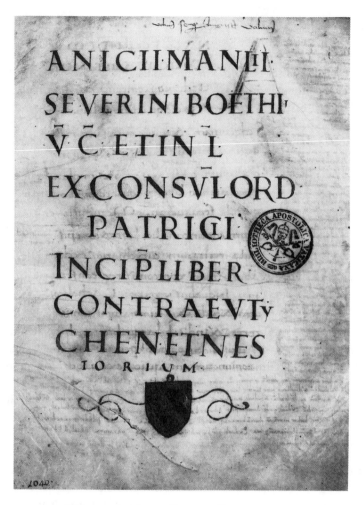

17. Biblioteca Apostolica Vaticana, Urb. lat. 532, fol. 1r

antique deluxe book was imposed late and never completely. One also encounters at Tours the insertion of ancient elements of classical origin that are unknown elsewhere, such as iconographic motifs drawn from imperial coins. Most of all, the new minuscule broadly dominates the graphic field of the codex at Tours, with the rustic capital also being used more than elsewhere at the expense both of uncial of Italian inspiration and of the regularized monumental capital, which arrived here relatively late. It is not easy, and perhaps not essential, to explain the reasons for such diversity. One might, however, hazard the hypothesis that early Carolingian Tours,

being a scriptorial center of ancient date that was well organized already
in the eighth century, felt the influence both of insular models and, above
all, of local tradition. There may also have been lacking the understanding,
instruments, and masters who—working in a court environment that was
probably newer, more open, and more differentiated—rendered possible
the use of purple, the exact constructive geometry, and punctual imitation
of different models of both books and graphics of greater or lesser antiquity.

Many of the stylistic characteristics of this first and still uncertain Carolingian monumental capital are also shared, if less obviously, by the contemporary uncial of roman derivation. As has already been suggested with regard
to the epitaph of Hadrian I, this uncial went back to the ancient filocalian
graphic tradition in what one might call its latest and most diffused version,
as revived and modified by Italian book production of the fifth and sixth
centuries. It is also here, particularly in some great deluxe codices of the
period, rather than in the epigraphy of the classical age or the *tituli Damasiani*, that were found the direct models of the early Carolingian monumental capital. A codex such as the purple Gospels of Trento (+Dublin and
London = *CLA* II, p. 17 and n. 437),[25] of Italian origin and attributed to the
fifth century, presents majuscule initials of uncial-capital type, richly "flowered" and characterized by obvious curling, that could easily be compared
with the equally ornate Gospels of Godescalc or the Arsénal. It is not by
chance, therefore, that Bernhard Bischoff and Carl Nordenfalk in 1965, in
the catalogue of the great exhibition of Aquisgrana, likened the so-called
Augusteus Virgil[26] and the Codex Arcerianus of the *Corpus Agrimensorum*[27]
to the Carolingian books produced at the highest level.[28]

In the Augusteus Virgil—that singular and enigmatic fragment from a
codex difficult to imagine in its entirety—one already sees the links between
two or more letters and the elevation of *L, F,* and *T* on the line, both typical
of the stone of Hadrian I, as well as the light forkings at the ends of some
letters (*C, G, S, V, Z*) that characterize the uncial and monumental capital
of the court school. But it is in the sixth-century Arcerianus A that we
discover still more direct analogies with the Carolingian examples: there

25. See the reproduction in *API*, 7, fasc. 52, pls. 94–96; also E. Cau, "Ricerche sui codici in
onciale dell'Italia settentrionale (secoli IV–VI)," *Ricerche medievali* 3 (1968): 20 and pl. IX.

26. *CLA* I, p. 13 and VIII, p. 9; for the relevant bibliography, see my article "Per la datazione." See also the important hints contained in G. Cavallo's review of the complete reproduction in *Rivista di filologia e di istruzione classica* 100 (1972): 511–18.

27. *CLA* 1347b. See the complete reproduction: *Corpus Agrimensorum Romanorum. Codex
Arcerianus A der Herzog-August-Bibliothek zu Wolfenbüttel*, ed. H. Butzmann (Lugduni Batavorum, 1970), and also the remarks in Petrucci, "Onciale romana," pp. 107–09.

28. *Charlemagne*, nn. 386–87 and pp. 207, 227–29.

capitals appear only in title or as initial letters, while the text, of obviously "roman" stylization, is in uncial. The heavily traced capitals of the Arcerianus A, moreover, have an abundance of letters higher than the others, as well as the obvious forkings at the end of the horizontal bars of some letters and the little tail added to the conjunction of the medial bars of the *M* that characterize the earliest Carolingian expressions of the type. Analogous characteristics can also be found in the monumental capitals inserted for the titles, *initia,* and *explicit* in other uncial or semi-uncial codices of the same period: examples include B.N. lat. 12205, containing the *Regula Magistri,*[29] and the Biblioteca Laurenziana's Paulus Orosius "confectus in statione magistri Viliaric antiquarii."[30] In both these cases, the capitals are used not as a text script as in the Augusteus Virgil but as a layout script in a manner analogous to the Carolingian usage. Also different is the case history provided by initials in the true sense of the word, whose vicissitudes between late antiquity and the early Middle Ages have been traced by Carl Nordenfalk in a book full of documented examples.[31] This case is different, to begin with, because initials, being isolated individuals, do not belong to a continuous written context, so that their pictorial-ornamental characteristics could be freely accentuated; they were also nearly always executed by persons different from the scribes, who generally were educated to other traditions and models. Nevertheless, the Arcerianus A contains some initials drawn by pen with abundant curls that offer a ready comparison to the analogous initials of the Arsénal Gospel.

Like uncial, therefore, Carolingian capitals fail to present a solid stylistic uniformity, being in this way a typical script of imitation. The manuscripts grouped with the so-called Viennese "Coronation" Gospels, also produced in court circles but by a different school whose Hellenistic-Byzantine inspiration is obvious in the miniatures, present a rather different and much more organically compact typification.[32] A first example of this group is provided by the eponymous codex,[33] the Viennese Gospels, whose opening pages present some splendid monumental capital letters that are perfectly geometrical,

29. *CLA* 633; see also *Regula Magistri. Edition diplomatique des manuscrits latins 12205 et 12634 de Paris,* ed. H. Vanderhoven and F. Masai, Publications de Scriptorium, 3 (Brussels and Paris, 1953), esp. pp. 13–26 and pls. I–IV.

30. *CLA* 298; see also A. Petrucci, "Un altro codice della bottega di Viliari," in *Studi offerti a Roberto Ridolfi,* Biblioteca di bibliografia italiana, 71 (Florence, 1973), pp. 399–406.

31. C. Nordenfalk, *Die spätantiken Zierbuchstaben* (Stockholm, 1970).

32. See W. Köhler, *Die Karolingische Miniaturen,* vol. 3: *Die Gruppe des Wiener Krönungs-Evangeliars. Metzer Handschriften* (Berlin, 1960); and also Porcher, *Impero carolingio,* pp. 92–98.

33. *CLA* 1406; Köhler, *Gruppe,* pls. 1–27.

traced with noncontrasting strokes, without forkings or ornamental curls at the end of the bars, and constructed with precise formal balance. Other examples belong to the Brussels Gospels,[34] whose initial page displays a capital that is, however, less harmonious in its proportions and tracing than those found further in the codex. Finally, deluxe codices often have normalized and austere monumental capitals like this alongside the more animated and ornate ones already described: this occurs, for example, in the famous Lorsch Gospels, divided between Rome and Bucharest,[35] where a capital with heavy tracing and abundant curls is accompanied by another that is dry and slender, belonging to all appearances to another and different stylization (fig. 18); it also occurs in the Gospels of Saint Médard of Soissons (B.N. lat. 8850),[36] where the normalized monumental capital presents the *M*-with the little tail turned to the left as an individual element within a canon now repeated faithfully. One can conclude from this that the normalized capital, after having appeared already perfect in the Coronation Gospels, was then adopted in the court school, where it competed with other, richer stylizations before finding better fortune and wider diffusion among the various centers operating for the Carolingian courts in the course of the ninth century.

But where could the inspiration and models have come from? How and why could they have been born, already perfect, in a school of book production tightly bound to the Byzantine-Greek artistic world? It is difficult to answer such questions, nor am I prepared to do so here and now, but I believe it may nonetheless be useful to venture some hypotheses with the understanding that they are merely provisional.

In the first place, I believe that it is very likely that a model and perhaps *the* model of the normalized monumental capital had been elaborated by the "scriptor regius Bertcaudus" whom Lupus of Ferrières mentioned in his 836 letter to Aginard as having reconstructed the "mensura . . . antiquarum litterarum, dumtaxat earum quae maximae sunt et unciales a quibusdam vocari existimantur" (measure of antique letters, or at least of those which are most noble and which are considered to be called uncials by some).[37] This con-

---

34. Brussels, Bibl. Royale, MS no. 18723; Köhler, *Gruppe*, pp. 85–93, pls. 40–48.

35. Divided into two parts: Alba Julia (Romania), Biblioteca Documentaria Batthayneum, and Biblioteca Apostolica Vaticana Pal. lat. 50. Reproduced in its entirety: *The Lorsch Gospels*, ed. W. Braunfels (New York, 1967). See also, Köhler, *Hofschule*, pp. 88–100 and pls. 96–116.

36. Köhler, *Hofschule*, pp. 70–82 and pls. 67–93; *Charlemagne*, n. 417, p. 249. Both types of capital also appear in the Codex Aureus of the British Library, Harl. 2788 (= *CLA* 198), for which see Köhler, *Hofschule*, pp. 56–69 and pls. 42–66.

37. See Bischoff, *Charlemagne*, n. 385a and pl. 36, and the same scholar's "Paläographische und literaturwissenschaftliche Beobachtungen zu Einhards Kreuzsockel," in K. Hauck, ed.,

18. Lorsch Gospels, second part, Biblioteca Apostolica Vaticana, Pal. lat. 50, fol. 8r

clusion tends to be confirmed by the fact that the first examples of such writing come from court circles, where Bertcaudus was *scriptor regius*; by Lupus's singling out of a strict canon (*mensura*) which cannot refer to the ornate monumental capital that is variously interpreted from example to example; and by the perfect correspondence between the known examples of the normalized capital and the ideal alphabet drawn in a codex contemporary with Lupus's letter, which Bischoff has identified as belonging to him.

Admitting all this to be true or likely, there remains the problem of the models that inspired Bertcaudus or his predecessors. Here, too, in my opinion, one must discard the usual hypothesis of epigraphic sources. Rather, it is probable that the *mensura* was obtained by a reelaboration in a normalizing sense of late antique book models executed using geometrical instruments (compass and straight-edge) that were different from those abundant with decoration and irregularities that we have called indirectly filocalian.

It is very probable—given that we are speaking here of hypotheses—that such models belonged to the group of codices using the so-called elegant or squared type of monumental capitals—an admittedly artificial and limited style but one of unbroken continuity and imposing dignity. Two very well known examples of this tradition are the Augusteus Virgil and the San Gall Virgil.[38] In particular, the monumental capital of the second and third San Gall hands presents undeniable points of contact with the normalized capital of the Carolingian court school: first, it has a tracing that is not strongly chiaroscural; the round letters (*C, G, O*) tend to perfect circularity; and, finally, instead of the indirectly filocalian curls and forkings at the ends of horizontal and vertical shafts, it presents those little straight complementary strokes that rather clearly contribute to the differentiation of "normalized" Carolingian capitals from different contemporary typifications.

Even if it may be difficult to accept—and impossible to prove—that precisely these codices or one analogous to them ended up in the hand of Bertcaudus and his disciples, their existence does, in my opinion, render more probable the hypothesis developed here that the different stylizations

---

Das Einhardkreuz. Vorträge und Studien der Münsterauer Diskussion zum Arcus Einhardi, Abhandlungen der Akademie der Wissenschaften in Göttingen, phil.-hist. Klasse, 3d ser. 87 (1974): 93–95.

38. For the San Gall Virgil, for which there is no complete reproduction, see *CLA* 977 and M. Geymonat, "I codici G e V di Virgilio," in *Memorie dell'Istituto Lombardo di Scienze e Lettere* 29 (1966): 289–438, esp. pp. 292–300. As a working hypothesis, I would distinguish at least three hands in the series of fragments preserved in the San Gall Stiftbibliothek: no. 1394, of which the first can be seen only in the first folio (pp. 7–8); the second in pp. 11–12, 39–40, 43–44, and 47–48; and the third in pp. 16–15, 20–19, 23–24, 27–28, 31–32. Attribution of pp. 35–36 remains difficult. For a general hint about the influence of this MS (together with the Augusteus) on the calligraphy of Tours, see Rand, *Survey*, p. 40.

of monumental capitals elaborated in Charlemagne's court circles were based on models derived from late antique books rather than from epigraphy. Examining the deluxe Carolingian book as a whole, moreover, including its particular characteristics and the function it served in the educated culture of its time, permits us to adduce other more general elements that support this formulation of the problem.

The deluxe Carolingian book is characterized by recourse to layout scripts of ancient origin; the reconstitution of a rigid hierarchy of graphic types; the frequent use of parchment colored even partially in red; the use of writing in gold or silver; a rich ornamentation and, often, an ample stock of illustrations, including full-page figured miniatures; patronage generally coming from high personages in the royal and imperial family and court; and texts of generally scriptural or liturgical content, with hagiographic or other subjects being rarer. It did not, however—at least for the first period that extended until the death of Charlemagne—constitute an artistic product standardized within precise parameters of either stylization or manufacture. Red-colored parchment was adopted in some cases and not in others. In some volumes only some leaves were colored, in others they all were. Chrysography, usually linked to purple parchment, sometimes is adopted even on white parchment. Among the products of the court school, there are obvious differences in both ornamentation and miniatures between the Vienna Gospels and the Tours Gospels groups. And the list could be extended.

Deluxe Carolingian books also present interesting considerations regarding the techniques by which they were manufactured, including the architectonics of the page and the resulting relationship between text and ornament. There is, for example, a notable diversity in formats. These extend from a medium-oblong model (Godescalc and Arsénal) to the model of the Gospels themselves that, although still oblong, is larger (with a page size averaging 365 × 250 mm., and 30–32 lines per page), while the three manuscripts of the Coronation group revert to a smaller size with squarer dimensions (about 310 × 240 mm., with 23–26 lines per page). One also encounters the oversized format belonging to some of the large Tours Bibles (about 480 × 360 mm., except the earliest example, San Gall no. 75, which is 537 × 393 mm., with 50–51 lines per page); a smaller format tending toward square was the rule for the Tours Gospels, with the height-width ratio of both examples approaching the 5:4 proportion theorized in a Tours text of the ninth century.[39] Other details worth noting include: the techniques for perforations,

---

39. See E. K. Rand and L. W. Jones, *Studies in the Script of Tours*, vol. 2: *The Earliest Book of Tours* (Cambridge, Mass., 1934), p. 88.

which were made within or close to the space used for writing;[40] the glimpses of still imperfect technique provided by the adjustments that scribes sometimes had to make, erasing part of a page's decorative frame in order to insert writing into a scheme of ornamentation that had been done in advance;[41] the experiments in creating a visual linkage between the illuminated page and the facing title page;[42] and so forth.

None of this denies that the deluxe Carolingian book, which constituted a novelty in the European cultural world of its times, reflected a political purpose. The use of purple-dyed parchment, in particular, which systematically reappears in the West after more than two centuries,[43] might encourage us to attribute to codices written for Charlemagne or members of his family and court the precise symbology of imperial power parallel to that which some scholars have seen in the rebirth of the monumental capital. This is especially so because purple, whether as coloring from cloth or ink, was reserved to the emperors by right in Byzantium. It is also known that Charlemagne and his court took up wearing of purple cloth after Christmas in the year 800 and that the solemn privileges issued by some of his successors (if not by Charlemagne himself) bear the imperial subscription in red according to the Byzantine custom of the chrysobollos.

It is, then, certainly appropriate that our specific research would take into account the relationship between politics and Carolingian deluxe books. But as was true with manuscript illumination that followed late antique sources, and with capitals that were all reconstructed by imitating sixth-century Italian models, so it seems to me that a simpler explanation for the use even of purple-dyed parchment and chrysography can be made in terms of the imitation of late antique practice that resulted from a general drive to the

40. For example, in the Gospel of St. Médard of Soissons (B.N. lat. 8850) and the London Codex Aureus, Harl. 2788.

41. Thus in the Codex Aureus; and one can also note the uncertain and irregular edging lines that recur in the Gospels of Godescalc.

42. The evidence is assembled by H. Roosen-Runge, *Farbgebung und Technik frühmittelalterlicher Buchmalerei. Studien zu den Traktaten "Mappae Clavicula" und "Heraclius,"* vol. 1 (1967), p. 33 and pl. I.

43. For the rebirth in Carolingian times of the use of purple (variously obtained) in the production of books, see I. Carini, *La porpora e il colore porporino nella diplomatica specialmente siciliana* (Palermo, 1880), pp. 31–32, 52, 60–63; W. Wattenbach, *Das Schriftwesen im Mittelalter* (Leipzig, 1896), pp. 132–39; E. A. Lowe, "The Morgan Golden Gospels: The Date and Origin of the Manuscript," in *Studies in Art and Literature for Belle da Costa Greene* (Princeton, 1954), pp. 266–79, repr. in *Palaeographical Papers, 1907–1965,* ed. L. Bieler, vol. 2 (Oxford, 1972), pp. 399–416; and H. Roosen-Runge and A. E. A. Werner, "The Pictorial Technique of the Lindisfarne Gospels," in *Evangeliorum quattuor Codex Lindisfarnensis* (Oltun and Lausannae, 1960), pp. 263–65.

antique and from the antiquarian and archeological tastes which were widely diffused in the early Carolingian world. In this regard, it is certainly interesting to note the poetic accompaniment with which Godescalc dedicated his Gospels to Charlemagne.

> Aurea purpurei pinguntur grammata scedis
> Regna poli roseo pate sanguine facta tonantis
> Fulgida stelligeri promunt et gaudia celi
> Eloquiumque dei digno fulgore coruscans
> Splendida perpetua promittit praemia vitae.
> En precepta dei colorata colore rosarum
> . . . . . .
> Sic doctrina dei pretiosis scripta metallis
> Lucida luciflui perducit ad atria regni.[44]

Golden letters drawn on leaves of purple, like the kingdoms of thundering heaven made blood-red, disclose the brilliant rewards of the star-bearing heaven, and an eloquence shimmering with a brightness worthy of God, augurs the splendid rewards of eternal life. Behold the commands of God tinted with the hue of roses. . . . In this way the teaching of God written in precious metals extends forward toward the shining palace of a light-filled kingdom.

While certainly aware of the symbolic value of the purple coloring of the leaves of his codex (partial as they were, since the margins were left white), Godescalc thus saw it in connection with the special dignity of the Gospels text rather than the status of the recipient.

Among the Italian (and Greek) codices of the fifth and sixth centuries that were used as models for the graphic and figural compositions that Carolingian artists inserted into their own, revived manufactures, there must have been some, if not many, that were lettered in gold or silver on purple-dyed parchment. Like every other characteristic of deluxe early Carolingian books, the use of purple and chrysography came to the masters of the court school not from an act of imperial will but from the mute eloquence of great models that came to Charlemagne's Gaul from the rich Italian reservoir, glowing with color, images, and imposing graphic compositions. In this regard, it suffices to recall the illuminated leaf representing an evangelist inserted into the Brussels Gospels (Bibliothèque Royale 18723) that Hans Swarzenski with brilliant insight recognized in 1940 as a late antique in-

---

44. In caroline minuscule at fols. 126v–127r; see *MGH, Poetae Latini aevi Karolini*, vol. 1, ed. E. Dümmler (Berlin, 1880), pp. 94–95.

SYMBOLIC ASPECTS OF WRITTEN EVIDENCE

sert;[45] the relatively high number of late antique deluxe manuscripts that come down to us; and the fact that eighth-century England with its wealth of "Roman" codices already (or still?—the question has some importance) exceptionally produced some codices on purple. Here too the Carolingian graphic renaissance can be described, in the phrase Aby Warburg applied to the fifteenth-century Italian renaissance,[46] as a "transmigration of images" that in the eighth and ninth centuries drew with it from Italy to Gaul an entire paradigm of late antique graphic and book models.

In the present case, however, the phenomenon was not so much a sudden leap of centuries as a slow crawl across that obscure and ambiguously rich stylistic period suggestively called "sub-antique,"[47] which so far as concerns the history of the book can be localized in Roman-Byzantine Italy of the seventh and eighth centuries and perhaps also in contemporary Romanized England. The use of purple leaves first appears in England in the Amiatina Bible (*CLA* 299),[48] and it reappears at a distance of a century or more in the Canterbury Gospels (*CLA* 214)[49] and in the Codex Aureus of Stockholm (*CLA* 1642).[50] While Ceolfrid's Bible beyond a shadow of a doubt derives directly from the Cassiodorean exemplar, in all probability the other two cases represent early ninth-century examples executed under direct Carolingian influence.[51] Also singular is the generous use of imitated rustic capitals in the Psalter made at Canterbury in the early eighth century, today Cotton Vespasian A I (*CLA* 193); the same manuscript also contains capitals evi-

45. "The Xanten Purple Leaf and the Carolingian Renaissance," *Art Bulletin* 22 (1940): 7–24; Porcher, *Impero carolingio*, p. 92.

46. "Italienische Kunst und internationale Astrologie im Palazzo Schifanoja zu Ferrara," in *Italia e l'arte straniera. Atti del X Congresso internazionale di storia dell'arte 1912* (Rome, 1922), p. 191.

47. By E. Kitzinger, taken up and cited by Erwin Panofsky in *Renaissance and Renascences in Western Art* (Uppsala, 1965), p. 43. See too, more generally, the illuminating article of Erjwin Rosenthal, "Classical Elements in Carolingian Illustrations," in *La bibliofilia* 55 (1953): 85–106.

48. One of the two pages in purple is reproduced in G. Biagi, *Reproductions from Illuminated Manuscripts: Fifty Plates from MSS. in the R. Medicean Laurentian Library* (Florence, 1914), pl. V.

49. Fols. 1, 30, 43, and 44 are in purple. Citing only some recent contributions relating to this MS, which has a fairly vast bibliography: S. M. Kuhn, "From Canterbury to Lichfield," *Speculum* 23 (1948): 591–629 and "Some Early Mercian Manuscripts," *Review of English Studies* n.s. (1957): 356–70; P. McGurk, "An Anglo-Saxon Bible Fragment," *Journal of the Warburg and Courtauld Institutes* 25 (1962): 18–34; D. M. Wilson, *Anglo-Saxon Ornamental Metalwork, 700–1100, in the British Museum*, Catalogue of Antiquities of the Later Saxon Period, I (London, 1964), pp. 22, 23, 25, 26, 27, and pl. V.

50. E. A. Lowe, *English Uncial* (Oxford, 1960), p. 22, pl. XXVIII.

51. I have not been able to examine directly Stockholm's Codex Aureus, but imitation of Carolingian models is suggested by the outlining of the gold capitals with a continuous red line in the Canterbury Gospels that, although absent in the insular tradition, is found in the earliest deluxe codices of the court school.

dently derived from sixth-century "Roman" models (compare the *A* of fol. 140v with some of those of the Wolfenbüttel *Corpus Agrimensorum* (*CLA* 1374b).[52] For northern Italy, one can mention the unique *Lexicon* Paris, B.N. lat. 9451 (*CLA* 580),[53] entirely written in silver uncial and caroline on purple parchment (probably tinted rather than dyed); it is perhaps more probably to be attributed to the end of the eight century than to the beginning of the ninth and was apparently tied more to "late antique" or even Italian graphic traditions (see the "Roman" symptoms in the uncial and the traces of Lombard jewelry in the highly elaborate ornamentation) than to direct Carolingian influence.

The early Carolingian deluxe book, with its symbolic language formed of writing, colors, images, and artistic manufacture, thus did not bear a message of imperial majesty, Augustan grandeur, and porphyrogeneous sumptuosity. Rather, it repeated, although in a profoundly different ideological context, the Christian model of the book-as-object—not a tool but a symbol of culture—that since the fourth and fifth centuries had represented the late classical world's most direct expression of the sacrality of biblical and liturgical texts. This model had been characterized by artificiality of script, usually unnaturally traced and rich in ornamental elements that enhanced the books' suitability for display and veneration at the expense of ease in reading and consultation, and by the use of materials to whose preciousness the luxuriousness of the external appearance of the book corresponded. It is certainly not by chance that the best and most complete examples of this ideal model belong to Theodorician Italy of the early sixth century, where several well-known and closely related Gospels were produced, among them the famous gothic Codex Argenteus;[54] that was also the Italy that had produced codices such as the so-called Augusteus Virgil and the Arcerian *Corpus Agrimensorum,* the canons of whose graphics were admired and revived in the Carolingian court environment. The Oriental art of the same sixth century had given life both to splendid sacred purple codices and to that masterpiece of graphic restoration and illustrative art, the Ambrosiana Iliad: certainly Greek codices were also in the hands of early Carolingian artists.

52. For the Psalter Cotton Vespasian A I, which Lowe attributed to the first half of the eighth century (see *English Uncial,* p. 21 and pls. XXVI–XXVII), it is known that the rustic capitals are by at least two hands, of which the first wrote fols. 2v–3v, 109r, 141v, and the second wrote fols. 4r–11v. On this, see esp. D. H. Wright, "The Italian Stimulus on English Art around 700," in *Stil und Ueberlieferung in der Kunst des Abendlandes,* vol. 1 (Berlin, 1967), pp. 84–92.

53. See R. Amiet, "Un 'comes' carolingien inédit de la Haute-Italie," *Ephemerides liturgicae* 73 (1959): 335–67; *Charlemagne,* n. 384, p. 218.

54. For references to deluxe gothic books, see A. Petrucci, "Scritture e libro nell'Italia altomedievale. I. Il sesto secolo," *Studi medievali* 3d ser. 9 (1968): 188–91.

Does this settle everything? Can we thus ascribe everything to a mechanical and reflexive process of retrieval, selection, and imitation of models, and to the unaware adaptation of messages and meaning? Perhaps not: and the proof is found if we push our investigation beyond Charlemagne's period into that of his immediate and eventual successors.

On 8 October 827 a Greek codex containing the works of Pseudo-Dionysius the Areopagite was solemnly deposited at St.-Denis. It had been sent as a gift to Louis the Pious by the Byzantine emperor Michael II. That night the book, which was believed to contain the works of Saint Dionysius, worked a total of nineteen miracles: such, at least, was the story told by Abbot Hilduin of St.-Denis when he wrote Louis about them several years later.[55] In both the episode and the expressions used by the narrator, one can see traces of a conscious cult of the book venerated as sacred relic: this is true despite the fact that the external appearance of this codex (it is today B.N. gr. 437)[56] is relatively modest and bears no element that visually conveys a sacral message.

Another codex of the same period, Spanish in origin but closely tied to Carolingian artistic experiments, shows how it was now possible to go beyond late antique models even within a traditional vision of the sacrality of the book containing the text of the Gospels, creating a richer expressive form that drew graphic polymorphism, multiple colors in the background and writing, and ornamentation into a new synthesis even as it presented itself as an instrument of new symbolic messages. This is the enigmatic Cava dei Tirreni Bible, attributed to the mid-ninth century,[57] which employs pages colored deep blue alongside pages colored red, and which alongside chrysography adopts writing in a variety of colors, from green to deep blue to red and even white. The writing itself can take the form of a cross, adopting an obvious symbolic figural appearance (one thinks of the contemporary figured poetic works of Raban Maur, to cite but one example) (fig. 19). Even the antiquarian element of graphic restoration is subtly invoked by employ-

55. The text of the letter is in *MGH, Epistolae Karolini aevi*, III, ed. E. Dümmler (Berlin, 1889), pp. 327–35. For the episode, see R. J. Loenertz, "La légende parisienne de Saint Denys l'Aréopagite, sa gènese et son prémier témoin," *Analecta Bollandiana* 69 (1951): 217–37; P. Lemerle, *Le premier humanisme byzantin*, Bibliothèque byzantine, 6 (Paris, 1971), pp. 13–16.

56. See H. Omont, *Fac-similés des plus anciens manuscrits grecs en onciale et en minuscule du IVe au XIIe siècle* (Paris, 1892), pl. XIV.

57. Cava dei Tirreni, Badia della SS.ma Trinità, MS 1. See E. A. Lowe, "The Codex Cavensis: New Light on Its Later History," in *Studies Presented to Kirsopp Lake* (London, 1937), pp. 325–31 (repr. in *Palaeographical Papers*, vol. 1, pp. 335–41); T. Ayuso Marazuela, "La Biblia Visigótica de la Cava dei Tirreni. Contribución de la Vulgata en España," *Estudios Biblicos* 14 (1955): 49–65 and 15 (1956): 5–56; B. Bischoff, "Kreuz und Buch im Frühmittelalter und in den ersten Jahrhunderten der spanischen Reconquista," in *Bibliotheca docet. Festgabe für Carl Wehmer* (Amsterdam, 1963), pp. 19–34, esp. p. 28.

19. Cava dei Tirreni, Monastery of SSms. Trinity, MS no. 1, fol. 8r

ing, in addition to rustic capitals, uncial, semi-uncial, and the so-called *b-d* uncial: the only known instance of the revival of this type after the fifth and sixth centuries. In other codices of the Carolingian period not tied to the court or to Tours, one encounters analogous phenomena of graphic-structural research stretched to exploit in new ways (and without excessive reverence for late antique models) the possibilities offered by the page, ornament, and script types. A well-known example is Theodulf's Bible, where one finds virtuoso micrographics in gold and silver on purple (Paris, B.N. lat. 9380 and Puy, Cathédral).[58] Another is the St.-Denis Gospels (Paris, B.N. lat. 9387), originally from northern France, written in gold, silver, white, and red on purple; one also finds some leaves colored blue.

One should note that the pure "normalized" capital is never used in such examples, which belong to graphic-book traditions that can be called "provincial" and divergent. But in the decades between the reign of Charlemagne and that of Charles the Bald, the restoration of the "normalized" capital was brought to completion. There were splendid examples produced at Tours under abbots Fridugisus and Adalardus, with capitals that are perfectly regular in design, proportions, and harmony of the tracing, even if Alcuin's Bible at Bern[59] still reveals some very light forkings and the Nancy Gospels[60] shows the unusual characteristic of having the horizontal bar of the *L* lightly curved upward that is also seen in both the San Gall Virgil and in sixth-century uncial codices attributable to northern Italy. The group of five deluxe codices, attributed to a school serving Lothar,[61] display a monumental capital characterized by irregularity of design and proportions and with heavy tracing. Outside of Tours, the "normalized" capital celebrated its triumphs in the most splendid codices produced by the school of Metz, specifically the Gospels B.N. lat. 9388 (fig. 20)[62] and Drogo's Sacramentary,[63] which are both by the same hand, where fanciful variants with rich interweavings appear.

But it is above all in the great codices commissioned by Charles the Bald

58. See L. Delisle, "Les Bibles des Théodulfe," in *BEC* 40 (1879): 5–47; *Charlemagne*, n. 424, p. 257. Very close to it, even if rather less rich in ornamentation and lacking purple leaves, is the Bible, Brit. Lib. Add. MS 24142, for which see *Catalogue of the Ancient MSS. in the British Museum*, vol. 2 (London, 1884), pp. 5–8, and a mention in Delisle, "Bibles," pp. 30–31.

59. Bern, Stadtbibliothek, MS nos. 3–4; see Rand, *Survey*, n. 73, p. 133 and pl. XC; W. Köhler, *Die Karolingische Miniaturen*, vol. 1: *Die Schule von Tours*, I (Berlin, 1930), pp. 375–76, n. 17, pls. I, 18; 19.

60. Rand, *Survey*, n. 79, p. 137 and pls. XCVII–XCIX; Köhler, *Karolingische Miniaturen*, vol. 1, n. 28, pp. 383–84, and pls. 35–39.

61. See W. Köhler and F. Mütherich, *Die Karolingischen Miniaturen*, vol. 4: *Die Hofschule Kaiser Lothars* (Berlin, 1971).

62. Köhler, *Karolingische Miniaturen*, vol. 3, pp. 134–42 and pls. 66–75, esp. 70a, 73b, and 75a.

63. Ibid., pp. 143–62 and pls. 76–91, esp. 79b and 80a.

20. Paris, B.N. lat. 9388, fol. 100a

that the two stylistic traditions of Carolingian monumental capitals finally
achieved a rather suggestive alternation of graphic forms. In the Bible of S.
Paolo fuori le Mura in Rome,[64] a work of Ingobertus, there are both very
pure normalized capitals and heavy "flowered" capitals with rich ornamental

64. Of the vast bibliography relative to this codex, I will cite some of the most notable and
recent contributions: P. Durrieu, "Ingobert, un grand calligraphe du IXe siècle," in *Mélanges
offerts à E. Chatelain* (Paris, 1910), pp. 1–12; C. Cecchelli, *La vita di Roma nel medio evo*, vol.
1: *Le arti minori e il costume* (Rome, 1952), pp. 477–515, 525–32 (with the unsustainable attribution
to the period of Charlemagne); E. H. Kantorowicz, "The Carolingian in the Bible of San
Paolo fuori le Mura," in *Late Classical and Mediaeval Studies in Honor of Albert Mathias Friend,*

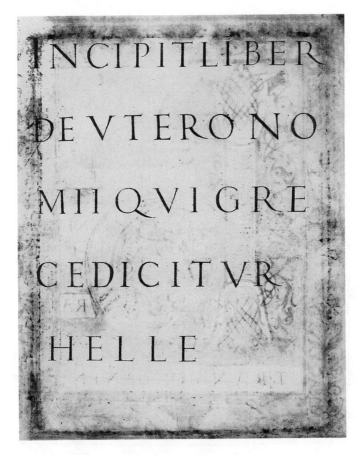

21. Rome, basilica of San Paolo, Bible of Charles the Bald, fol. 57r

elements, while other pages bear a capital with thin tracing enriched by
elegant forkings (figs. 21, 22).[65] But this and other great codices of Charles

---

Jr., ed. K. Weitzmann (Princeton, 1955), pp. 287–300; H. Schade, "Studien zu der Karolingischen Bilderbibel aus St. Paul vor der Mauern in Rom," *Wallraf-Richartz-Jahrbuch* 21 (1959):
9–40; J. E. Gaehde, "The Bible of San Paolo fuori le Mura in Rome: Its Date and Its Relation
to Charles the Bald," *Gesta* 5 (1966): 9–21; reproductions in *API*, IV, fasc. 32. More generally, for the deluxe codices executed for Charles the Bald, see Porcher, *Impero carolingio*, pp.
141–58.

65. For the "flowered" capital, see the reproduction in *API*, IV, fasc. 32, pls. 6 and 11. One
can observe that the ornamental elements are added in different colors, white, yellow (fols.
60v, 76v) or even dark blue and green (fol. 76v); for the normalized capital, see ibid., pls. 9
and 10; there are alternating rows written in thin capitals with barely perceptible forking and
in capitals with heavier stroke and more evidence forking, e.g., fol. 7r, repr. ibid., pl. 4.

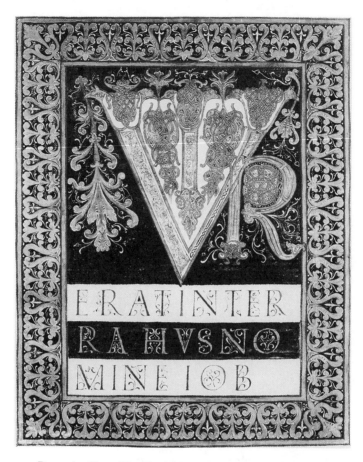

22. Rome, basilica of San Paolo, Bible of Charles the Bald, fol. 76r

the Bald, such as the analogous Codex Aureus of Munich (Gospels of St. Emmeram of Ratisbon, Clm. 14000),[66] represent a synthesis of the preceding stylistic tradition that goes well beyond the capitals. These books really constitute a summation of all the elements that went into deluxe books—from graphics to polychromatics, from illustrations to ornaments, from often imposing format to page layout—into an organically new expressive discourse.

66. Integral reproduction: *Der Codex Aureus der Bayerischen Staatsbibliothek in München*, ed. G. Leidinger (Munich, 1925). The codex has been restored: see P. Gichtel, *Der Codex Aureus von St. Emmeram. Die Restauriernung des Cod. lat. 14000 der Bayerischen Staatsbibliothek München* (Munich, 1971).

SYMBOLIC ASPECTS OF WRITTEN EVIDENCE

All the elements of tradition and of imitation lose their individuality as they are reelaborated and modified, finding themselves fused for the first time in a figural discourse that embraces the entire page whatever its composition. In this sense, Ingobertus was entirely justified in boasting of having reached and surpassed, by conscious intellectual effort (*tenore mentis*) the Italian calligraphers (the *Graphidae ausonii* , as he called them) who were the authors of the models by which until then the Carolingian graphic tradition had been more or less directly inspired.[67] Of the figural discourse itself one might say that, having begun from distant insular precedents and experiments such as the Bible of Cava dei Tirreni, it tended now to achieve an overall visual effect in which the text lost all analytical-discursive relevance, with the iconography of writing becoming a purely figural fact like ornamentation, color, images, and the play of space.

As for the techniques of execution and overall manufacture of the "imperial" codices made for Charles the Bald, many of these derived directly from Tours. Comparing the Bible of San Paolo with some of the most important Tours codices results in a significant list: pages no longer entirely colored purple but striped or in a single column (Paris, B.N. lat. 250, the Bible of Roricus, etc.);[68] the enormous format typical of the Tours Bibles;[69] probably the practice of executing full-page miniatures on parchment folios prepared separately and in ways different from others (see the Bible of Grandval);[70] the practice of tracing the design (with ink? or charcoal? or both?) in preparation for drawing the great normalized capitals (already seen in the Bible of Roricus, fol. 83v, and in that of Vivianus, fol. 4r);[71] and so forth. Naturally, in the two great codices of Charles the Bald mentioned

67. The text of the poem of Ingobertus is in *MGH, Poetae aevi Carolini* III, 1, ed. L. Traube (Berlin, 1886), pp. 257–64. See Durrieu, "Ingobert"; Gaehde, "Bible," esp. pp. 15–16; note the opinion of B. Bischoff (p. 15, n. 30) that the caroline minuscule of the text comes from Reims.

68. According to a recent hypothesis of Carl Nordenfalk (*Codex Caeareus Upsaliensis: An Echternach Gospel-book of the Eleventh Century* [Stockholm and Uppsala, 1971], pp. 83–84), this use in Carolingian manuscripts would have derived from late antique examples containing pages of incipits with rows of writing enclosed between decorated horizontal stripes, as in Vienna Nationalbibliothek cod. lat. 847 (*CLA* 1491), originating in Ravenna and attributed to the sixth century. Thus, see also Hermann, *Frühmittelalterlichen*, n. 4, pp. 39–42.

69. For the format of the Tours Bibles, see above; the Bible of S. Paolo measures 440 x 355 mm.; the Codex Aureus of Munich 420 x 330 mm., a format thus slightly smaller than the average of the great Tours Bibles.

70. In the S. Paolo Bible, all the folios containing full-page miniatures are on detached membranes with an appearance different from the others, being glossier and grayish in color; one can see the same thing, as far as I have been able to determine, in the Bible of Grandval, London, Brit. Lib. MS Add. 10546 (see esp. fol. 352).

71. In the Bible of S. Paolo, one can see traces on fols. 85r, 100v, 101r, 108r, 115r, and 116r; examples of the illuminated initials are visible on fols. 327v and 328r.

above, the S. Paolo Bible and the Codex Aureus of Munich, the very exceptionality of the results obtained indicates a process of production that was particularly complex and consciously differentiated.

Yet this new synthesis was probably not the result of furious stylistic research alone. Also involved, and perhaps of overriding importance, was a deliberate will to transform the expressive instruments inherited from the subantique and Carolingian tradition, transcending the semantic values of the symbolism of the sacred text to arrive at a conscious, new symbolism of imperial power, whose emblems were even collected in certain representations found in the same codices. The determination to achieve a superior stylistic unity thus corresponded directly to the imperial patronage that, indeed, was continuously and explicitly referred to by the illustrations and texts, without there any longer being the mediation of written discourse (as one might call it) that in Charlemagne's time was still fully evident, as in Godescalc's poem. These effects, moreover, were achieved despite the fact that these two productions differ notably in their graphic and technical aspects, not only presenting different basic scripts (uncial in the Codex Aureus, caroline minuscule in the S. Paolo Bible) but even differentiating page layout and insertion of ornament, probably also to adjust for the different lengths of the respective texts.

Such a modification of stylistic language and ideological message could find its explanation in Charles the Bald's and his court's policy of restoration and cultured "grandeur." This was a policy whose ideological content could not and must not be confined to the learned ecclesiastics of the Carolingian court or the Roman curia: it had also to reach the wider audience of the lay ruling class—still mostly illiterate and thus outsiders to books—and (if only indirectly) even the vast strata of urban population who somehow encountered the manufactured forms that were the expressive bearers of that ideology. In seems to me that it is in such a perspective that the precise reference to the symbolism of the book, inserted by Berengarius and Liutardus in the song celebrating Charles the Bald that surrounds the image of the enthroned sovereign, acquires its deepest significance: "Istius imperio hic codex resplendet et auro" (This codex is resplendent in gold and his rule). Nor can it seem strange that the spokesmen for this policy, on Christmas Day 875 in the Rome of John VIII, were objects such as the wooden chair of Saint Peter[72] and a book such as the S. Paolo Bible: this last both bringing to a

---

72. Perhaps it will suffice to refer here only to "La cattedra lignea di S. Pietro in Vaticano," four studies by M. Maccarrone, A. Ferrua, P. Romanelli, and P. E. Schramm, in *Memoria della Pontificia Accademia Romana di Archeologia* 10 (1971), and in the collection of G. Arnaldi in *La cultura* 3 (1974): 336–47 (esp. 344).

culmination and transcending a book and graphic tradition that for centuries in the Latin and eastern Mediterranean had represented the ideal model of the sacred book and of its religious message made into a unity of word and sign.

7

READING IN
THE MIDDLE AGES

THE THOUSAND YEARS INCLUDED in the Middle Ages constitute a particularly important period for a study of reading conceived as the techniques and behaviors, both individual and collective, comprised in an act of reading that itself must be seen as having psychological-physical, cultural, and social aspects. Indeed, the models and conditions of reading usual in late antiquity were radically transformed during the Middle Ages. This period also saw the formation and diffusion of modes of reading that would be those of the modern age and of the cultural universe distinguished by printing with movable type.[1]

In late antiquity, the models and techniques of reading that had been dominant in classical culture had already been modified by two innovations that had taken form and spread progressively within Christian culture and communities. The first of these was the division of the text of the Gospels into "cola et commata": those brief textual segments whose isolation made reading easier and more accessible even to semiliterates who did not have much experience of books. This innovation had been introduced by Jerome to serve, as he said, "utilitati gentium," in reality being an aid (as Cassiodorus

Originally published as "Lire au moyen âge," in *Mélanges de l'Ecole Française de Rome* 96, no. 2 (1984): 603–16.

1. On reading in the Middle Ages, see H.-J. Martin, "Pour une histoire de la lecture," *Revue française d'histoire du livre* 46 (1977): 583–609; G. Severino Polica, "Libro, lettura, 'lezione' negli Studia degli ordini mendicanti (sec. XIII)," in *Le scuole degli ordini mendicanti* (Todi, 1978), pp. 375–413; P. Saenger, "Silent Reading: Its Impact on Late Medieval Script and Society," *Viator* 13 (1982): 367–414 and "Manières de lire médiévales," in *Histoire de l'édition française*, vol. 1: *Le livre conquérant. Du Moyen Age au milieu du XVIIe siècle* (Paris, 1982), pp. 131–41.

recalled)[2] to the "simplices fratres" for whom it was the only means by which they could "pronuntiare sacratissimas lectiones . . . inculpabiliter." The other innovation was the invention of miscellanies—collections of various texts of different authors copied one after the other. Although the texts were sometimes bound together by a common theme (in coherent or organized miscellanies), they could also simply be juxtaposed without any apparent logic. This innovation, having appeared in the Coptic-Christian communities of Egypt in the course of the fourth century, was then transmitted to the early Middle Ages; there is no doubt that it constituted a profound and significant transformation of the traditional model of reading based on the unitary book containing a single work or at most the works of a single author.[3]

Late antiquity had similarly bequeathed different modes of reading to the early Middle Ages. Cassiodorus clearly distinguished the "sedula lectio" in which he himself engaged (*Inst.* I, *praef.* 8) from the "simplicissima lectio" of the less cultured brothers (ibid., 9). The first kind of reading was a cultural operation by means of which a scholar, working alone or with collaborators of his choosing, took possession of the text for purposes of self-instruction, comment, or collation. The second kind of reading was an essentially liturgical operation, sometimes public and thus "pronunciata" with voice raised, in contrast to the first which was (almost always) silent or solitary. The wonder Augustine expressed when in 384 he saw Ambrose read "tacite" (*Conf.* VI, 3) has recently led certain historians to accord too much importance to the difference between reading aloud, seen as typical of the classical world, and silent reading supposedly invented in the Middle Ages, or at least by Christianity. In fact, the practice of "tacite legere" was already current in the ancient world (Horace, *Sat.,* II, V, 68).

The situation concerning the Middle Ages, moreover, is far more complex than it appears at first glance. One can distinguish three reading techniques that were broadly diffused and used deliberately for different purposes: silent reading, "in silentio"; reading at a low voice, called murmuring or rumination, which assisted meditation and served as an aid to memorization; and, last, reading aloud, which required, as in antiquity, a particular technique and was very similar to the practice of liturgical recitation and chant. Each of these techniques corresponded to a precise function and was used in specific circumstances and milieus—the first and probably the second occurring in the solitude of the cell, and the third in public, in the presence of the community. In the world of Christian culture, all three were broadly influenced by the techniques and practices of liturgy and prayer.

2. *Inst.* I, *praef.* 9 and I, XI, 4.
3. See above, Chap. 1.

In reality, it would seem that the most important phenomenon in the domain of early medieval written culture had less to do with the contrast between silent and vocalized reading than with the obvious gap—although one that has been little stressed until now—between practices of writing and practices of reading. Everyone who has a direct acquaintance with early medieval manuscripts knows how defective these were as instruments to facilitate the average reader's reading and comprehension of the text. The widespread use of continuous writing, without spaces to separate the words; the indiscriminate use of capitals, which often give neither guidance nor orientation; punctuation that was rare, arbitrary, and with little or no differentiation, or that was simply absent: all these made reading difficult, even for well-educated readers. The overall impression is that there was no effort to shorten the time required for reading, for indeed everything contributed to keep reading extremely slow, attentive, almost stumbling. Thus, one of the fundamental characteristics of the activity of reading in the early Middle Ages lay in the slow mechanism of spelling out words.

All this resulted from a conception that saw writing not as in the service of reading but as an end in itself. In this perspective, writing obeyed its own rules of composition and its own rhythms of execution, without considering at either a theoretical or practical level the effect these had on the practice of reading. The use of continuous writing, for example, responded to necessities of an aesthetic order: by maintaining a continuous presence of black on the line, it guaranteed that the page would have an overall harmony based entirely on the balance produced by the alternation of the black of the written bands and the white of the bands left empty. It is not by chance that continuous writing had always been systematically adopted for uncial and semiuncial, the two traditional scripts of late antiquity.

Paul Saenger has recently argued a different thesis in this connection. Claiming that word separation was "the contribution of the early Middle Ages to the evolution of western written communication," he ascribes its first appearance in a partial fashion to manuscripts executed in the eighth century in the British Isles.[4] A summary inquiry applied to a number of facsimile collections, however, shows that in reality the situation in the early Middle Ages was more confused and complex than Saenger's suggestive but brief observations would suggest. There were, in effect, two widely used practices at that time: that of continuous writing and that, to which recourse was had especially by scribes of limited talent, of introducing separations

---

4. "Silent Reading," p. 377; see also the paper of M. B. Parkes, "The Contribution of Insular Scribes of the Seventh and Eighth Centuries to the 'Grammar of Legibility,'" in *Grafia e interpunzione del latino nel medioevo* (Rome, 1987), pp. 15–30.

into groups of letters in a fashion that was irregular and arbitrary. Often, indeed, the break came in the very middle of a word, at great harm to the reader.

It is true that a regular separation of words does appear in certain manuscripts of the eighth and ninth centuries. But this was not an exclusively insular practice; it occurs as well in German manuscripts, some from centers founded by the Irish but also some from centers of autochthonous origin. The practice also appears in some Swiss Rhenish manuscripts and in a certain number of manuscripts from northern Italy. These were probably zones where, as in the British Isles, limited knowledge of Latin had hastened the invention of instruments permitting easier reading of the text. In the Carolingian period the two practices were in use simultaneously. In southern Italy, the separation of words appears between the ninth and tenth centuries but became widely diffused and obligatory only in the first half of the eleventh.

On the whole, then, one has the impression that the scribe of the early Middle Ages was scarcely sensible to the problems and practice of reading. This indifference can only come from the limited experience he himself had with the practice. In fact, the scribe of the early Middle Ages was destined and trained (if he received any training at all) for writing rather than for reading, which explains the high number of raw, unskilled, and uneducated scribes that characterize the production of books in the early Middle Ages.[5] It is thus not surprising that the chronicler Ekkhard IV of San Gall tells us that in the second half of the tenth century his homonymous predecessor Ekkhard I assigned to copy books those young brothers whom he judged to be less intelligent and less adapted to study: "et quos ad literarum studia tardiores vidisset, ad scribendum occupaverat et lineandum" (and those whom he saw came later to the study of letters, he employed in writing or lining).[6] The fact that this occurred in a monastery like San Gall, which at that time was a very active center for producing books, renders this practice still more significant.

The subscriptions that some scribes affixed to their manuscripts when their work was done confirms that during their work the copyists of the early Middle Ages paid little attention to the needs of reading—or of readers. In fact, they rarely address their natural interlocutor, the reader. When they do, moreover, they never join the reader in dialogue, never evoke the reasons and sense of their work, and especially never show the least interest in the

5. See above, Chap. 5.
6. *Casuum Sancti Galli Continuatio I auctore Ekkehardo IV* in *MGH, SS II* (Hannover, 1829), p. 122.

use for which it was done. The only clearly expressed intention is to obtain prayers for the good of their soul in exchange for the pains that they have taken.

More generally, the early Middle Ages appears as a period in which the minimal need to read corresponded to and was paralleled by a marked illiteracy in reading. One has the overall impression that there was an important category of semi-illiterates, lay and ecclesiastic, who in one fashion or another were capable of writing something—the subscription to a brief text—without having any familiarity with reading and books: thus, the number of readers was still more restricted than the number of persons able to write. This conclusion only confirms, from a different angle, the characteristic divide between reading and writing practices just discussed.

Having said this, one must add that circumstances in the early Middle Ages scarcely provided much incentive to read. Books were kept in places that usually were poorly adapted to reading, nor did there generally exist spaces specially equipped for that purpose: one read in the places reserved principally for other activities, such as the cell, the refectory, and the cloister. As an arduous activity, reading was consequently rather rare and even, surprising as it may seem, a marginal activity in the context of early medieval civilization. One does witness an increase in the production and circulation of books during the Carolingian period; the ninth and tenth centuries also must have seen more reading, as witnessed by the frequency with which books were borrowed. But these shifts were not sufficiently radical to alter the general conditions of reading, which remained quite laborious despite the adoption of the new unified script, caroline minuscule, that permitted an objective improvement in the model of reading. Other modifications occurred in the course of the eleventh century that manifestly aimed at facilitating the reading and comprehension of the text: a progressive and expanding use of separated writing; the use of the hyphen for words not ending on a line; the use of the double apex when two *i*'s came in succession; the use of the majuscule form of the *s* when the letter was found at the end of a word.[7] These mark the arrival of new cultural times, when new roles and new functions would be created for books and writing in a society that itself was being transformed.

In the twelfth and thirteenth centuries, the framework of written culture underwent profound changes due to a variety of well-known factors that can be listed rapidly as including: the general increase in the diffusion of reading

---

7. See A. Petrucci, "Istruzioni per la datazione," in "Censimento dei codici dei secoli X–XII," *Studi medievali* 3d ser. 9 (1968): 1115–26.

and writing; the progressive increase in the production of written documents
and private acts of writing;[8] the marked (although difficult to measure) increase in the production and circulation of books; and the creation of new
cultural structures and institutions (advanced schools, universities). The more
intense circulation of written products that resulted from these trends in turn
provoked in society a need for reading that was considerably stronger than
previously. In its wake there also appeared a specific demand for written
products that were organized in a way to facilitate rather than impede reading itself, a tendency that was also furthered by the emergence among the
most educated readers of a new relationship with the text and the progressive
affirmation of new modes of reading. As Malcolm Parkes notes, "During
the course of the twelfth century the monastic culture gave way to the culture
of the schools. There were new kinds of books—a more technical literature—and new kinds of readers. The monastic *lectio* was a spiritual exercise
which involved steady reading to oneself, interspersed by prayer, and pausing
for rumination on the text as a basis for *meditatio*. The scholastic *lectio* was
a process of study which involved more ratiocinative scrutiny of the text and
consultation for reference purposes."[9] It was precisely to answer this type of
need that concepts such as *ordinatio* and *divisio* of the text were introduced
into the program of the new model of reading. Although these had been
quite foreign to the text/book relationship in the early Middle Ages, Jordan
of Saxony in 1220 placed them at the basis of what he called the *forma
tractatus*: the text/book of scholastic/university culture.

The twelfth and thirteenth centuries, therefore, saw a radical transformation of the model, techniques, and general conditions of reading. The
scholastic/university book differed from its early medieval predecessor at
several points. It was generally of large format and thus heavy, hard to manage, and difficult to transport; it also needed solid, fixed support when being
read. Writing was laid out in two relatively narrow columns, with more
compressed text, so that one line of text corresponded closely with the visual
field of recognition or fixation:[10] the quantity of text that could be taken in
at a single glance. The text was carefully articulated in a series of divisions
and subdivisions (chapters, paragraphs, subparagraphs) more detailed than
in the past, all for the purpose of rendering comprehension and especially
consultation easier: according to Vincent of Beauvais, the "capitulatio" was

8. See M. T. Clanchy, *From Memory to Written Record: England, 1066–1307* 2d ed. (Oxford,
1993), pp. 44–80.

9. "Influence of the Concepts of Ordinatio and Compilatio in the Development of the
Book," in *Medieval Learning and Literature: Essays Presented to R. W. Hunt* (Oxford, 1976),
p. 115.

10. J. Taylor, *Insegnare a leggere e scrivere* (Milan, 1976), p. 25.

made so that "operis partes singule lectori facilius elucescant" (the parts of the work would be manifest to the individual reader).[11] The articulation of the text was placed in relief and emphasized by a rich series of graphic interventions and tools including rubrics, paragraph marks, initials and majuscules of different size, running titles, reminders, indices, and alphabetical tables, all of which enclosed, delimited, and cut up the text, rendering it thus accessible in small portions that could easily be found again. Thanks to numerous abbreviations, reading became incomparably more rapid than before and often was transformed into a practice—consultation—specifically belonging to the professional researcher. It is therefore not surprising that a typical representative of scholastic culture such as Peter Lombard used expressions such as "statim invenire," "presto habere," and "facilius occurrere" when he spoke of the relationship he wished to maintain with a text.[12] Reading thus became a practice that one could organize and determine in advance, having as its objective the cultural preparation and the didactic and scientific activities of the new professional intellectual, whether lay or religious: professor, jurist, physician, theologian, notary.

No longer separated from writing, reading became instead still more closely bound to it. People read *to* write: this is the sense of the *compilatio*. They read and wrote together when commenting and annotating.[13] They wrote while reading when composing, because every text was—necessarily—based on the *auctoritas* of its predecessors and on the permanent use of citation.[14] Thus, at the beginning of the twelfth century, archivist and chronicler Guibert de Nogent linked *perpetuitas legendi* and *continuatio scribendi* in the same process, as complementary and necessary stages of an intellectual's activity.[15]

In practice, these changes went beyond techniques of reading, touching as well its mechanical conditions, its places and spaces, the material means used, the behaviors and attitudes of readers. Libraries, as we know, were transformed. In the course of the thirteenth century there appears a completely new kind of place dedicated to reading and study in common that

11. Cited by Parkes, "Contribution," p. 133.

12. Richard H. Rouse and Mary A. Rouse, "*Statim Invenire*: Schools, Preachers and New Attitudes to the Page," in *Renaissance and Renewal in the Twelfth Century*, ed. Robert L. Benson and Giles Constable (Cambridge, Mass., 1982), pp. 201–25.

13. For the reader "legens et rescribens," see Severino-Polica, "Libro, lettura," pp. 394–95.

14. For the four ways "faciendi libros," of the scribe who "scribit aliena, nihil addendo, vel mutando," the "compilator" who "scribit aliena, addendo, sed non de suo," the "commentator" who "scribit et aliena et sua," and finally, of the "auctor" who "scribit et sua et aliena, sed sua tamquam principalia," see Bonaventure, *Commentarium in I librum Sententiarum*, in *Opera Omnia*, vol. 1 (Ad claras aquas, 1882), pp. 14–15.

15. M. C. Garand, "Le scriptorium de Guibert de Nogent," *Scriptorium* 31 (1977): 3.

indeed becomes essential: one room, of variable length on a basilical plan, equipped with benches disposed horizontally in parallel rows, and the books arranged in rows and attached by a chain. This is the typical library of the mendicant orders, the new model for reading in common. Laymen could also enjoy these novelties because the orders' libraries often functioned as libraries for universities of higher culture, welcoming visitors who came from outside the orders.[16]

The existence of such places meant that all intellectuals saw their modes of private reading change, because it was precisely the reunification of writing and reading into a single practice that permitted intellectuals to express their claims and obtain more space for their work than they had had before— spaces that were also better organized and better equipped. The Esdra who, in the Amiatina Bible of the beginning of the eighth century was represented, in conformance with "ancient" models, sitting on a stool, knees resting on a little bench, carrying a manuscript on his knees, gave way to the image of a clerk wearing eyeglasses, installed in a solid chair before a vast writing bench which protected and isolated him. He was surrounded by desks intended for activities of reading and writing, shelves, open and closed books, notebooks, foolscap, and all other writing materials.[17]

In reality, the very ideology of reading, which in the early Middle Ages had been linked to the religious practice of *ruminatio* of the divine word, underwent a total transformation in the new universe of official culture, henceforth dominated by the image of public teaching. John of Salisbury contrasted private reading, which he defined as an "occupatio per se scrutantis scripturas," to magisterial reading, which generally took place in public and joined teacher and student: "docentis et discentis exercitium."[18] This latter style of reading, the *lectio*, was fundamentally the same as university scholarly research. It was a reading that, while dividing and commenting on texts, fixed them in an authoritative manner and imposed on them a hierarchy. One read to others actively, but one read through someone passively. Reading was given and it was received. The *lectio*, with its fixed rules and unequal exchange, became the predominant European model of individual and common reading of the thirteenth and fourteenth centuries.

It was not the only model, however, for in the thirteenth and fourteenth centuries, in all of Europe but most especially in the towns and communes

16. See below, Chap. 10.

17. See A. Petrucci, "Gli strumenti del letterato," in *Letteratura italiana*, vol. 1: *Il letterato e le istituzione* (Turin, 1982), pp. 2, 3, 6, 7.

18. See the reference in Severino-Polica, "Libro, lettura," pp. 377-78.

of Italy, the increasing literacy of lay people gave birth to literary works in vernacular languages for them to read. The production of books in vernacular languages grew steadily, spreading into more and more regions.

The production of books in vernacular languages demonstrates that a demand existed. And if a demand existed, that was because there was a reading public. But on the whole this was not the public of official culture in Latin. Certainly there were judges, notaries, and clerks who owned and read books in vernacular languages: Petrarca himself did so, even if he felt he had to defend himself for it. But they were a minority. The great mass of those who read works in vernacular languages were essentially monolingual literates who did not know Latin but had nevertheless learned to read and write: they were merchants, artisans, shopkeepers, artists, accountants, shop or banking employees, as well as some workers and some women. In their reading, these people could not refer to any traditional model susceptible of being transmitted by repetition or other formal instruction. They could not adopt the learned model, which was too difficult, complex, and costly for them. By force of circumstances, they thus had to invent new modes of reading that, in ideology and practice, were different from those of learned people, modes that were independent of any institution, rule, norm, and ritual and—in a word—free.

Different readers do not in themselves account for the different styles of lay/bourgeois reading in comparison with those of official culture. There were differences as well in the means by which books were produced. The book in a vernacular language was most often written in the milieu where it was read, by readers themselves who recopied texts for their own use and that of their children or their friends. There was still more difference in the physical appearance of the reading matter, which generally took the form of books written on paper, with a medium format, in nontypical cursive scripts preferably laid out on the whole page. The text was presented without commentary, with simple illustrations or ornamentation drawn by pen and colored with inks or inexpensive colors. Finally, there was a difference in the places where books were kept and read. According to customary usage, although recurring by analogy rather than a direct inheritance from the early Middle Ages, books in vernacular languages—always rare—were kept in the family chest with important documents, account books, and all the papers of the household. As for the act of reading, it was done at home, the shop, the counter, wherever it was possible. Belonging to the sphere of leisure and free time rather than work, this activity had no special place.[19]

There was also another mode of existence for books and the practice of

19. See Petrucci, "Biblioteche antiche," pp. 543–46.

reading that, although transmitted from generation to generation, stood apart as the exclusive preserve of a particular social class: the aristocracy. Courtly reading in the later Middle Ages differed markedly in practice from scholastic or bourgeois reading for many reasons linked to both physical book models and personal behavior patterns. Physically, the books that fulfilled courtly commissions and usages were made of parchment, of medium or small format, written in formal script laid out in two columns, illuminated or ornamented more or less richly depending on the particular case but, like the bourgeois model, lacking commentary. Moreover, the practice of courtly reading, again like the bourgeois model, was never restricted to particular places or locations. Indeed, it had available to it the broad social spaces of courtly life: salons and large bedchambers and, outside, the open spaces of the courtyards, gardens, and parks. "The lady had two couches of rich silk installed in the great garden and had brought there whoever played music, read, or engaged in fencing."[20] In effect, courtly reading came to insert itself as a complementary element into a more complex and organic *paideia* including the arts of conversation, music, and the body; it was often accompanied by physical exercises such as walking, games, dancing, and fencing, or it could alternate with such activities, being then followed by music. Finally, while the reading of the clerk or the merchant remained almost invariably a purely masculine activity, courtly reading engaged women as well as men, as we recall from the common reading of Paolo and Francesca immortalized by Dante (*Inferno* 5, ll. 127–38).

In Florence at the turn of the fourteenth and fifteenth centuries, "a band of arrogant youths"[21] headed by Niccolò Niccoli effected a radical return to antiquity in the domain of studying classical texts and producing books. The promoters of this movement were all bourgeois or petits-bourgeois. But they resolutely rejected models of books current in contemporary mercantile vernacular culture to seek out a model three or four centuries earlier: the books from the Romanesque period, still written in caroline minuscule, that were totally different from the books of the scholastic/university period. This effort had some precedents in the late fourteenth-century activities due to certain humanists, most notably Petrarca; but it had never before been pushed to its fullest consequences. What resulted was a complete renewal of a kind of book that displays the following characteristics: reduced (small or

20. *La tavola ritonda e l'istoria di Tristano* , vol. 1 (Bologna, 1864), p. 419.

21. Felicitously expressed by E. H. Gombrich, "From the Revival of Letters to the Reform of Arts: Nicolò Niccoli and Filippo Brunelleschi," in *Essays in the History of Art . . . to R. Wittkower* (London, 1967), p. 82.

medium) format, sometimes almost square; an absence of commentary that liberated the texts from stifling interpretations; disappearance of the fixed and visible system of dividing and organizing the text; and a revolution in graphics resulting from the substitution for gothic textura of a minuscule imitated from the caroline while a capital of roman type replaced the upper-case letters of gothic style. Finally, the abbreviations that had been so abundant in university tradition practically disappeared.[22]

The consequences of these changes for modes of reading were very important. Reading, deprived of the devices that had been installed to make it faster, had to return to a slow and reflective rhythm, concentrating on the text that was now the sole master of the page. Consultation of books, deprived of the subsidiary instruments that university culture had furnished, had to modify its rhythms and functioning. But the most important innovation, and that most weighted with consequences, was the replacement of a compact graphic system whose elements were closely knit together along the line by a ventilated system in which words, but especially letters, seen and fixed as independent signs, were henceforth separated from each other. Later this phenomenon would become one of the characteristic modes of reading specific to printing. But at the beginning of the fifteenth century it apparently sprang rather from this new, more rational form of visual perception, one that, according to Walter Ong, constituted one of the innovations of humanism, a perception that was also expressed by a better balance of black and white on the page, on the lines and between the lines of the new model of reading.[23]

These changes did not entail comparably radical modifications in the conditions of reading which, in contrast, remained bound to the model of the preceding period. In practice, modes of reading in the fifteenth century continued to obey the rules elaborated in the preceding period in the milieu of scholastic/university culture, at least as regards the physical conditions of reading: furniture, equipment, the disposition of places for reading, etc. The respect for tradition in this aspect of intellectual life is apparently explained by the fact that the humanist, in his role as intellectual, renounced neither the prestigious model of the university professor nor the static, authoritarian, and hierarchical reading that was its corollary. From this point of view, the decisive break with the past was produced only in the third quarter of the fifteenth century when the consequences were felt of three innovations that

22. See the synthesis in A. Petrucci, "'Anticamente moderni e modernamente antichi,'" in Petrucci, *Libri, scrittura e pubblico nel Rinascimento. Guida storica e critica* (Bari, 1979), pp. 21–36.

23. W. J. Ong, "System, Space and Intellect in Renaissance Symbolism," in *Bibliothèque d'humanisme et renaissance* 18 (1956): 228.

had taken place in the domain of written culture: the creation of state libraries, founded on the humanistic model by some of the greatest princes
and sovereigns of Europe and Italy; the coexistence of manuscript and
printed books in the system of reading; and, finally, the birth of the new lay
book of small format: the *enchiridion* or the "pocket" book of the new gen-
erations of readers.

In such a context, the experience that an Angelo Poliziano must have had
of reading seems particularly significant.[24] This intellectual, modern in so
many ways and clearly different from most of his contemporaries, treated
the world of books as an open and inexhaustible reservoir, diachronic and
plurilingual in its immense possibilities of development. But at the same
time he maintained a relationship with books that was freer, more supple,
and less concerned with ownership; it was often realized outside of any
institutional framework or any fixed rituals. This reading sometimes was
accompanied by other physical and intellectual activities, as we see in two
extracts from his letters written in vernacular:

> "Ieri sera cominciamo a leggere un poco di s. Agostino. E questa lezione
> risolvessi alfine nel musicare e in iscorgere e dirozare certo modello di
> ballerino che è qua." (Yesterday evening we begin to read a little Saint
> Augustine. And at the end this reading turned into playing music and
> jumping up and polishing a certain model of dancing practiced here.)[25]
> "Visitiamo questi orti, che ne è piena la città Pistoia e qualche volta la
> libreria di maestro Zambino, che ci ho trovato parecchi buone cosette,
> et in greco et in latino." (We visit these gardens, in the very heart of
> the city of Pistoia, and sometimes the bookstore of master Zambino,
> where I found several good items in both Greek and Latin.)[26]

Poliziano was a professor; he was also the greatest textual philologist of his
time. And yet in his fashion of reading, in the suppleness of the relationship
he maintained with books and texts, one easily recognizes the hedonistic
ambitions that were traditionally part of aristocratic education and that one
finds in lay and bourgeois reading in the printing epoch. In a word, it is the
reading of a cultivated person of the modern epoch.

What has just been said shows clearly how new tendencies and practices
dawned in the world of written culture of the Middle Ages, both among the

---

24. Petrucci, "Biblioteche antiche," pp. 551–54 (below, pp. 231–35).
25. Letter of 8 April 1476 to Clarice Orsini, in A. Poliziano, *Prose volgari inedite e poesie
latine e greche edite e inedite* (Florence, 1867), p. 47.
26. Letter of 31 Aug. 1478, p. 61.

cultural avant-garde and in recently literate classes who for the first time had wholesale access to books. In the beginning, these tendencies and practices were adopted employing old models of reading whose links to preceding cultural systems made them impractical for the new usages. This is why the promoters of new practices soon sought to modify the model of reading then in use, and thus to imagine, produce, and impose a new type of book. It was only in a second stage that the diffusion of the new model of reading produced, little by little, a modification of the instruments and places of reading.

The history of the slow and progressive formation and propagation of the humanistic mode of reading supports this interpretation. In 1366, Petrarca, in a letter to Boccaccio, extolled the virtues of the ancient caroline minuscule that, by its complete simplicity, represented for him the ideal of writing. It was, he wrote, "castigata et clara seque ultro oculis ingerens" (plain and clear and offering itself to the eyes) (*Fam.*, XXIII, 19, 8). The objectives were thus clear and the tendencies evident from the beginning. Yet another thirty years were needed before a group of avant-garde intellectuals brought to realization the new model of book to which Petrarca aspired, and it was still longer before, under the influence of different circumstances, there were changes in the places and, by extension, the very ideology of reading. Thus liberated from the comfortable but rigid schema of the scholastic *lectio,* reading was finally transformed into a freer (and more problematic) relationship with the printed text.

8

MINUTE, AUTOGRAPH, AUTHOR'S BOOK

T HE TERMS THAT MAKE UP the title of this paper—*minute, autograph, author's book*—propose difficult problems of defini-tion. Indeed, the terms indicate textual phenomena and prod-ucts, or different phases in the production of the text, each of which can find an exact characterization only when located in a historical perspective and placed in relationship to concrete situations. But historical study of the material components of textual analysis is made more urgent by two current concerns: on one side, there is the steadily increasing interest of several disciplines in acts of writing; on the other, there are the perspectives opened by the philology of modern and contemporary texts into the field of genetic criticism and textual studies, where we have learned to assess textual proc-esses in relationship with the operations of writing and the material editorial conditions that are at their base. In particular, it seems evident that studying the participation of the author in the work of writing his or her own text and analyzing when and how such participation changed over time would constitute a notable contribution both to better understanding the processes by which complex texts are produced and to the criticism of those texts. Such studies, moreover, can also serve to make more precise for each his-torical epoch and situation what were the relationships between writing and reading, and between book and text, that constitute the deepest nature of any higher written culture.

This chapter, however, does not intend to be a general theoretical or

Originally published as "Minuta, autografo, libro d'autore," in *Il libro e il testo*, ed. C. Questa and R. Raffaelli (Urbino, 1984), pp. 399–414.

methodological discussion: defining and understanding means first of all marking the temporal and spatial limits of the phenomena in question. I have therefore chosen to fix attention on a particular period of European and Italian intellectual history, specifically that running from the end of the eleventh century to the mid-fourteenth, because at that juncture, within the framework of an overall growth and expansion of written culture, the world of graphic production in Western Europe underwent multiple dramatic and far-reaching changes. I believe that it will be particularly fruitful for our purposes to analyze three phenomena over this several-hundred-year span, or rather three problems that relate directly to the terms announced in the title, in some measure making a discursive transposition of those terms into inquiries. These phenomena-problems are:

1. The ways in which, precisely between the eleventh and fourteenth century, the author's direct participation in the material production of his own texts begins to be seen and then is gradually extended, at least in some sectors of European written culture, both in editorial phases and in phases of turning a text into a book; this last aspect constitutes the problem, complex because it is multiform, of the "author's book."

2. The characteristic typology that the materials of editorial preparation came to take on in relationship with the delineation of a process for drafting complex texts that, in contrast to the past, was articulated over several phases of writing that were predominately or completely autograph; further, because these materials varied markedly both in their nature and in the times given over to editorial work, they thus ended up enjoying a certain autonomy from each other, with all of them being intended for preservation, at least after a certain moment.

3. The influence that may have been exercised on this process by the model of documentary practice, which itself became broadly diffused precisely during the twelfth and thirteenth centuries, that had the notary articulate the drafting of the private and semi-public acts of which he was normally the sole author and writer into several phases that were entirely autograph despite being distinct in time and in textual and material characteristics.

It is generally agreed that the traditional system of dictation by which late antique and early medieval protagonists of written culture drafted complex texts admitted little participation in the actual writing by the authors, apart from their eventually (but not always) participating personally in the phases of correction; the first writing out of a text, moreover, whether or not corrected by the author's hand, was generally entrusted to materials intended to be obliterated (wax tablets) or destroyed (waste scraps of parchment). I do not believe that this interpretation of the facts is substantially wrong, despite the fact that it has never in recent times been rigorously verified and might be understood in less absolute terms than has usually been done. But it is certain that only for the eleventh century and especially for the twelfth does one begin to have considerable numbers of manuscripts of medieval authors that are partially or wholly autograph. It is thus precisely in this period that one must locate the beginning of a substantial modification of this "writing relationship" that somehow and in certain circumstances links the author to his own text.

This is not the place for a census of medieval author's autographs and in particular those of the eleventh and twelfth century that have so far been recognized: that undertaking was completed more than sixty years ago by Paul Lehmann and was repeated rather recently by Monique-Cécile Garand.[1] Here, rather, the interest lies in specifying the personal and social characteristics of these authors, the nature of the text transmitted, and the typological characteristics from the viewpoint of writing practices and material production that they reveal under that lens of graphical and codicological analysis which, as Derolez observed, is the only means "able to provide us with the hyphen between those two great moments in the genesis of a text: composition and publication."[2]

Garand has already observed that most of the authors included in the census were monks whose work connected them with the library, archive, or school of their monastery; she also noted that most of the texts they produced consisted of "universal, regional, or local chronicles, annals, and the lives of saints or great personages" and thus belonged to two specific disciplinary sectors—history and hagiography. One can add that there were

---

1. P. Lehmann, "Autographe und Originale namhafter lateinischer Schriftsteller des Mittelalters," in *Erforschung des Mittelalters*, vol. 1 (Stuttgart, 1959), pp. 359–81 (orig. in *Zeitschrift des deutschen Vereins für Buchwesen und Schriftum* 3 [1920]: 6–16). M.-C. Garand, "Auteurs latins et autographes des XIe et XIIe siècles," *Scrittura e civiltà* 5 (1981): 77–104. Recently, F. Gasparri has restated the problem of the contrast between an oral system of dictation and a written, autograph system in "Textes autographes d'auteurs victorins du XIIe siècle," *Scriptorium* 35 (1981): 277–84. Also important are the contributions of A. Derolez, "Quelques problèmes méthodologiques posés par les manuscrits autographes: Le cas du Liber Floridus de Lambert de Saint-Omer," in *La paléographie hébraique médiévale* (Paris, 1974), pp. 29–36; and by E. Ornato, "L'edition des textes médievaux conservés dans des manuscrits autographes," in *Les manuscrits. Transcription, édition, signification* (Paris, 1976), pp. 37–57. For the general expansion of written culture in Europe between the eleventh and fourteenth centuries, see the useful and stimulating book by M. T. Clanchy, *From Memory to Written Record: England, 1066–1307*, 2d ed. (Oxford, 1993); and *Gli autografi medievali. Problem paleografici e filologici*, ed. P. Chiesa and L. Pinelli (Spoleto, 1994).

2. "Quelques problèmes," p. 29.

two lay authors who also had careers concerned with administration and documentation: Goffredo of Viterbo, imperial notary of Frederic I, and Pietro da Eboli, courtier of the Norman Kingdom of Sicily. Similarly, the listing of the types of texts transmitted by autograph manuscripts can be augmented by the organic collections of documents put together as compilations in some great Benedictine monasteries: one might recall at least the works of Gregorio di Catino and Peter the Deacon. With regard to the typology of the autograph codices produced in this period and by these particular categories of authors, it is doubtless also true, as Derolez and Garand have already shown, that one must recognize distinctions both according to the intention of the individual writer, who may have produced the book for himself or for preservation in the common center, and according to the stage of drafting of the text evidenced by each product.

A clear identification of the textual function of each piece of evidence is rather difficult, in part (it seems to me) because their differences result precisely from the basic characteristic that they have in common: the diversity of the experiences and circumstances in which their author-producers worked. Some of these authors, whose educations still linked them to the practice of dictation, were forced to write by their own hand because of the momentary or prolonged absence of helpers; others wrote because of the restricted nature of the texts to be transcribed or drafted; and still others were accustomed to making use of helpers only irregularly, then intervening again by their own hand where and when they thought it expedient. It is hard to know how aware any of them were that there was a special value in the author's autograph participation in the writing of his own text, especially since many of them continued to employ dictation whenever they could or in alternation with autograph writing, as Thomas Aquinas still did in the mid-thirteenth century. But it is certain that, practically at the beginning of the period under examination, a tireless writer such as Guibert de Nogent could clearly define the two practices by implicitly contrasting what he called "continuatio scribendi" to oral composition done by dictation and thus "sola memoria, sola voce, sine manu, sine oculis" (by memory and voice alone, without hand or eyes).[3]

These and other indications remind us that we are dealing with a process that, by revolutionizing intellectual practices and rendering them more complicated, ended up touching the physical behaviors of practitioners and profoundly modifying their habits. The contrast between voice and hand, between memory and eyes—expressed in Guibert de Nogent's happy and eloquent formula—testifies to how the gradual increase in autograph behav-

3. Cited by Garand, "Auteurs latins," p. 86, and "Le scriptorium de Guibert de Nogent," *Scriptorium* 31 (1977): 3.

iors from the beginning was situated in the context of a complex and vast transformation of the intellectual professions themselves. For it is not by chance that almost at the end of this process, in the mid-thirteenth century, Bonaventura da Bagnoregio distinguished four modes of *facendi libros*: that of the *scriptor*, or scribe who "scribit aliena, nihil addendo vel mutando" (writes the work of others, adding or changing nothing); that of the *compilator*, who "scribit aliena, addendo, sed non de suo" (writes the work of others, makings additions that are not his own); that of the *commentator*, who "scribit et aliena et sua" (writes the work of others and his own work), but only as secondary material; and finally that of one who "scribit et sua et aliena, sed sua tanquam principalia" (writes his own work and that of others, but principally his own) and who thus alone "debet dici auctor" (ought to be called an author). Bonaventura therefore placed this last image, essentially the new intellectual of scholastic/university culture, at the top of a hierarchical progression based entirely on the practice of writing, linking the scribe and the author without any break in continuity as it embraced and defined the entire panorama of possible intellectual activities within the institutional and physical framework of the operations of writing.[4]

Consequently, precisely because the autograph codices of the eleventh and twelfth centuries (and in part those of the following century) constitute direct evidence of this profound process of transformation, they present some common characteristics worthy of the greatest attention beyond the formal differences that distinguish them:

1. In almost all the cases examined, and especially when comparing treatments and compilations of a historical-documentary character, it is evident that the codices were meant to be one of a kind in that the relevant texts were intended to be preserved in the very place where they were produced without further reproduction except as an exceptional case;

2. Whether the autograph is total or partial, almost all the codices in question are characterized by successive corrective or supplementary intervention by the author's hand that can be grouped in multiple "campaigns of modifications," to adopt the descriptive formulation of Ezio Ornato;

3. Such interventions were executed with "slow" and often "invisible" techniques, that is, with additions that were lined, framed, and of minute size and with corrections executed predominantly by erasure;

4. For the new intellectuals, see the fine synthesis of Jacques Le Goff, *Les intellectuels au moyen âge* (Paris, 1957), who cites Bonaventura, *Commentum in I Librum Sententiarum*, in *Opera omnia*, vol. 1 (Ad claras aquas, 1882), pp. 14–15.

such techniques are typical of book techniques, with erasure in particular being tied to thick and resistant writing material such as parchment.

One can thus define the "author's book" as having the function of an archival codex of the text, a characteristic shared by the majority of the autograph manuscripts of the period under examination despite the formal diversity of individual instances. From another angle, this image also correlates directly with the development of another phenomenon, that of the "progressive text" intended to be redrafted and enriched by the author in successive phases of writing all done by his own hand. It thus seems undeniable that the model of the author's book and the practice of the progressive text, at least in this period and in the concrete examples that survive, were both direct consequences of increasingly frequent autograph interventions by the author in the writing of his own text.

Already in the eleventh and twelfth centuries, therefore, such interventions had profoundly modified the very process of redacting the text to be transmitted, at least to the extent of prolonging it over time in terms not precisely definable. Even if limited to a restricted number of cases, this phenomenon cannot be undervalued because it introduced radical modifications into the relationship between author and text. But the majority of these "author's books" did not create traditions. They were not reproduced, being instead kept in the very place where they were produced like a kind of jealously reserved written memory, which leads to the supposition that at least in some cases they ended up acquiring a certain patina of "authenticity" with overtones of genuinely juristic value linked to the prestige of the place of conservation and the predominately autograph character of its writing. In this perspective, autograph codices kept in unique copies in the very institutions in which or for which they were written can be considered not so much "minutes" or "originals" as "authenticated stages" of a specific text. Naturally, that also applies in the case especially frequent in the immediately succeeding period (thirteenth and fourteenth centuries), in which for each text one can have multiple and successive "author's books" wholly or partially autograph.

Because the range of case histories offered by partially or entirely autograph author's books from the eleventh and twelfth centuries is fairly wide, choosing examples that have some indicative value is particularly difficult. Let it therefore suffice here to refer to Garand's already cited article, which is well provided with eloquent plates, limiting ourselves for reasons of brevity to one example from the end of the twelfth century, to which we shall juxtapose, for contrast and comparison, another from the mid-thirteenth century.

The *Liber ad honorem Augusti*, compiled by Pietro da Eboli between 1195 and 1196, comes down to us in codex 120 of the Burgerbibliothek of Bern.[5] It is divided into two parts: the first, comprising books I and II, was written by a copyist but has subsequent autograph interventions by the author; and the second, comprising a third book, was written by a hand different from the first scribe that Massimo Miglio has recently shown to have been that of the author himself. The codex is supplied with a splendid series of full-page miniatures illustrating the historical events narrated by the poetic text, with captions also done by the author's hand. The author himself, having conceived of the work in only two books and having had the manuscript prepared as a finished deluxe codex (perhaps as a presentation copy), subsequently modified its orientation for obvious political reasons by adding a third book in his own hand and by intervening in the text of the preceding part. The corrective interventions, generally limited to one or a few words, or to a verse, were executed on erasures; additions were arranged neatly in the margins or on leaves inserted at the appropriate places. But in this way the codex, from being a finished product, was turned by the author's own hands into a working model. Pietro da Eboli was fully aware of this, to the extent that he extended his corrective labors to the newly compiled and completely autograph third book itself, in several cases leaving open the possibility of variants, making interlinear insertions of the proposed new reading above the old text, but without canceling it. Because the work had no later manuscript tradition, we can venture the hypothesis that the unique author's book that transmits it was preserved as evidence of a prolonged operation of redrafting and rewriting that conferred on it some patina of authenticity and that made its existence worth prolonging into our times.

More complex and also more instructive for our purposes is the case represented by Vat. lat. 7260, which constitutes the entirely autograph "author's book" of the famous *Chronica* written between 1279 and 1288 by Salimbene de Adam of Parma.[6] This is a relatively small codex, written by Fra Salimbene in a neat, clear gothic script laid out in two columns studded in the margins with more or less lengthy textual additions made by the author himself at different times. Because the codex also bears frequent corrections

---

5. See the edition of *Liber ad honorem Augusti*, ed. G. B. Siragusa (Rome, 1906) and *Studi su Pietro da Eboli*, Studi storici, 103–05 (Rome, 1978), and in particular the essay of M. Miglio, "Momenti e modi di formazione del 'Liber ad honorem Augusti,'" pp. 119–46.

6. For Salimbene de Adam it is sufficient to refer to the *Cronaca*, ed. G. Scalia, 2 vols. (Bari, 1966); Vat. lat. 7260 is described in vol. 2, pp. 987–1003.

of obvious copying errors, one must deduce that it was itself a copy of a preceding redaction. And because internal references inserted into the marginal additions direct us not so much or only to individual passages of the text but also to individual leaves of the codex in accord with a numeration applied by Salimbene himself, one must also deduce that the author considered the codex itself to be the unique witness and depository of the text as well as an exemplar for personal use. By this means, Salimbene retained for himself the possibility of continuing to make new interventions while assuring others (the reading public? the friars?) of the authenticity of what was written.

Having worked as archivists or librarians charged with preserving public and private acts, and having used those acts to prepare their historical and documentary works, many authors of eleventh-, twelfth-, and thirteenth-century autograph books must have known the practices by which notaries and chancery copyists produced documentation. For private acts, these practices were defined with increasing exactness by rigorously requiring an autograph prepared by a drafter juridically qualified for preparing documents: the notary. In fact, beginning in the early Middle Ages and especially in the regions of Italy under Lombard law, the notary differed from the ecclesiastical compiler of texts by traditionally being the *scriptor* of the documents he drafted. Precisely in the twelfth century, when subscriptions in the hands of the parties and witnesses were eliminated, such autographs became total—a development that corresponded perfectly to the notariate's conquest of the *publica fides,* or autonomous capacity to establish the credibility of the documents drafted, and to the parallel creation of the *instrumentum publicum.* At the same time, one sees the development and definition of a second, also typically notarial practice of drafting detailed and articulated minutes for documents that had an autonomous juridical value.

Here, too, was a case of perfecting a practice used for a long time in different forms, since already in the eighth century Italian notaries had written out brief notices of essential points on the verso of parchment leaves, with the original document itself then drafted on the recto. From this starting point, across a long and complex evolution between the eighth and twelfth centuries, one arrived first at the drafting of *imbreviature* (genuine minutes separate from the originals), then to gathering them in files, and finally to their registration in volumes called cartularies or protocols. These facts, to whose clarification many scholars have made contributions even recently, are well known. But what matters here is less the overall process, which culminated in the twelfth century with the creation of the *instrumentum publicum* drafted in several phases spaced out in time, than certain aspects of notarial practice that remarkably and perhaps not entirely by chance resemble those of contemporary literature.

These aspects, moreover, are wonderfully witnessed in the documentation of Genoa, the oldest in Italy, whose collection of notarial protocols begins with that of Giovanni Scriba embracing the years 1154–64. One finds, in fact, that already in the first half of the twelfth century there had been established at Genoa a rational process of documentation articulated in three successive phases: first, the notary took down data relative to the contract on a small paper leaf or in a small book of paper called a "manual"; then, after a certain lapse of time, these notes were developed into an actual minute (the *imbreviatura*) written out in a larger paper register called a cartulary or protocol that itself was valid at law; finally, if one of the parties requested it, he drafted the *instrumentum publicum* on parchment.[7]

Several aspects of these practices seem especially important for our purposes and worthy of reflection:

1. the drafting of the text of the *instrumentum*—having become steadily larger and richer in formulas, clauses of warranty, and specifications of rights—in several phases separated in time and all entirely autograph by the notary;

2. the use of rapid and visible techniques (crossing out, smudging with the finger) distinct from the slow, disguised techniques of scriptoria producing books for the intervening corrections and additions executed by the notary, often *currenti calamo,* on the text of the preparatory drafts;

3. the preservation of the final minute constituted by the *imbreviatura* (the authenticated stage of the text par excellence) by the author of the text himself, who sometimes even went so far as to keep the early rough drafts written out rapidly in the manual or on loose leaves;

4. the use of paper, a new and less expensive writing material that in the twelfth century was certainly imported to Genoa rather than made there, as the medium on which the whole preparatory process of the text was accomplished (fig. 23).

These elements are important both for the novelties they introduced into the writing practices of Western Europe and for their obvious parallels to

7. On the birth of the *instrumentum publicum* and of the notarial practice of the triple redaction of the act, see G. Costamagna, *La triplice redazione dell'instrumentum genovese* (Genoa, 1961); Costamagna and M. Amelotti, *Alle origini del notariato italiano* (Rome, 1975), pp. 205–82; for the case of Rome, see A. Pratesi, "I 'dicta' e il documento privato romano," *Bullettino dell'Archivio Paleografico Italiano* n.s. I (1955): 93–109.

23. A thirteenth-century Florentine notary's notebook. Florence, Archivio di Stato, Not. A.C., c. 568ª, f. 44r.

the analogous and contemporary practices of autograph writing in the world of "literary" culture that we discussed above. Indeed, there is no doubt that both processes—consisting on one hand of the gradual assertion of the author's autograph participation in the drafting of the complex texts of official culture and on the other of the affirmation of the new notarial *instrumentum publicum*, with its articulated formation—belonged to the same overall movement that rapidly transformed the world of written culture. This was a world in which the most complicated intellectual exigencies of the new philosophy and law, and the general need for greater written production of both documents and books, required immediate, practical answers. It was precisely in the twelfth and thirteenth centuries that such solutions were found and then rapidly accepted in both fields.

Beyond such coincidences of a general character, however, there are other still more precise points that in my opinion cannot be denied:

1. The qualification of the text of the *instrumentum* as a text in some measure "progressive," admittedly within the limits of a set scheme and formulary, was expressed by that limited but evident freedom to intervene, add, and correct which notaries automatically claimed for themselves in the course of the drafting process—a freedom that was deplored by the thirteenth-century jurist Odofredo when he complained that the notaries "detrahebant et adiungebant ad sensum suum et creditoris" (subtract and add to their sense and that of the creditor).[8]

2. The analogy of function and nature (even if not of typology) that came to be established between the "author's book" as we have defined it and the notarial protocol in which the notary added rubrics, left empty spaces for the later insertion of the imbreviatura of certain deeds, arrayed annotations in the margins, effected corrections and additions, and employed a complex system of cancellation signs (the *lineatura*) and sigla that almost constituted a personal code to document for himself the drafting stage of each document.

If the practices for writing documents developed by Italian notaries in the course of the twelfth century present some analogies with the writing practices of the contemporary world of written higher culture, the influence of the completely new procedures and instruments that the notariate had de-

---

8. Cited by M. Moresco and G. P. Bognetti, *Per l'edizione dei notai liguri del sec. XII* (Genoa, 1938), p. 58.

veloped seems still more decisive in the period immediately following. These innovations, documented by the same sources, were:

1. the transformation of the preparatory stages of the text, or at least the minute or *imbreviatura* that was the last of them, into a text with the value of an original meant to be carefully preserved even after the original document had been drafted and delivered to the parties;

2. the autonomy and even physical differences that the preparatory stages enjoyed with respect to the finished text in that both the manual and the cartulary were on paper rather than parchment, in the form of a register rather than leaves, written in a fluid cursive with many abbreviations and sigla rather than the ordered and generally clear chancery minuscule employed in the *instrumentum*, and including numerous corrective interventions and additions that obviously could be admitted only exceptionally and in special form into the version *in mundum*;

3. last but not least, the use of paper as the material ancillary to the writing operations, functionally destined not only to the writing out of the first rough and provisional drafts but also, as often occurred, of personal notes, accounts, pen tests, and so forth.

All these innovations were taken up by late medieval and modern literary practices, in some measure continuing to characterize them in forms that were perpetuated practically unchanged until the first mechanical processes—the typewriter. In such a perspective, one cannot underestimate the importance of the practice of preserving the minutes instead of destroying them, especially since it witnesses a profound modification in the mentality of the *scriptor-auctor* who was now brought into an ongoing if latent connection with his productions and conditioned by the infinite, always present possibility of returning to a finished or abandoned text. It is pertinent in this connection to note the remark of the Russian poet Osip Mandelstam that "the indestructibility of the rough draft is a dynamic law of the work of art," in the sense that a literary text acquires the temporal density of progressive elaboration only by preserving an always potentially active matrix. No one, I think, can deny that this practice, as applied to the text of the *instrumentum*, was introduced in the Latin West, precisely in the form that it would maintain for centuries, by Italian notaries in the twelfth century. On the other hand, one could also say that written European culture's adoption of paper as a writing material itself carried a substantial innovative charge, because paper both changed the material conditions for operations of writing and made it possible to articulate the processes of redacting texts in a rather more varied fashion than had been true in the past. Contrary to what is commonly thought, paper was not adopted in literate Europe because of a heightened need to read, but because of a heightened and more articulated need to write.

The notariate never played a more active and decisively innovative role in Italian culture—either as a professional category or as individual practition-ers—than in the period corresponding to the full flowering of communal society and to the thirteenth and fourteenth centuries. Precisely in this period notaries—each of whom drafted an enormous number of acts—perfected the use of the innovative instruments and practices that their predecessors had introduced in the twelfth century. Our archives are full of examples, such as the protocol of the Florentine notary Biagio Boccadibue (1298–1314), which is available in a recent edition.[9] Still more complete is the material of notary Massarello di Pellolo, active in Perugia between 1361 and 1404, that Attilio and Imma Bartoli Langeli prepared for the Franciscan exposition held in 1982.[10] This material includes notes, *bastardelli*, protocols, and *instrumenta* that sometimes seem to involve four distinct successive stages: the first rough draft on loose sheets; the full writing out in *infilza* or in the *bastardello*; enrollment of the draft in the protocol, which in practice could also have gaps or be reduced to notes *pro memoria*; and the definitive redaction *in mundum* that involved a final phase of textual interventions and elaborations.

Only a broad census of the Italian and European literary autographs of the thirteenth and fourteenth centuries, together with a scrupulous codicol-ogical and graphical analysis of individual evidence, could fully reveal the extent to which intellectuals foreign to the world of documentation arrived at their writing and drafting practices by experiences analogous to those of the notaries or by more or less direct influences. Since the research now in progress on the part of many scholars of the period in Italy (especially the lively group guided in Milan and Padua by Giuseppe Billanovich),[11] in France (let it suffice to mention the name of Gilbert Ouy), in Britain, Germany, and the United States continues to produce results in abundance, for my present purpose I will limit myself to discussing the autographs of two im-portant literary individuals from fourteenth-century Italy: Francesco da Bar-berino and Francesco Petrarca.

9. *Biagio Boccadibue (1298–1314)*, ed. L. De Angelis, E. Gigli, and F. Sznura, vol. 1 of *I notai dell'età di Dante* (Florence, 1978). See also notary Palmerio di Corbizo da Uglione, *Im-breviature. 1237–1238*, ed. Luciana Mosiici and F. Sznura (Florence, 1982), whose introduction contains interesting observations on the process of corrections and additions in the protocol.

10. In *Francesco d'Assisi. Documenti e archivi. Codici e biblioteche miniature* (Milan, 1982), pp. 43–45.

11. See the journal *Italia medioevale e umanistica*.

Francesco da Barberino (d. 1348) was the contemporary of both Dante and Petrarca and, like the latter, was the son and grandson of a notary; he was a notary himself for some time, as well as a judge and doctor of laws. He is the earliest example of a literate medieval Italian who expressed himself in Italian as well as in Latin and for whom it is possible to study the elaboration of a text through original manuscripts that have come down to us. Two partially autograph codices survive for his well-known *Documenti d'amore,*[12] a didactic work in vernacular verse with comments in Latin that passed through several phases of drafting, mostly with direct participation of the author; in fact, Francesco stated in one note of the Latin comment that there was not in "hoc libro littera nec figura, que, ante alicuius transcriptum, per me ad minus non fuerit tracta quater" (this book a letter or figure that was not traced at least four times by me before anyone else's transcription). The older of the two codices we possess, Barb. lat. 4077, contains the poetic Italian text, part of the translation into Latin prose, the beginning of the comment, and sketches for twenty-seven miniature illustrations. It is written only in part by the author, who made himself the coworker of the two copyists; Francesco, moreover, subsequently returned to the text, using the slow system of erasure and rewriting to carry out corrections and modifications (some of considerable length) that touched both the originally autograph part and those written by other hands. The other codex, Barb. lat. 4076, presents a different and more complex case. It is a direct copy of the first, complete in both text and comment, and also bears the definitive version of the illustrative cycle executed by an artist of high quality. But it is not entirely in the author's hand, as has generally been thought following the old view of Egidi, for paleographical analysis reveals that it is rather the work of several copyists (figs. 24, 25).

The hypothesis that Barb. lat. 4076 was entirely autograph rested on interpreting some phrases contained in the comment as marking the interruption and resumption of the work of writing, which thus would have been effected by the author himself. But in fact these phrases, being firmly incorporated in their context, constitute either functional references to the text, as when Francesco proposes to *redire ad literam* (an expression erroneously interpreted by Egidi as referring to writing, although it doubtless indicates the Latin text), or they are rhetorical appeals to the readers to stress the articulation of the text in the style of public readings or cycles of lessons: hence, the parallels Egidi suggested between these expressions and Petrarca's

12. See *I documenti d'amore di Francesco da Barberino secondo i manoscritti originali*, ed. F. Egidi, vol. 4 (Rome, 1927), pp. XVI–XXVIII.

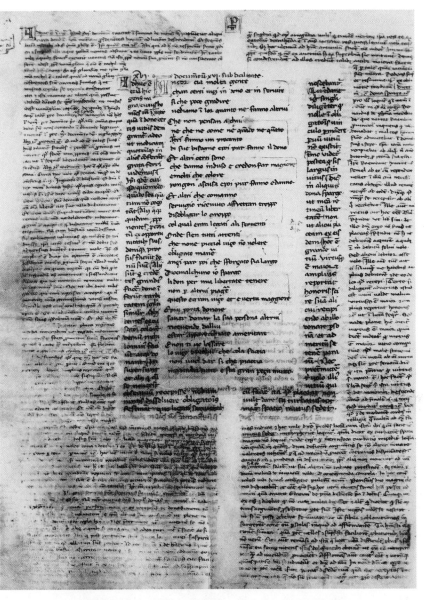

24. Biblioteca Apostolica Vaticana, Barb. lat. 4076, fol. 18v

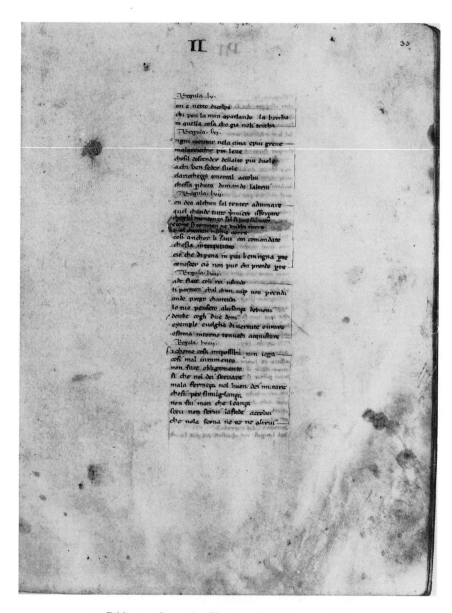

25. Biblioteca Apostolica Vaticana, Barb. lat. 4077, fol. 35r

marginal notations in the sheets of minutes of the *Rime* (which I will discuss shortly) do not stand up. Barb. lat. 4076 is thus shown to be what it really is, an "author's book" whose writing, impagination, and ornamentation were accurately constructed on the model of the preceding codex and which was intended to receive a definitive redaction of the text; it was precisely the high level of professionalism needed for this task that led the author to have the copying done by others, although under his supervision. All the same, even in this deluxe codex Francesco ended up making interventions in his own hand with a meticulous and varied work of correction by erasure that mainly affected the Latin text and related comment (written by several hands at a later time) but more rarely even the poetic text in vernacular. By their extent, complexity, and duration over time, these interventions modified the very nature of the book, transforming the deluxe codex, perhaps meant to serve as a donation copy, into an archival author's book or authenticated stage of a still and always open text.

Although he employed them, Francesco da Barberino was in open warfare with the copyists of his time: following a humanistic topos that would also be dear to Petrarca and Salutati among others, he accused them of corrupting the "subtle" texts that their "crass" brains could not understand. Perhaps this was why he was directly interested in the problem of manufacture, layout, and structure of highly articulated and complex books such as those contained in his *Documenti d'amore,* to the extent that he did not hesitate to regulate every step of their construction and even to place his own hands on them. Even so, as far as we know, he never arrived at seeing an entirely autograph process, in which an author would be occupied in the work of writing his own text from the first rough draft to the exemplar or exemplars for circulation, as being an end in itself, although that would be to some extent the exact parallel to the notarial *instrumentum publicum* which was entirely an autograph of the author.

Resolutely setting out upon this road, however, was that other notaries' son and grandson, Francesco Petrarca. To his acute sensibility for the world of books Petrarca joined a shrewd experience and precise will to change graphic practices that was sustained by a genuine religion of writing which expressed itself in a perpetual desire to rearrange and change his own texts. With regard to the *Bucolicum carmen,* which Petrarca consigned in 1357 to a final, autograph version in Vat. lat. 3358 and then ceaselessly reelaborated until 1366, Nicholas Mann observed that the "innate and intrinsic dynamism of the text contained in this manuscript is at once a paradigmatic example of the author's literary activity and a demonstration of the inadequacy of the notion of the literary text as something static: whether before or after the first fixing by writing on parchment, the eclogues were constantly subjected to modifications".[13]

This is not the place to recall Petrarca's many whole or partially autograph manuscripts, nor the innovative quality of his writing.[14] For our purposes a brief, illustrative examination will suffice of that text whose stages of redaction can be most easily discussed in their material and graphic characteristics: the *Rerum vulgarium fragmenta*. Writing about it to his brother Gherado, perhaps as early as 1349, Petrarca remembered with apparent precision the effort of continual textual reelaboration that his *nugae* had already cost: "quotiens sillabas contorsimus, quotiens verba transtulimus, denique quod non fecimus ut amor ille . . . plausibiliter caneretur?" (How many syllables have we twisted, how many words have we transposed, what in short did we not do to make that love pleasingly sung?) (*Fam.* X 3, 21–22). The direct evidence of such creative labor by the writer, which in actuality lasted beyond the date of the letter and was interrupted only by death, is conveyed to us in two manuscripts: Vat. lat. 3196, the so-called draft codex, and Vat. lat 3195, the so-called Canzoniere original (figs. 26–29).[15] The first of these is not really a codex but resulted from the casual binding of nine folios and two loose sheets coming from the paper archive of Petrarca's work; it contains the "anecdotes of a perpetual perfectibility" (as it was happily put by Gianfranco Contini)[16]—the sketches, first drafts, provisional collections or vernacular poetic components and even of a letter (the *Fam.* XVI 6). Beyond being swept by crossouts, corrections, and additions, the paper leaves of Vat. lat. 3196 also contain a series of large and small afterthoughts and annotations in Latin that Petrarca placed in the margins and the white spaces, bearing precise chronological references to the stages of drafting of individual texts,

---

13. "The Making of Petrarch's 'Bucolicum Carmen': A Contribution to the History of the Text," *Italia medioevale e umanistica* 20 (1977): 127–82, esp. 130.

14. For the script and a provisional list of Petrarca autographs, see my *La scrittura de Francesco Petrarca*, Studi e testi, 248 (Città del Vaticano, 1967), and esp. Albinia de la Mare, *The Handwriting of the Italian Humanists*, vol. 1 (Oxford, 1973), pp. 1–16. For Petrarca's letters, superlative examples of multiple redactions, in addition to the splendid and still valid pages of G. Pasquali, *Storia della tradizione e critica del testo* (Florence, 1952), pp. 457–465, see Francesco Petrarca, *Epistole autografe*. Introduction, transcription, and reproduction edited by A. Petrucci (Padua, 1968).

15. The best technical treatment of these two manuscripts is still E. H. Wilkins, *The Making of the 'Canzoniere' and Other Petrarchan Studies* (Rome, 1951), esp. pp. 75–79 and 107–98. See also the integral facsimile reproductions: *Il codice Vaticano Lat. 3196 autografo del Petrarca*, ed. M. Porena (Rome, 1941), and *L'originale del Canzoniere di Francesco Petrarca, codice Vaticano latino 3195*, ed. M. Vattasso (Milan, 1905).

16. "Saggio d'un commento alle correzioni del Petrarca volgare," in his *Varianti e altra liguistica. Una raccolta di saggi* (Turin, 1970), p. 5.

Tuttol di piango. & poi la notte quando
trouomi in prato. & a dolorarsi menali
Jn tristo humor uo li occhi & consumando
laltimo si de lamorosi strali
Lasso che pur talun a la lenu sole
di questa morte che si chiama uita·
Che pieta u . . el mio fido soccorso

En se serua te . . . .
Prenden . . . e . . . miseri mortali·
Cosi spendol . . o tempo . . . .
el corr i doglia· & son stral a . . . . . .
Mi tengon . . ogni . . . .
& un luna ombra a la lenu . o gial piu co . . .
. . la lenu . sa . . . del nimal m . . . .
. . . . nel socol & no . . . .

Gia stesu co si . . . . . . querela
chun foco & i pieta sessi sentire
& lempia nube che l afredda & uela
o sessi quell altru i odio uenir
Or no odio p lei p me pietate
Tal su mia stella· & tal mia cru . . sorte
Che quandi sia di questa . . . .

En . . . .
Al . . . . gela·
Rompess . . . .
Che lesti ont . . . .
Certo che quel no uo questo no posso·
Ma ento la . . . . . sua belta . .
Sa pial nolo che dolce e la mia morte

Ra quantunque leggiarie donne & belle
Col suo beinuso suol del laltru sar . .
Amor pur chalor . . . . . nu sauelle
si aluuer bello· & poi l ueder . . . . . .
Come nacun a . . el la luna . el sole
Aluo mio & l inteller . . le parole
Tanto & piu sien le cose oscure & sole·

Sui ga costa dal modo no . . . . . .
Quel che sal . . . de le . . on stelle·
Dice di quanto questa in terra . . . . .
peru uertu . elmio regno co . . . .
si lacre uenta . a la terra herbe & . . . .
& al mar . . olleste i pesa & lona . .
Se morte l . . . .

Jl cantar nouo el pianger delli augelli·
el mormorar de liqui . cristalli
quella che neue . l uolto . oro i capelli
desuam al suon delli amorosi balli
Cosi mi sueglio a salutar l auror .
Ne primi anni . la ngliato . & son . chom
leuarsi i seme· en un p . to . en una hora·

Jn sul di sanno retenui le uelli
Giu p turre i freschi r . u . & uelli
Nel cui amor no sur mai igrin ne salli
pettinado al sue uecchio i bianchi uelli
el sol che seco· & pui laltru . ondio siu
J glio ueduto alcun giorno ambed . .
Quel sar l estelle & questo sparir lui

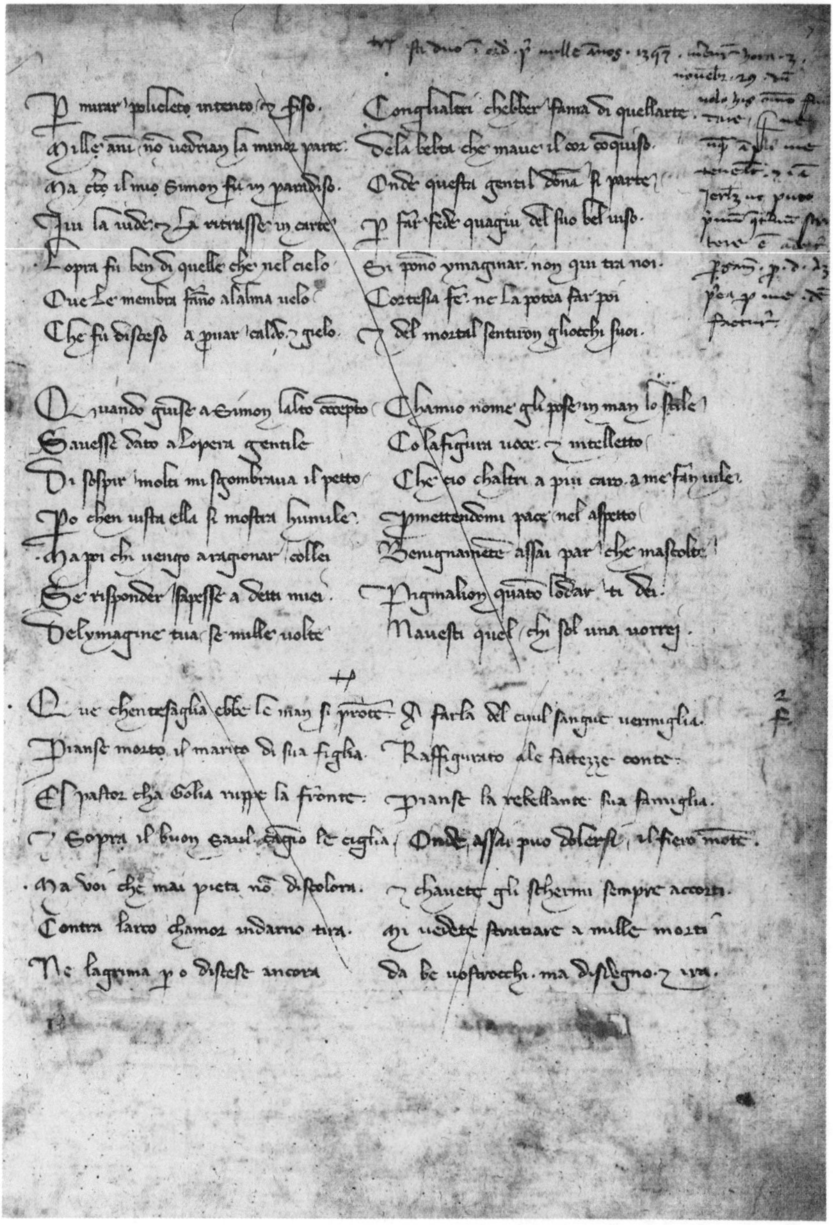

[Biblioteca Apostolica Vaticana, Vat. lat. 3196, fol. 7r — manuscript in Italian chancery cursive. Diplomatic best-reading below.]

[top marginal note:] † p[er] dì ... in mille anni · 1397 ...

Per mirar Policleto intento e fiso
Con gli altri ch'ebber fama di quell'arte
Mille ani non uedrian la minor parte
de la belta che m'aue il cor coquiso
Ma certo il mio Simon fu in paradiso
Onde questa gentil dona si parte
Iui la uide: e la ritrasse in carte
p far fede quagiu del suo bel uiso
L'opra fu ben di quelle che nel cielo
Si pono ymaginar, non qui tra noi
Oue le membra fanno a l'alma uelo
Cortesia fe ne la potea far poi
Che fu disceso a prouar caldo e gielo
del mortal sentiron gli occhi suoi

Quando giuse a Simon l'alto ccepto
Ch'a mio nome gli pose in man lo stile
Sauesse dato a l'opera gentile
Colla figura uoce e intelletto
Di sospir molti mi sgombraua il petto
Che cio ch'altri a piu caro a me fan uile
Po chen uista ella si mostra humile
ymettendomi pace nel affetto
Cha poi chi uengo a ragionar collei
Benignamente assai par che m'ascolte
Se risponder sapesse a detti miei
Pigmalion quato lodar ti dei
De l'ymagine tua se mille uolte
M'auesti quel chi sol una uorrei

Que chen tesaglia ebbe le man si prote
El farla del ciuil sangue uermiglia
Pianse morto il marito di sua figlia
Raffigurato a le fattezze conte
El pastor cha Golia ruppe la fronte
Pianse la ribellante sua famiglia
e sopra il buon Saul cangio le ciglia
Onde assai puo dolersi il fiero monte
Ma uoi che mai pieta nõ discolora
e hauete gli schermi sempre accorti
Contra l'arco ch'amor indarno tira
mi uedete straziare a mille morti
Ne lagrima po discese ancora
da be uostrocchi ma disdegno e ira

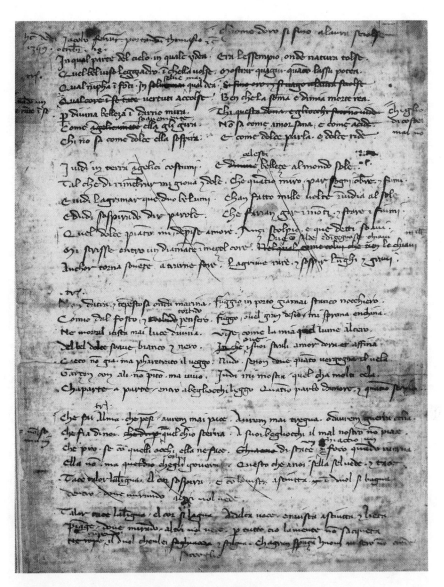

28. Biblioteca Apostolica Vaticana, Vat. lat. 3196, fol. 5v

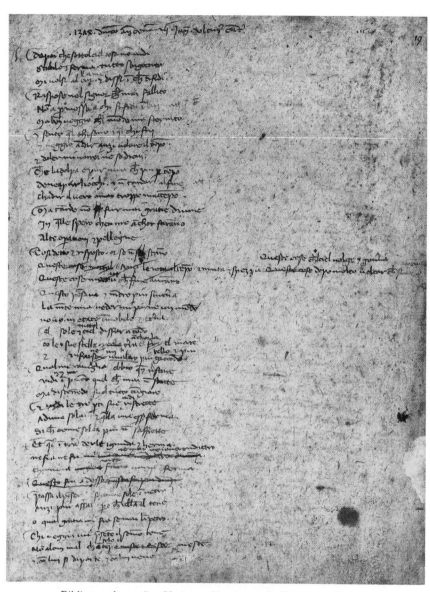

29. Biblioteca Apostolica Vaticana, Vat. lat. 3196, fol. 19r (paper insert)

observations on his own conditions of writing, on the motivations for poetic inspiration, and even observations of a rhetorical and stylistic nature.

All this is well known, and it would be out of place for me to speak of it at length. What matters here, however, is the incontestable fact that one encounters in the writing habits of Petrarca the vernacular poet more than one point of contact with contemporary notarial practices:

1. the sketches written in an extremely rapid flowing hand on loose paper leaves, with many corrections executed using fast techniques for crossing out and with frequent brief chronological annotations providing exact datings for the phases of the writing, that immediately call to mind the analogous paper pages of notarial manuals or *bastardelli* containing the first drafts of acts;

2. the so-called collections for reference (probably in orderly paper fascicles) containing the fair copies of components not yet in definitive form that were written out in an elegant chancery minuscule; these in turn call to mind notarial protocols containing the definitive minutes of acts: for example, the protocol of Lapo Gianni for the years 1298–1328 now in the Archivio di Stato of Florence;[17]

3. the custom of placing Latin notes in the margins, witnessing the various phases of elaboration of the text, or even the dry notations such as *tr(anscriptum)*, that correspond to the notarial practice of placing in the protocol summary marginal notations on the state of the elaboration of the act and on its eventual redaction *in mundum*;

4. finally, the system of crossing out the components that were transcribed elsewhere with great oblique strokes—sometimes parallel, sometimes crossed, sometimes divergent—that corresponds exactly to the same system adopted by notaries to cancel the text of the document in the *bastardello* or protocol when it has been copied elsewhere or developed *in mundum*, or after the related juridical action was over.

If Vat. lat. 3196 collects the "minutes" of the *Rime*, Vat. lat. 3195 constitutes their "original": actually, this is a complex codex with a long history, in which Petrarca initially had his scribe and disciple Giovanni Malpaghini copy the opening sections of the first and second parts of the collection and then, after the flight of his pupil, continued himself by completing the writing out

17. Archivio di Stato di Firenze, Notarile Antecosimiano L 76; see the reproductions from it in A. Petrucci, *Notarii. Documenti per la storia del notariato italiano* (Milan, 1958), pl. 49 and pp. 101–03.

in a patient work of copying, displacements, additions, corrections, and reorderings from October 1368 until at least the beginning of 1373 and probably until his death. Ernest Wilkins calculated that, excluding minor interventions, Petrarca worked on this codex in his own hand in twenty-seven different periods in his last years of life, within which one can distinguish forty-eight "working times": a constant, repeated, and total undertaking, therefore, that again transformed the nature of this codex from the author's book into an archive book, consecrated by an always impending labor of writing and rewriting. It suffices to see some pages of this unique book to perceive the textual modus operandi of the great poet as in an X ray. Indeed, we are far from the practices of fluent writing appropriate to the minute and the documentary tradition. Here, Petrarca moves within that other writing tradition of books, and he naturally was aware of and respected its rules and rhythms—I would almost say its liturgy. He corrected, modified, added, substituted, and displaced his texts with attentive and slow techniques, mimicking as closely as possible the practices of scribes. His aim was always to give the reader an author's book that in appearance lived up to a model of the book.

With Petrarca, indeed, the practice of the complete autograph proposed by the notarial model found its summation in an ideal based entirely on the book. The many perfect "author's books", containing texts of his works written out in his own hand, must have constituted models for an organic and quite personal proposal for reforming the system of book production, the functionality of the literary book, and the connection between book and public: we are here far removed from the world of notaries with their paper notebooks. But despite this distance, I continue to believe that Petrarca's writing and textual experience, in its great richness and the exemplary problems it poses, confirms the hypothesis ventured here that in medieval Europe, between the twelfth and fourteenth centuries, one of the principal factors inspiring first the autograph participation of authors in the material manufacture of their works and then the articulation of literary discourse in several phases of writing was the example offered by notaries and their professional (and entirely autograph) practices of drafting, registering, and preserving documentary texts. Admittedly, the evidence here adduced may be judged more indications than proofs, because practically all of the research in this field, which alone can furnish a more exact and complete framework for the realities of the practices and the products, is yet to be completed.

9

READING AND WRITING
VOLGARE IN
MEDIEVAL ITALY

THE MANUSCRIPT BOOK
New Books and New Techniques

I N T H E course of the twelfth century the manuscript book gradually acquired a steadily increasing importance and diffusion in
the education and culture of the higher classes of Western Europe. Book
production grew notably in numerical terms. Although it is impossible to
state precisely the percentage of increase, the accuracy of my statement is
amply demonstrated by the fact that many more twelfth-century codices
survive in modern libraries than those attributable to the eleventh. It is not,
therefore, by chance and perhaps without exaggeration that Saint Bernard
of Clairvaux (d. 1153) stated, in a text lamenting the rapid diffusion of Abelard's works: "Libri volant" (books fly).[1] Admittedly, the rapid circulation and
reproduction of written texts had to and did occur in well-defined social
spheres and within specific categories of intellectual technicians: "clerks",
almost all of them in orders. Indeed, Saint Bernard had in mind a circulation
confined to a circle of lettered clerks—men who read books, attended advanced schools, and studied, and who were familiar with the practice of
cultural and philosophical disputations; all of them were able to write as well

---

Originally published as "Il libro manoscritto" and "Le biblioteche antiche," in *Letteratura
italiana*, ed. A. Asor Rosa, vol. 2: *Produzione e consumo* (Turin, 1983), pp. 499–524, 528–54.

1. *Epistulae* CLXXXIX *(PL* 182: 355); cited in G. Severino Polica, "Libro, lettura, 'lezione'
negli 'studia' degli Ordini mendicanti (sec. XIII)," in *Le scuole degli Ordini mendicanti (secoli
XIII–XIV)*, Convegni del Centro di Studi sulla Spiritualità Medievale, XVII (Todi, 1978),
p. 393.

as read and speak Latin, the universal language of educated Europe at the time.

This category of persons, being more or less directly linked to the great religious schools, the first universities or the great monasteries, constituted a public that was substantially homogeneous; it also steadily grew numerically in every region of Europe—from France, where intellectual activity was particularly lively, to Norman England, to Italy in both the center-north and the south, and to Spain, which was being liberated from Moslem rule. Already around 1115 Guibert de Nogent could compare the scarcity of eleventh-century masters with the frequency with which *vagantes* clerks were encountered in the villages and cities of his time.[2] This progressive numerical growth constituted the principal incentive for the revival and steady growth of book production; but it was not the only cause, because the European manuscript books of the twelfth century did not consist entirely of the scholastic books of biblical exegesis or philosophy or civil law that nourished the university "clerk." Indeed, the manuscript book of Western Europe in the twelfth century constituted a complex reality embracing a varied typology of products and responding to many functions.

First, there was the Bible. There was a vast production of Bibles and Gospels—with or without a commentary, with or without the introductory and supplementary texts of Saint Jerome—in every region of Europe over the entire span of the century. Generally these books were of large format, with the text laid out in two columns, comments in smaller lettering, running titles, miniatures, and decorated initials. Then there was the Divine Office. This century saw the steadily increasing production of the liturgical texts needed for the daily functioning of old and especially newly founded churches and monastic centers in both city and countryside; these texts as well were diffused in exemplars that usually combined large format and accurate execution. Whether old or new, monasteries and churches also had need of patristic texts, especially but not exclusively of Augustine and Jerome, and of the encyclopedias and treatises used for study and the professional preparation of moderately educated ecclesiastics; these texts, too, were reproduced and diffused in codices of large or medium format that were manufactured to a high standard. But higher culture, as imparted in the great religious schools and in the new-born universities, needed still other, more specific texts and thus other books; thus there resulted a specialized production of juridical, philosophical, and medical works, of translations from Arabic and Greek, and of Latin classics, all aimed at a public both more restricted and vastly more mobile and dispersed. This public, moreover—

2. See Ph. Wolfe, *The Awakening of Europe* (Harmondsworth, 1968).

which consisted of the great cultural centers of Europe of the time—not only read but produced texts; consequently, there also existed a production of books due to the great intellectuals and masters of the time, from Saint Bernard to Abelard, from Peter Lombard to John of Salisbury, to the new *literati*, poets, and chroniclers writing in Latin.

Many of these books, for both study and work, gradually took on a particular, homogeneous appearance, being remade according to the model adapted to slow reading, to meditative and repetitive study, and to marginal annotation that was characteristic of the didactic habits of the time: the model of the large "desk" book was a massive volume (more than thirty-five or forty centimeters high), with text laid out in two columns and broad external and internal margins available for comments and annotations.[3]

One must mention, finally, the more limited but diffused didactic exigencies for teaching boys the first steps of elementary learning or the intermediate study of rhetoric, for such pupils had to be provided with Psalters, comprehensive Latin grammars, and miscellanies of classical authors and of the Fathers. These books were smaller in size than others, in external appearance being also less carefully done and thus less costly.

As usual, therefore, books had different functions corresponding to the various requirements of the potential and actual public, from which in turn were modeled the various typologies of the products. Thus, in twelfth-century Europe, the process of producing the book-as-object underwent a notable evolution, which had its expression in the adoption of new techniques for writing and layout of the text, preparing the leaves and the fascicles, and the binding of the volumes. In all these areas, executing books became much more uniform and thus more rapid than it had been before, and consequently also capable of responding promptly and effectively to the diversification and growth of the demands of the market.

For writing, adoption of the pen with point cut obliquely, which spread progressively within Europe from the mid-eleventh century (and which lay at the origin of the transformation of caroline minuscule into gothic textura), permitted individual graphic signs to be broken into a great number of short, juxtaposed strokes: a technique that permitted different scribes to achieve very uniform results and the greatest impersonality of the product. Along with other devices such as placing letters closer to one another and separating words, this technique also contributed to making the words easier to recognize, thus accentuating the overall legibility of the text. Further contributing to the legibility of the text and permitting it to be better memorized—

3. J. Destrez, *La pecia dan les manuscrits universitaires du xiii͏̈ et du xiv͏ᵉ siècle* (Paris, 1935), p. 46.

essential requirements for books intended mainly for study—was its subdivision into a series of passages whose groupings and divisions were graphically marked by devices such as red titles, colored paragraph signs, projecting majuscules, and initials that were enlarged to a greater or lesser extent.[4] Also having the purpose of making possible a still more rapid reading was another technique that contributed strongly to modifying how the writing appeared in the European book of the twelfth and thirteenth centuries: the adoption of a more extensive and complex system of abbreviation. Instead of being entirely written out, practically every word was written only partially, with special signs being added that permitted the expert reader to complete the text mentally. With the whole operation of reading now being highly synthesized on the page, it could be finished in less time than had been required in the past.

Since the text in schoolbooks was usually accompanied by a commentary, the margins had to have enough space for affixing either a continuous commentary or at least some notes from reading and study. The text was thus laid out in two rather tightly written columns that were displaced upwards and toward the center of the white space in a way that left free the lower and outside margins of the page. But it was also useful to have a rather precise delimitation between text and comment; for this reason, from the end of the twelfth century the text was laid out below rather than above the first of the guide lines, in such a way that the principal writing ended up caged and geometrically marked out between the lines, thus avoiding any risk of being confused with the more or less incidental supplemental texts meant for the margins.[5] This was probably also why "dry lining," which left on the parchment only a groove that although visible to the scribe was barely noticeable to the reader, was replaced in the twelfth century by clearer, more noticeable lining in lead,[6] and then later by lining done in a pale ink.

As the writing and text changed, so also did the book as a whole. Each codex was composed of several fascicles made of several leaves of parchment that were folded and sewn. And indeed it seems that it was exactly in the eleventh and twelfth centuries that there appeared in Europe a revolutionary

4. For the writing techniques of the Gothic period, see R. Marichal, "L'écriture latine et la civilisation occidentale du Ier au XVIe siècle," in Centre International de Synthèse, *L'écriture et la psychologie des peuples. XXIIe semaine de synthèse* (Paris, 1963), pp. 236–41. One must also refer to the notable technological changes that occurred in many areas in twelfth-century Europe; see L. White, Jr., "Cultural Climates and Technological Advance in the Middle Ages," *Viator* 2 (1971): 171–201, esp. 195.

5. The phenomenon is noted by N. Ker, "From 'Above the Top Line' to 'Below the Top Line': A Change in Scribal Practice," *Celtica* 5 (1960): 13–16.

6. Thus J. Vezin, "Les manuscrits datés de l'ancien fonds latin de la Bibliothèque Nationale de Paris," *Scriptorium* 19 (1965): 86–87.

technique in the preparations for writing by which some copyists learned to write on uncut leaves of parchment, practically "laying out" the text as the first typographers did centuries later, in imitation of the manuscripts. This was another technique—although probably not one that was widely diffused—that served to make the work of copying and the manufacture of the book more rapid and uniform. Manufacturing books was brought to completion, then as later and even as today, by the binding, an operation that was slow and complex in the early Middle Ages because of the use of wooden boards for covers and because of the long, complicated manual stitching of the fascicles. Again, this period sees the operation of stitching made much quicker by the adoption of new, ingeniously innovative techniques. This involved stitching with a frame that simplified and mechanized (in its proper sense, that is, by adopting a machine) the last phase of the process of manufacturing a book, an innovation that had a widespread and immediate diffusion throughout Western Europe.[7]

Yet it was not only in the techniques nor even in the marked increase in numbers produced that the process of manufacturing manuscript books was modified between the end of the twelfth and the first decades of the thirteenth century. Also changed were the very places where the production occurred and the social status of the operators, with the process being definitively both urbanized and laicized. The new public for books became increasingly the urban public that attended the new universities; and the adoption of new techniques introduced both a rigid separation between the various phases of the work into the productive processes and a demand for specialized competencies that, while certainly not unknown to the old early medieval monastic writing centers, were probably never adopted there to such a regular and organic extent. Within a brief time, these new modes of execution and new techniques of production contributed to transferring the principal seats of production closer to the universities that were the principal places of consumption. One result was the close connections between the centers of commerce (stationers' shops) and those where books were produced; another was the new figure of the lay worker-scribe—the "mechanici et manuales librorum" of which Gerson later wrote.[8] Represented variously by students needing money, by notaries or priests wishing to round out their income, by literate urban artisans, and by women or boys able to write, these worker-scribes worked alone, usually at home, none of them being capable

7. For the impagination of codices, see L. Gilissen, "La composition des cahiers, le pliage du parchemin et l'imposition," *Scriptorium* 26 (1972): 3–33. For sewing with a frame, see P. Bozzacchi, "Il codice come prodotto e come oggetto di restauro," *Bollettino d'informazioni dell'Associazione Italiana Biblioteche* 17 (1978): 25–28.

8. J. Gerson, *De laude scriptorum tractatus*, ed. J. S. Smith (Rouen, 1841), p. 1.

of completing by themselves all of the operations necessary for the production of the finished book. These different operations were done in different places and entrusted to different, mostly lay hands, each with a specific competence: parchment makers, scribes, rubricators, illuminators, binders. Only the entrepreneurial bookseller linked them together.

With the thirteenth century, university institutions inserted themselves into this process, both for economic reasons related to managing the interests of their own corporations of masters and students, and for ideological reasons related to the control of written texts and their diffusion. In this way the so-called pecia system of production was born, articulating the different roles of all participants (the worker-scribe, the bookseller, the institution of the university in its capacity as administrator, the private individual as patron or purchaser); as used in Paris and Bologna at least, it was based on official exemplars deposited with recognized booksellers, on a fixed charge per copy that was forcibly kept low, on the work of numerous copyists, and on the loan of exemplars kept loose (in pecia, to be precise) to permit a more rapid copying of individual works.[9] Transformation of the book into a commodity; transformation of the work of copying into labor commissioned and paid according to public tariffs, with the corresponding emphasis in the copyists' subscriptions on the motif of the physical effort of writing; clear hierarchalization of different types of books—and of scripts—and of their respective functions: these are the most evident consequences of the embryonic process of industrialization of book production that we have just discussed.

Compared with the total mass of production, the number of manuscript books produced by the pecia system was not that great; and not all books repeat the dominate model of the "desk book." But there is no doubting that all, or nearly all, books produced in Western Europe during the twelfth and thirteenth centuries had two basic elements in common: they were composed of parchment leaves and bore texts in Latin. Few indeed were the codices in vernacular languages (and only from outside Italy), and only with the Duecento do books written on paper begin to appear.

Volgare *Books and Their Public*

In Italy of the last quarter of the twelfth century, between the age of Frederick Barbarossa and that of Innocent III, books were written in Latin, Greek, Hebrew, and perhaps (in Sicily) in Arabic, which was certainly used

9. For the pecia system, see, in addition to Destrez, "La pecia," G. Fink-Errera, "La produzione dei libri di testo nelle università medievali," in G. Cavallo, *Libri e lettori nel medioevo. Guida storica e critica* (Bari, 1977), pp. 13–65, 284–302.

for writing documents. But books were not then written in vernacular, as was done at the time in other European countries. Nevertheless, vernacular culture—which until this time was exclusively oral—did begin to leave more or less broad and durable traces, passing into writing in more or less occasional ways and beginning to be read as well as written.

In reality, in all of Europe—and thus even in Italy, although later than elsewhere—the process of cultural promotion and conquest of social status by which vernacular languages passed from being "subsidiary private languages"[10] to arrive at forming a literary public[11] can be divided into two successive phases. The first was constituted by landing at what one may call the "state of writing," by which a language, having until then remained merely oral, came to be recognized as being "writable" and actually was written by means of attributing to it a system of graphic signs in use and the indispensable textual "formality," even if initially at rudimentary levels. The second phase, which is more significant for us, is the conquest by vernacular languages of the right to "canonization in books," by which complex texts in vernacular come to be consciously and organically written in book form by themselves (that is, without being mixed or juxtaposed with other texts in "noble" written languages). The modes and forms of this process of canonization in Italy constituted a chapter of great importance in the history of written culture and of the book; they were also a highly significant moment for the formation and transmission of the prose and poetic texts in *volgare* that mark the beginning of the cultural patrimony that we are accustomed to calling Italian literature.

As in France,[12] so also in Italy, the oldest literary texts were transmitted in the form of adventitious and occasional additions generally made in the final "guard" pages of codices containing Latin texts. This was the case for the *Ritmo cassinese,* an addition of an early thirteenth-century hand in beneventan script, including many errors of transcription, on a leaf of the eleventh-century manuscript Cassinese 522.32.[13] It was also true for the *Ritmo*

10. Borrowing an expression of A. Roncaglia, "Le origini," in E. Cecchi and N. Sapegno, eds., *Storia della literatura italiana,* vol. 1: *Le origini e il Duecento* (Milan, 1965), p. 213.

11. One must refer here to E. Auerbach, *Literatursprache und Publikum in der lateinischen Spätantike und im Mittelalter* (Bern, 1958); trans. by Ralph Manheim as *Latin Literary Language and Its Public* (New York, 1965).

12. See G. de Poerck, "Les plus anciens textes de la langue française comme témoins de l'époque," *Revue de linguistique romane* 27 (1963): 1–34.

13. For this and the other "archaic monuments" of Italian literature, see G. Folena, "Überlieferungsgeschichte der altitalienischen Literatur," in H. Hunger et al., *Geschichte der Textüberlieferung der antiken und mittelalterlichen Literatur,* vol. 2: *Überlieferungsgeschichte der mittelalterlichen Literatur* (Zurich, 1964), pp. 325–35. The *Ritmo* in particular is reproduced in *Archivio paleografico italiano* 10, pl. 5; edited in G. Contini, ed., *Poeti del Duecento* (Milan and Naples, 1960), vol. 1, pp. 3–6; vol. 2, p. 790.

laurenziano, added to the final pages of a *Martyrologium* of the twelfth century by a slightly later hand (end of the twelfth to beginning of the thirteenth
century);[14] and for the *Ritmo su Sant'Alessio*, added by two hands of the
beginning of the thirteenth century in a codex of Ascoli Piceno,[15] and for
the example, actually more religious in nature than literary, that seems to be
the oldest of all: the formula for confession of Sant'Eutizio of Norcia, added
by the same hand as the main writer of the book in the final leaves of
manuscript B 63 of the Biblioteca Vallicelliana of Rome, a late eleventh-
century manuscript.[16]

The casual and adventitious character of interpolating such vernacular texts
into the context of Latin books seems obvious. But the practice is also indicative of a deliberate intention to register these texts for the purpose of
preserving them, even if by a procedure that was out of the ordinary, with
a character almost resembling documents more than books, and necessarily
in unique copies. Moreover, these instances took place using already made
books, and thus occurred in book environments: in Montecassino itself for
the *Ritmo cassinese*; in another Benedictine monastery, Sant'Eutizio of Norcia, for the confession formula; probably there were also other cases (such
as those minor ones documented by Baldelli[17]) in monastic sites furnished
with books and having the capacity and habit of writing. But, above all,
these episodes were due to writers accustomed to linking written registration
of a literary text with the book-object, even if only by means of addition and
interpolation. It is thus helpful to acknowledge that there existed an ecclesiastical or rather monastic medium for the survival of these first vernacular
texts by means of registration in books. Yet we are still dealing with survival
without further reproduction and without any possibility of circulation: in
short, a survival more of documentary-archival type than of book type, despite the physical place chosen for the registration.

On the other hand, it is rather probable, if only by suggestion from the
Provençal model, that either within the environments producing poetry or
outside of them there was also some recourse in Italy to a first registration
of more or less extensive poetic texts on loose leaves of parchment: in short,
the famous "breu de pergamina" of Jaufre Rudel.[18] It is likely that this was

---

14. Repr. in *Archivio paleografico italiano* 1, pl. 17; edited in Contini, *Poeti del Duecento*, vol.
1, pp. 3–6; vol. 2, p. 790.

15. Repr. in *Archivio paleografico italiano* 6, pls. 33–35; edited in Contini, *Poeti del Duecento*,
vol. 1, pp. 15–28; vol. 2, p. 793.

16. Repr. in E. Monaci, *Facsimili di antichi manoscritti per uso delle scuole di filologia neolatina*
(Rome, 1881–92), pls. 19–20; edition and commentary in A. Roncaglia, *Origini*, pp. 214–16.

17. See the articles gathered into the first part of I. Baldelli, *Medioevo volgare da Montecassino
all'Umbria* (Bari, 1971), pp. 5–163.

18. Remembered by G. Folena, "Tradizione e cultura trobadorica nelle corte e nelle città

the means used in the twelfth and thirteenth centuries by troubadours and Provençal poets, both non-Italians active in Italy and Italians writing in Provençal; such nonbook forms of registration may also have represented the earliest phase of the lyrics of the school of Sicilian poetry, of which we have no original manuscripts in the sense that they came directly from the environment where the texts were produced. Finally—given that the personages of the chansons de geste were well known in various regions of the peninsula as early as the eleventh century—one cannot exclude the possibility that there was also some circulation in Italy of the so-called *jongleur* manuscripts, of which the famous Oxford manuscript of the *Chanson de Roland,* dating from the second quarter of the twelfth century, may well represent an example;[19] these would have been codices of small format and careless appearance, roughly written and lacking any ornamentation, that were intended to furnish the text of the poems to the performers who declaimed them and thus reserved for the use of a restricted category of professionals.

The casual and adventitious registration of vernacular texts in a Latin book context to which it was foreign solved the problem of preserving the text itself but not that of reproducing and diffusing it. Writing more or less brief vernacular texts on loose leaves or membrane rolls, or even the exceptional recourse to notebooks or small codices for registering more ample poetic texts meant for recitation, similarly solved only the limited problem of fixing and perpetuating the texts themselves within the very restricted professional circles that produced them; the texts were normally communicated to the outside world by the oral forms of declamation and song. Neither system, to the extent one can even speak of a system, could resolve the problem of a regular transmission in writing of vernacular texts to a literate public able and wishing to read them: to replicate, in short, even if in different forms, the route of producing and distributing texts (producing a book—its reproduction and diffusion—reading) that belonged to official written culture in Latin.

---

venete," in G. Arnaldi and M. Pastore Stocchi, eds., *Storia della cultura veneta,* vol. 1: *Dalle origini al Trecento* (Vicenza, 1976), p. 456. See also D. S. Avalle, *La letteratura medievale in lingua d'oc nella sua tradizione manoscritta* (Turin, 1961), p. 47 and fig. 2a, and p. 48 (now available in a new edition). An example from Germany is discussed in Richard Rouse, "Roll and Codex: The Transmission of the Works of Reinmar von Zweter," in Richard and Mary Rouse, *Authentic Witnesses: Approaches to Medieval Texts and Manuscripts* (Notre Dame, Ind., 1991), pp. 13–29 (orig. publ. in *Münchener Beiträge zur Mediävistik und Renaissance-Forschung* 32 [1982]: 107–23).

19. Oxford, Bodleian Library MS Digby 23. For the dating, see most recently Ch. Samaran, "Sur la date approximative du Roland d'Oxford," *Romania* 94 (1973): 523–27. More generally, see M. Delbouille, "Les chansons de geste et le livre," in *La technique littéraire des chansons de geste. Actes du colloque de Liège, 1957* (Liège, 1959), pp. 321–27.

And yet that new public did exist in the thirteenth century, and in Italy as well as in France, Germany, and Spain. Moreover, it was a public of literates who could read and write, and who could read and write in the vernacular more easily than in Latin. Much if not all has already been said about this public's social composition and geographic distribution, its links with communal urban society and with mercantile activity; it is not necessary to repeat here a picture already in large part known.[20] But it may be worth the effort to highlight the coincidence of some elements not previously examined for possible, significant correlations. To begin with, there is the fact that with the conquest of the "right to write" by Italian vernacular (or Italian vernaculars) in the twelfth and still more the thirteenth centuries, there was reborn in Italy after an eclipse of nearly eight hundred years a relatively new figure in the panorama of Western medieval written culture: the literate person free to write apart from any precise social function or constricting juridical obligations. No longer would one write only in performance of responsibilities as a master, scribe, or clerk, or because one was a judge, notary, functionary, or professor, or even because one was a witness or guarantor of a legal action: one wrote only because one was literate, that is, one wrote because one was able to do so. In the second place, these literates who were "free to write" did so in vernacular, outside the bounds of the language-institution of official culture, and they produced evidence written not as books but explicitly inspired by documentary models (letters, receipts, account books, books of memoirs in the form of a register, and so forth); moreover, they always wrote in cursive and never in the textura scripts that belonged to books. Finally, this phenomenon was chronologically and functionally parallel to the already discussed industrialization of the processes of book production in urban areas and their professionalization by means of advanced techniques. In Italian society of the thirteenth century, the worker-scribe became almost the contrasting mirror image of the literate who wrote by choice; and while the first was constrained to use almost exclusively Latin, the second wrote predominantly in vernacular.

In reality, the panorama of Italian book production of the Duecento was also shaped and diversified by other factors, some of which resulted directly from a certain conservative backwardness of our national written culture seen as a whole. In mid-century, while Frederick II lay dying in his beloved Puglia, the situation in the kingdom was one of complete multigraphism. As in the preceding century, Greek, Arabic, and Hebrew were being written in addition to Latin. In the narrower field of Latin scripts, this situation was

20. See, most recently, F. Cardini, "Alfabetismo e livelli di cultura nell'età comunale," *Quaderni storici* 13 (1978): 488–522.

accompanied by the coexistence of gothic text script, minuscule, and chancery and notarial cursives with various other graphic typologies tied to centuries-old traditions and ancient cultural centers (Montecassino, Naples): these included beneventan script for books and curial script for documents. Nor were there centers of book production elsewhere in the peninsula capable of exercising an effective hegemony over others by imposing a single model (as Paris did in France). Bologna developed its own stylistic interpretation of gothic textura (the *littera bononiensis*) and its own model of the university book, which it imposed on Padua and the new University of Naples. But in Rome and perhaps also in the larger Tuscan centers, production of the most prestigious books was still largely entrusted to ecclesiastical centers. Meanwhile, a rich and varied production of codices of a "courtly" type was developed in the aristocratic courts of the Paduan plain and the Veneto; these manuscripts contained poetic texts in Provençal that were accurately written in textual gothic, finely illustrated, and destined for private reading rather than for study. A final element of both novelty and instability was constituted by the introduction of a writing material that differed from parchment in being less costly and manufactured with greater speed, less labor, and less expense: this was paper, which was first used for private and documentary (notarial protocols) purposes, and then also in books.

In such a situation, characterized on one hand by the absence of a dominant book model or center of book production recognized as being a leader, and on the other by the coexistence of varied traditions and influences, the emergence of vernacular literature (both prose and poetry) could only constitute a strong element of tension and contradiction; this was especially so because this literature still lacked its own physical container and felt pressure from an unstable public of what I have called "free literates" who were able to write and read, that is, to produce and consume texts. Indeed, these tensions would receive final resolution only three centuries later, with the diffusion of printing with movable characters.

Books, Writers, and Readers

The first problem was that of choosing a model "text container" which could, naturally, have taken shape as a type of book. Given the fluidity of the situation and the novelty of the texts and the public, it might seem that models other than the traditional ones were also conceivable: of the type, for example, of those already used for the "professional" circulation of French and Provençal poetic texts, or of documentary type, and so forth. Actually, however, one must conclude that no choice other than books was really possible. Although the culture of the new public was not based on books, with documentary models generally being more familiar and used, and although the process of industrialized book production seemed both removed from the needs of those who read *volgare* and was too costly for them, the book-form still had the prestige, of which all literates had to be more or less aware, of being the only instrument for conserving and transmitting moderately extended written texts (or shorter ones gathered together). Moreover, the circulation of rolls or loose leaves or the small notebooks of troubadours and jongleurs—supposing this occurred in Italy—could not have constituted a true alternative model to the book-form. Precisely in connection with the industrialization of the productive process, the book-form in late medieval European society (not only that of Italy) had assumed a series of fixed values that were fundamental to the whole graphic-communicative system. It was at once an economic value of investment or commerce, a symbol of prestige, and an instrument of study. In its very exterior typology, it represented the hierarchy of culture and of society itself, involving the whole patrimony of ideologies and permitting their controlled distribution.

Transmission of written texts that were not documents could not have occurred except through the book-form, which was the only means by which the texts themselves could achieve the ideological and social legitimacy that they needed. Thus, even new texts in vernacular languages had to submit to it to win the right to enter into the limited universe of written transmittability. But the book-form did not present a single model. It existed in several distinct varieties, and indeed there was a recent model drawn from the world of documentation that could be adapted to the book-form. This was the register, which was closer and more familiar to the new writers because it had been used not only by notaries but also by merchants and artisans for account books and record books compiled in vernacular and written in cursive.

Coming from the very end of the thirteenth century are three books that constitute almost emblematically the first evidence of an answer to the problem of the organic written transmission of the oldest poetic corpus in Italian: the three famous *canzonieri*, two of which are preserved in Florence (Biblioteca Nazionale Centrale, Banco Rari 217 and Biblioteca Mediceo-Laurenziana, Rediano 9), and the third at Rome (Biblioteca Apostolica Vaticana, Vat. lat. 3793).[21] These monuments are too well known to need description here. But it may be useful to call attention to the fact that they

21. It suffices to refer to B. Panvini, "Studi sui manoscritti dell'antica lirica italiana," *Studi di filologia italiana* II (1953): 11–26, 28–31, 33–40, to which should be added at least *Mostra di codici romanzi delle biblioteche fiorentine (Firenze, aprile 1956)* (Florence, 1957); and now R. Antonelli in *Letteratura italiana, Le Opere*, vol. 1: *Dalle origini al Cinque cento* (Turin, 1992), pp. 24–44. For the Banco Rari MS, see p. 81, and for the Laurenziana, p. 6.

propose two different types of books with vernacular text that would have great fortune in the course of the fourteenth century. The first, "courtly reading" type of book is represented by the two Florentine canzonieri. One of these (Rediano 9), of Pisan origin, was probably gathered by an admirer of Guittone, who had belonged to the Cavalieri di Santa Maria, (the so-called Frati Gaudenti) and contains a section in prose; the other (Banco Rari 217) is of Florentine origin and richly illustrated. Both are made of parchment, being of careful manufacture and medium-small format (height between 23 and 24 cm), without any apparatus or commentary, and were written in a gothic textura by a scribe of a notably professional level. The other, "register-book" type is represented by the canzoniere Vat. lat. 3793, which displays a manufacture and nature completely different from the other two (fig. 30). In fact, this is a manuscript of medium height (27 cm) whose thickness (24 fascicles and 376 pages) is much greater than the others; it was written in cursive by several nonprofessional hands (of which one was the most important), and probably put together over several stages, starting as loose fascicles. Lacking ornament, lining, or rubrication, it seems on the whole of rough manufacture.

The courtly reading book in vernacular is broadly represented in the Po valley of the same period and the Trecento proper by the production of illuminated codices bearing collections of Provençal lyrics[22] or French texts of knightly epics.[23] The oldest examples of this production are exactly contemporary with the two Tuscan canzonieri of Italian lyrics preserved at Florence, with which they present obvious typological affinities in format (rarely exceeding 30 cm in height), in the accuracy of the execution entrusted to capable professionals, in the exclusive use of gothic textura, and in having illuminated illustrations.[24] Sustained by specific centers of refined culture and modern and cosmopolitan tastes (among which were the aristocratic courts of the Da Romano, the Da Camino, the Da Carrara, and later also the Visconti and the Gonzaga), and produced by professionals of high ability working in complex environments, the courtly Italian codex of the thirteenth and fourteenth centuries represented both a certain sign of social prestige and a kind of economic investment for the aristocratic classes of the northern cities. Moreover, it enjoyed a passionate public and a wide circulation, as one can understand from Petrarca's pointed remarks ("Ecco quei che le carte

---

22. G. Folena, *Tradizione e cultura trobadorica*, pp. 457–66.

23. L. Renzi, "Il francese come lingua letteraria e il franco-lombardo. L'epica carolingia nel Veneto," in G. Arnaldi and M. Pastore Stocchi, eds., *Storia della cultura veneta*, vol. 1, p. 568.

24. As already acutely observed by Folena, *Tradizione e cultura trobadorica*, p. 466.

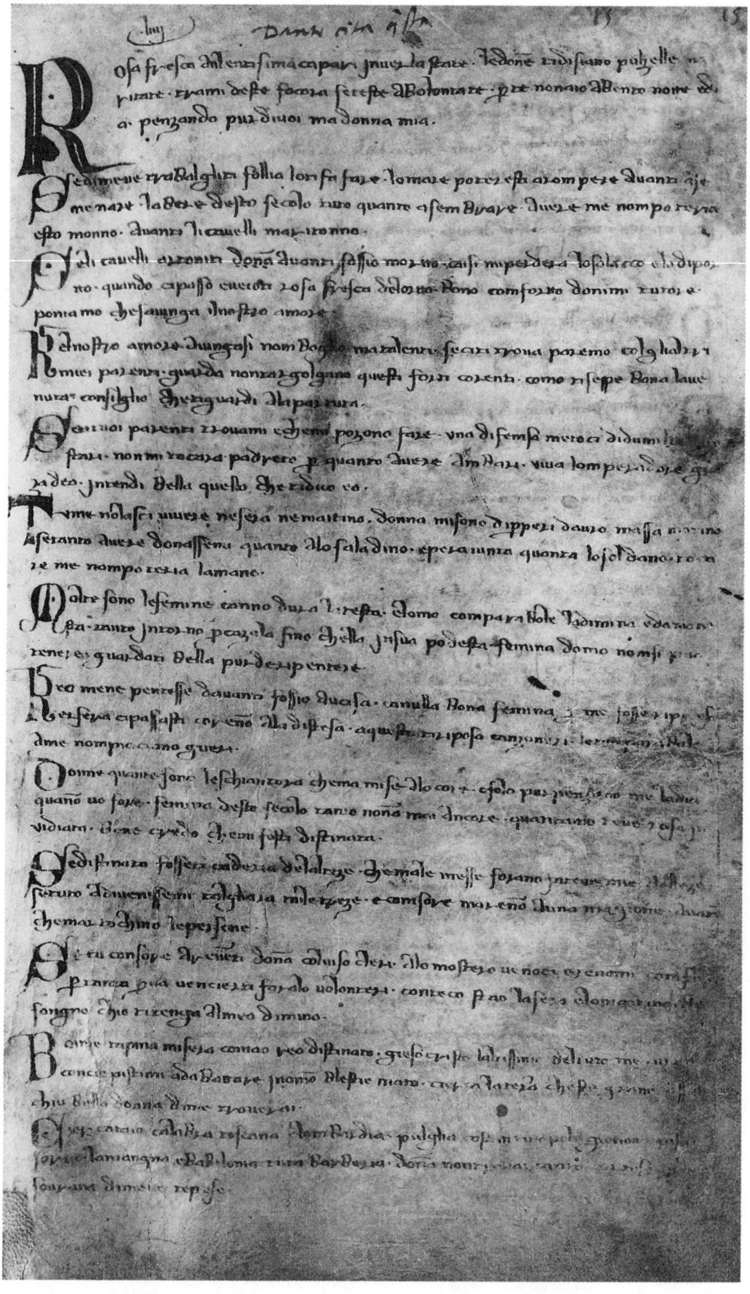

30. Biblioteca Apostolica Vaticana, Vat. lat. 3793, fol. 15r

empion di sogni, / Lancillotto, Tristano e gli altri erranti, / ove convien che'l vulgo errante agogni"[25]) as well as from Dante's episode of Paolo and Francesa, who were indissolubly bound to a refined rite of courtly reading.

The register-book, which is the other type of vernacular book that gradually achieved an identity, is less easily defined than the first because it always remained a private product, written directly by consumer-readers for their own use, and thus was tied more to local and individual experiences than to actual artisanal traditions. It was essentially a phenomena that depended on that new and more extensive "freedom of writing" already mentioned as typical of the literates of the vernacular culture of Italian urban society of the time, and it found realization in many typologies that, while differing in a variety of features, had certain elements in common: the use of cursive writing (chancery minuscule, and later also mercantile minuscule); the steadily increasing use of paper; moderate (and never very large) formats; often careless manufacture; the absence of comments or reader's notes; and the presence in the same volume of several texts with different natures (fig. 31).

In the course of the Trecento, it becomes possible to distinguish two subtypes at the extremes of the typology of the register-book that had broad diffusion and performed precise socio-cultural functions: the deluxe register-book, produced professionally for private patrons; and the *zibaldone*, or hodgepodge book, whose most characteristic examples retain the book-form only in its outward appearance as a container of folded leaves. Belonging to what I have called the deluxe register-book are some of the most famous and oldest fourteenth-century codices of Dante's *Commedia*: first and foremost the two written by ser Francesco di ser Nardo da Barberino, from 1337 (fig. 32) and early 1348, respectively;[26] the Landiano manuscript of Piacenza of 1336;[27] to which one can add the Biblioteca Laurenziana MS 40.16, Cortona 88, and Laurenziana 40.22—this last manuscript from 1355 being the most recent of those cited here (fig. 32).[28] These are all parchment codices of medium-large format (mostly 32 to 37 cm high), some with illuminations and of the highest calligraphical level, but all written in cursive, specifically the chancery minuscule that became the writing of personal and documentary use for every moderately educated person of fourteenth-century Italy.

25. F. Petrarca, *I trionfi*, III, vv. 79–81.

26. For the work of ser Francesco, see U. Marchesini, "I Danti del Cento," *Bullettino della Società Dantesca Italiana*, 1st ser. 2–3 (1890): 21–42; and also E. Casamassima, *La prima edizione della Divina Commedia (Foligno, 1472)* (Milan, 1972), pp. 61–63; and L. Miglio, "Per una datazione del Biadaiolo fiorentino (Ms. Laur. Tempi, 3)," *La bibliofilia* 77 (1975): 12–20.

27. See the complete facsimile: G. Bertoni, ed., *Il codice landiano della Divina Commedia* (Florence, 1921).

28. See the summary description of the oldest MSS of the *Commedia* in G. Petrocchi, ed., *La Commedia secondo l'antica vulgata* (Milan, 1966), pp. 57–91.

31. Niccolo da Poggibonsi, *Libro del passagio d'oltremare*, for a paper "register-book" copied by Simone di Paolo using a semicursive script with mercantile elements. Florence, Bib. Naz. Cent., MS Panciatichi 78, fol. 8v

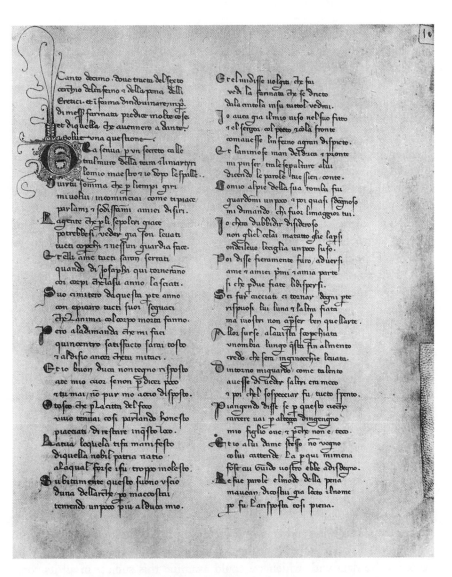

32. Milan, Bib. Trivulziana 1080, fol. 10r

To these Dante codices one can easily add analogous manuscripts with vernacular or, more rarely, Latin texts. One can mention here at least the well-known Laurenziana Biadaiolo of Domenico Lenzi[29] and the two doc-

29. For this MS, see L. Miglio, "Per una datazione."

umentary codices from Siena, the Caleffo dell'Assunta (a register-book with an imposing format—43 cm high) and the Statuti della Mercanzia.[30] But one must emphasize that such deluxe but not courtly products define not solely or principally the environment that produced them and placed them in circulation but also the patrons who commissioned them.

In their capacity as members and rectors of confraternities and hospitals, which were often linked by kinship ties to high-ranking ecclesiastics, many laymen belonging to mercantile, artisanal, or professional social strata also figured among those who commissioned deluxe books of liturgy or Scripture. The books themselves, however, remained a purely ecclesiastical product. But these patrons were also often influential members of guilds whose statutes and books of matriculants constituted in many Italian cities the prototypical deluxe register-book—a product that was and remained for this century an essentially bourgeois phenomenon.[31] In communal regimes the Arti were institutions that, if not strictly public, were always at least semipublic. Yet individual merchants and artisans did not restrict themselves to commissioning or buying deluxe books for the corporations or confraternities to which they belonged. They often also bought for themselves, naturally preferring works in *volgare* of devotional-moral, literary-fantastic, rhetorical-historical, or even technical character. In this way, the deluxe register-book, in addition to an eminently public function that was reserved to a handful of exemplars, also had a private use fulfilled by most of the products that extended not only to the acculturation of the individual patrons but also to the ennoblement of their homes, and of their business tables and desks.[32]

Shifting our attention from patrons to workers one notes that, unlike other economic activities, the process of producing manuscript books (both Latin and vernacular) for profit did not find in fourteenth-century Italy a precise or clearly defined localization within the corporate alignment of the Arti. This situation, which for that era constituted an obvious factor contributing to the haphazardness and lack of structure in book production and even to the informality of commerce in books, is the principal reason that today we lack precise data with which we could examine this subject in all its com-

30. For the Caleffo, compiled between 1334 and 1336 and containing documents relative to the Commune of Siena, see V. Federici, *La scrittura delle cancellerie italiane dal secolo XII al XVIII* (Rome, 1934), p. 35 and pl. 58; for the Statuti, of 1342–43, see [G. Muzzioli], *Catalogo [della] Mostra storica nazionale della miniatura* (Florence, 1953), no. 379, p. 244.

31. On this phenomenon, see L. Miglio, "Considerazioni ed ipotesi sul libro 'borghese' italiano del Trecento. (A proposito di un'edizione critica dello 'Specchio umano' di Domenico Lenzi)," *Scrittura e civiltà* 3 (1979): 309–27.

32. On the libraries of Italian merchants and artisans of the communal era, see Ch. Bec, *Les marchands écrivains. Affaires et humanisme à Florence, 1375–1434* (Paris and The Hague, 1967), pp. 407–15.

plexity. And, in fact, we know very little of the connections binding the lay illuminator, who was almost always also a painter and the owner of a shop, to the lay but sometimes religious scribe who executed the text in the type of script (generally chosen by the patron); and, except for university books, we know but little more about the connections between patrons, booksellers, and scribes.[33]

A summary census done for this study of scribes of vernacular Italian texts[34] reveals barely thirty-five names for the whole fourteenth century, most of them in the second half of the century. But only two of these can be considered to have been scribes by trade: one is the well-known and already mentioned ser Francesco di ser Nardo da Barberino, who as a copyist specialized in producing Dante's *Commedia* in the form of the deluxe register-book but who was also a notary; the other (excluding Antonio da Fermo, who executed the Landiano *Commedia,* of whom nothing else is known) is a Paolo Tosi da Pisa, who however belongs to the very end of the fourteenth century and continued to work until 1429. All others seem to have written for themselves, for their own family, sometimes for a friend, but not for pay.

It is these scribes who were the creators, especially from the second half of the century on, of the other subtype I mentioned: the *zibaldone,* or hodge-podge book, which was destined to dominate private book production in vernacular languages until the fifteenth century. These were always paper codices of small or medium format, lacking lining or any real ornamentation beyond simple pen designs, written in cursive (first in chancery minuscule, later and steadily more frequently only in mercantile minuscule scripts), and containing an astonishing variety of poetic and prose texts, including devotional, technical, and documentary texts, which were juxtaposed apparently without any specific criteria (fig. 33). These books seem, at first glance, the product of successive, multiple degradations: thus, with them one sees the private vernacular miscellaneous book made into a disorderly accumulation of texts; parchment was abandoned for paper, a baser material; in place of miniatures, a surrogate was sought in drawings; instead of the chancery minuscule used to produce documents in Latin, recourse was made to the humbler, more cursive mercantile scripts reserved for private and professional activities of businessmen and for writings in *volgare.* All this is true to a certain extent. But in this varied and complex phenomenon, encountered especially in northern and central Italy (for example, in Florence and Venice)

33. There is useful material in G. Orlandelli, *Il libro a Bologna dal 1300 al 1330* (Bologna, 1959), esp. pp. 7–37, Orlandelli's study of the *Contratto di scrittura* in Bolognese notarial doctrine.

34. Based on Bénédictins de Bouveret, *Colophons de manuscrits occidentaux des origines au xvie siècle,* 5 vols. (Fribourg, 1965–79).

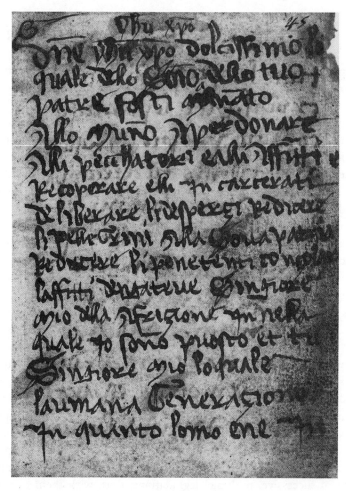

33. A *zibaldone* written by many hands but mainly by the Roman noble Stefano
Baroncelli. Biblioteca Apostolica Vaticana, Reg. lat. 352, fol. 45r

but present in every city in Italy,[35] there is also to be seen something else
more important. In the first place, there is the manifestation of an essentially
nonbook mentality, appropriate for those whose graphic culture consisted
especially of writing for business and private documentation, in which the
book-form, now reduced to the register-book, figured essentially as the container of evidence of more or less diverse times and natures. This attitude

35. For this phenomenon, see M. Cortelazzo, "La cultura mercantile e marinaresca," in
Storia della cultura veneta, vol. I, esp. pp. 674, 677.

also explains the frequently protracted time of composition of such products and the participation of several members of a family in this activity: exactly as with account books and *ricordanze*. But the *zibaldone* register-book, in its very singularity, also constitutes both the evidence for and instrument of a definite desire for extra-scholastic and autodidact acculturation that was both professional and ideological: a desire particular to artisan merchants of four-teenth- and fifteenth-century Italy who not by chance (as it might seem) wrote gate tolls and currency exchange rates in their *zibaldoni* alongside medical recipes, devotional tracts, lauds, and love lyrics, thus summing up on a brief, paper horizon of humble appearance the fundamental benchmarks of their culture and of their own presence in the society of the time.

Desk-Books and Author's Books

Italian society of the Trecento did, however, have precise terms for the ec-onomic value of book-forms: terms that lent themselves to identifying gen-eral types of that commodity-product, which could also be assigned value from a fiscal perspective. We can see this in a 1379 *gabella* of Perugia, which provided for the sum of three soldi to be paid as the toll for bringing into the city "livera grosse ecclesiastice, messale, breviarie, bibbia e simigliante" (big ecclesiastical books, missals, breviaries, Bibles, and the like); two soldi for "livera de leggie" (books of laws); likewise two soldi for grammar books of small format and for the "livero de Da[n]te o simiglie" (books of Dante and the like), which were considered to be a category of their own; and, finally, for the "squartabelghe e scripture" (small books and writings), only six denari.[36] In short, even deluxe register-books were not as a category com-pared to the largest "libri da banco" or desk-books, and if they took the form of a *zibaldone* they fell to the level of loose written sheets or private docu-mentation.

Boccaccio (d. 1375) had been dead for some years when the Perugia *gabella* was issued. This fact is relevant here because it seems possible that he con-sciously attempted to raise books with texts in *volgare* to the dignity of the ruling model of book production of the time—the desk book in gothic tex-tura script with all its physical and symbolic attributes. Actually, Dante had already thought of his reader as seated at a desk ("or ti riman, lettor, sovra 'l tuo banco" [but remain, reader, on your bench]),[37] evidently imagining the codices that would contain the *Commedia* as books not different from those in Latin that he and other intellectuals of the time habitually read at desks:

36. In B. Migliorini, *Storia della lingua italiana* (Florence, 1961), pl. IX.
37. *Paradiso* X, v. 22.

parchment, of large format, written in formal "littera textualis."[38] We know that this did not happen, that the earliest and principal manuscript diffusion of the *Commedia* was realized through other types of books characterized by cursive scripts, and that this was the common fate of the century's other great *volgare* texts such as, especially, the *Decameron,* which was diffused mainly in codices executed in chancery or mercantile minuscule, manuscripts of rough manufacture and for private use.

But this is not what the author wanted. Giovanni Boccaccio was scribe of his own works and also of the works of others, and one who did not lack definite professional ability. In particular, he was master of many typologies both graphic (from mercantile to chancery minuscule to gothic textura) and of books and documents (from the desk-book to the register-book to the cursive *zibaldone,* from the use of palimpsests to that of the short vernacular business letter constructed "alla mercantile"). But it was probably only after the decisive encounter with Petrarca and the resulting radical modification of his cultural orientation that he confronted, more concretely than had been done before, the problem of the diffusion in books of vernacular texts and of this physical typology.[39] The first codex of Dante's *Commedia* in Boccaccio's hand (Toledo, Cap. 104.6) and his splendid Dante-Petrarca anthology (Biblioteca Vaticana, Chigi L V 176 and L VI 213) already reveal the insertion into the deluxe register-book (average height: 28 cm) of an element belonging to higher categories of book-forms; this is the gothic textura script, which he adopted constantly whether for texts in Latin or in vernacular (excluding, obviously, the Florentine paper *zibaldone,* Biblioteca Nazionale Centrale, Banco Rari 50), whether these texts were his own (see the *Teseida,* Laurenziano Acq. Doni 325) or by others. His second *Commedia* (Riccardiano 1035), from 1363–66, was more than 30 cm high and bore drawings of a new type—true illustrations. But it was especially in the only exemplar left to us of the *Decameron* in his own hand, belonging to the last years of his life, that Boccaccio revealed his plan for promoting vernacular literature to the dignity of the university/scholastic desk-book.

Hamilton 90 of the Staatsbibliothek of Berlin is a codex of large format (37 cm high x 26 wide), and of notable thickness (today 122 leaves, but it

38. For Dante and his book culture, linked to scholastic-university models, see E. R. Curtius, *Europäische Literatur und lateinisches Mittelalter* (Bern and Munich, 1978), pp. 329–35.

39. For the handwriting of Boccaccio, see A. de la Mare, *The Handwriting of Italian Humanists,* vol. 1 (Oxford, 1973), pp. 17–29; and also the acute observations of E. Casamassima, "Dentro lo scrittoio del Boccaccio: I codici della tradizione," *Il ponte* 34 (1978): 730–39. For the autograph manuscripts, see G. Auzzas, "I codici autografi. Elenco e bibliografia," *Studi sul Boccaccio* 7 (1973): 1–20; and *Mostra di manoscritti documenti e edizioni: VI centenario della morte di Giovanni Boccaccio (Firenze, Biblioteca Medicea Laurenziana, 22 maggio–31 agosto 1975),* vol. 1: *Manoscritti e documenti* (Certaldo, 1975).

34. Staatsbibliothek zu Berlin—Preußischer Kulturbesitz, Hamilton 90, fol. 80v

originally had 134), written entirely in Boccaccio's hand in a thick and minute textura laid out in two columns (fig. 34). The text is impaginated and articulated in the manner proper to university/scholastic books, with large margins, use of rubrics, initials of alternating colors, paragraph signs, and majuscules touched with color; the only concession to the whim of the writer seems to be the little drawings that frame the reference marks at end of a fascicle within fine portraits of characters in the Decameron. The codex was evidently prepared over a rather long period of time; originally it was thought of as a deluxe book to give to some powerful person, but as it came to be executed with increasingly less care, it was reduced to being a domestic exemplar for rereading and correction. To the end, however, it retained the fundamental characteristics of the desk-book.[40]

Boccaccio's proposal, which turned toward the past rather than the future and was entirely enclosed within the vision of a book system in force in the world of his youth, had practically no followers after his death. The few codices of the *Decameron* in gothic textura (such as Milan Trivulziano 2263, written by the already cited Tosi in 1405) approached the courtly book rather than that model of the great book of official and institutional Latin culture which had been dear to the author. In this Boccaccio shows himself strangely distant from the teaching of his great master Petrarca, whose extreme sensitivity to the problems of the book and writing was rendered more acute over time, both from the direct contact with non-Italian productive experiences (especially those of France) and from his own collecting mania. As is well known, Petrarca criticized the gothic textura script of his time in several passages in his works, efficiently singling out its negative characteristics: the excessive artificiality of design, the compactness of letters placed side by side, the minuteness of the signs. And he contrasted it with the clarity, sobriety, and elegance of ancient caroline script, to which he called attention as a model for a new graphic style and which he himself tried to realize in his "half-gothic" bookhand.

But Petrarca did not stop at challenging the ruling script of his time from a purely graphic-aesthetic point of view. In his maturity and old age he even managed to undercut the hierarchy of book-types that then dominated the world of book production by inventing a new model and putting it to work. This was the small and manageable "libretto da mano" that he mentioned and praised explicitly in a letter to Luigi Marsili from the year he died.[41] He left at least two memorable examples of this book-type in his own hand: the autograph of the *Bucolicum carmen* of 1357 (Bib. Vat., Vat. lat. 3358) and the first of the two autographs of *De sui ipsius et multorum ignorantia* (Berlin Staatsbibliothek, Hamilton 493) from eleven years later. Both are about six-

---

40. On the autograph of the *Decameron*, see A. Petrucci, "Il ms. Berlinese Hamiltoniano 90. Note codicologiche e paleografiche," in C. Singleton, ed., *Decameron. Edizione diplomatico-interpretativa dell'autografo* (Baltimore and London, 1974), pp. 647–61.

41. Letter to Luigi Marsili, 7 Jan. 1374, in *Seniles* XV, 7.

teen centimeters high and barely eleven centimeters wide. Here, too, it is necessary to add that the proposal advanced by Petrarca for a small "reading book"—easy to hold in one's hands and accurately but clearly written—goes well beyond the external aspects of a purely formal challenge of the hierarchy of book-types belonging to the Gothic world. This challenge, indeed, was only one element of the polemic that Petrarca conducted, both by his daily practices as a writer and producer of his own books and by express declarations in works and letters, against the very foundations of the contemporary system of book production, challenging the rigid practices of the division of labor and the key figure of the worker-scribe.

The basic motives of Petrarca's position are enunciated with great clarity both in chapter XLII (*De librorum copia*) of the treatise *De remediis utriusque fortunae* on which he worked at Milan in 1373, and in a letter to his brother Gerardo the next year.[42] In the treatise Petrarca directly accuses the whole society of his time, from public authorities to individual scholars, of doing nothing to nourish any sensitivity for cultural problems and of not seeing that scribes had the technical preparation that they needed. The scribes, indeed, "were not restrained by any law, did not pass any exam, nor were chosen by any judgment"; the result, he concluded, was that "anyone who learned to paint something on parchment or to hold a pen in his hand could be taken for a scribe." According to Petrarca, this situation created a state of confusion in the transmission and diffusion of texts, and grave dangers for their very integrity, to the extent that, he asserted, "you could not recognize the very writings that you had composed." In the letter to Gerardo, moreover, he criticized the practice of the division of labor that in his opinion was responsible for incorrect texts. "With us," he affirmed, "there are those who prepare the parchment, others who write the books, others who correct them, others who illustrate them, and finally still others who bind them and decorate the outside surfaces."

For Petrarca and those who shared his views, nothing remained of the system for producing books or of the scale of typological and sign values that sustained it at the ideological level. Thus it was necessary to refound the process of producing manuscript books by returning to its origins, first resolving the basic problem of the relation between author and text and only then addressing the problem of the relationship between text and public. The mechanism of industrial production of books found in the great centers

---

42. A provisional edition of the chapter *De librorum copia*, edited by G. Contini, is in *Mostra di codici petrarcheschi laurenziani (Firenze, maggio–ottobre 1974)* (Florence, 1974), pp. 73–81; the letter to his brother Gerardo of 25 April 1374 (*Familiares*, XVIII, 5) is in V. Rossi, ed., *Le familiari*, 4 vols. (Florence, 1933–42), vol. 3, pp. 282–83.

of Gothic Europe paid practically no attention to authors and excluded them from any participation in the process of reproducing and diffusing texts. This too was an aspect about which Petrarca complained, denouncing the indifference of scholars for their works, which they entrusted to ignorant hands. "Liberal intelligence," he observed, "aspires to higher things, leaving the humble behind; thus the books of the learned, like the fields of the rich, give the appearance of being less cultivated than those belonging to others."

The resolution of the problem that Petrarca proposed was contained in the product that we can call the "author's book": the codex written by the very hand of the creator of the text, intended for a limited circulation and a reproduction guaranteed by other "author-colleagues," if one can so describe the friends and disciples who constituted his preferred first public. The author's book represented the culmination of a long process of textual elaboration over all of which the author himself exercised strict control by means of writing the various stages entirely in his own hand, from the first draft on paper to the last page of the definitive codex; this last, indeed, often turned into an archive-codex for an open work, receiving corrections, additions, and reconsiderations. This was a process that Petrarca had put to use for all of his written works from the most complex and demanding creations, which took him decades and were never finished, to letters. He has left us direct, eloquent testimony of this process in several codices of his hand and especially in those two manuscripts containing the *Canzoniere*: the paper minutes (Vat. lat. 3196) and the so-called *originale* on parchment (Vat. lat. 3195).

In the work and thought of Petrarca, the author's book could not be other than the best "reading book," because the perfect textuality, directly emanating from the author and warranted by his autograph, was (and always remained) the guarantee of absolute legibility for the reader. In this way, the circle was closed and the problem was, apparently, resolved. But not for the select few; in reality, only for a bare handful of readers.[43]

Writing to Read

It was, therefore, Petrarca who proposed the reform of book production and typologies that had not been provoked by the advent of texts in vernacular languages, which had generated instead a settling downward of existing categories of products. Petrarca's concerns applied only to the high levels of the

43. For Petrarca's script and his attitude toward books, see A. Petrucci, *La scrittura di Francesco Petrarca* (Città del Vaticano, 1967) and De la Mare, *Handwriting*, pp. 1–16. For his process of autograph elaboration of texts, see N. Mann, "The Making of Petrarch's Bucolicum Carmen: A Contribution to the History of the Text," *Italia medioevale e umanistica* 20 (1977): 127–82.

productive system, for cultured production (for cultivated readers) in Latin. (Petrarca's one great "author's book" in vernacular—the original canzoniere Vat. lat. 3195 [see fig. 26]—was really a story in itself.) Nonetheless, the reform proposed by Petrarca took hold only as it affected script, with the success of the "half-gothic" stylization; it had little effect on the book as a commodity, because for the most part production continued to be carried out according to the old models and systems. And yet Petrarca's proposed models, while difficult to put into effect in the cultural society of the Trecento, remained as an ideal and warning for the future and would in some measure be taken up by Italian intellectuals of the late Quattrocento.

But this was later. In reality, Petrarca already had clearly understood at least one of the reasons for the crisis that threatened book production in his century: the fact that the productive system, with its mechanical and repetitive impersonality and with the limitations it imposed on the repertory of books produced, no longer responded to the demands of an emerging public consisting of socially important men with refined educations. Such a public was represented by Petrarca, his friends, disciples, and correspondents, and by learned ecclesiastics and laymen, masters, notaries, judges, and officials scattered almost everywhere in Italy as elsewhere in Europe. But this new public demanded a new repertory of titles, which itself meant that a precise identification and a different function of books and of reading were needed, and with them a new book typology that would imply new modes and systems of production. At the very end of the Trecento in north-central Italy, all this gradually did come into being, at first in rather limited environments. The decisive development came in Florence at the turn of the fourteenth and fifteenth centuries through the work of Niccolò Niccoli, a merchant self-made into a humanist, and of the youthful Poggio Bracciolini, still less than twenty years old and already a highly accomplished scribe.

In the history of written culture there do not seem to have been changes or innovations, no matter how radical, that were not inspired by earlier, perhaps centuries-old models. And this was the case with the type of book, truly novel for its layout and script, that Niccoli and Poggio elaborated and produced privately in Florence with the help of Coluccio Salutati during the last years of the Trecento and the first of the Quattrocento. The model aspired to be, and for the most part was, an exact reproduction of the codices for study written in Italy between the eleventh and the beginning of the twelfth century. Lovingly reproduced from these codices were format, systems of lining, disposition of the writing, ornamentation (the famous initials "a bianchi girari") and finally, or especially, the script: the "castigata et clara" caroline, already praised by Petrarca, which was reproduced by means of a stubborn process of almost photographic imitation and which was called "antiqua" with some pride. The script was, in fact, at once old and new, a reevocation that quickly showed itself to be extraordinarily vital and in two or three decades was diffused virtually everywhere in Italy.[44]

In the process initiated by the two Florentine reformers, one a bibliophile and the other a professional scribe, there were two elements, which we could call structural, that challenged the existing productive system. The first consisted of the radical (even if gradually applied) revolution in writing techniques imposed by old caroline models, in the course of which both the pen cut at an angle (*a punta mozza*) point and the writing fragmented into short juxtaposed strokes that it produced were repudiated, to be replaced by the centrally cut pen and a writing that was more freely drawn and less bound to the mechanical repetitiveness of the worker-scribe. The second element consisted of the dislocation of the centers of new book production, constituted by specialized booksellers or even of individual scribes, which instead of being situated alongside universities, as they had been in the past, were now found in the capital cities of the new culture—Florence and later Rome—or attached to the courts of patron princes and their libraries. Thus the scribes frequently moved from one place to another within Italy, wherever drawn by economic convenience, such as the foundation of a new library or the summons of a commission.

The new books—of medium format sometimes tending a bit toward the square, with text laid out on the full page, with few abbreviations, and especially with new script and new ornamentation—contained exclusively texts in Latin, especially classical authors, translations from Greek, or texts by humanists (fig. 35); rarely was there anything else, at least for the first decades, although this was in part because other products were still commissioned or acquired through the old means and in conformance with old models. Vernacular books, indeed, continued to be produced according to the formal schemes of the preceding century. This was also the case for liturgical books or books tied to university culture, whose productive systems had not been altered at all because there had not been any demands for change from the public of ecclesiastics, teachers, scholars, and professionals who used these books daily.

Indeed, the new model book, which for decades had virtually nothing to do with vernacular texts, may even have had a negative effect on their diffusion by contributing to the gradual elimination of their own most prestigious vehicles and instruments: the register-book and the courtly book. This

---

44. The most recent critical contributions are in De la Mare, *Handwriting*, pp. 30–84; see also A. Petrucci, *Libri, scrittura e pubblico nel Rinascimento. Guida storica e critica* (Bari, 1979), esp. pp. 21–36.

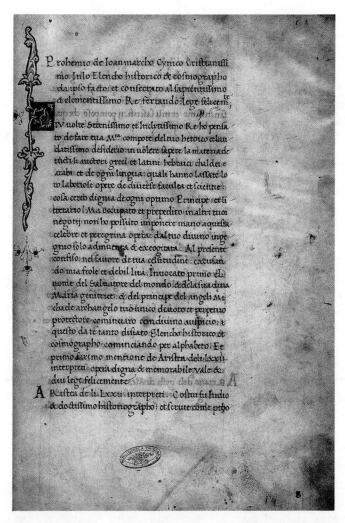

35. Giovanni Maria Cinico, *Elencho historico et cosmographo*, author's autograph presentation copy, ca. 1481–1491. Biblioteca Apostolica Vaticana, MS Chigi M. VIII 159, fol. 1r

occurred naturally and automatically when the old model vernacular book, patronized for both reading and prestige, came to lose its natural public— an effect produced on one hand by the conversion to humanistic culture of the more important representatives of the great mercantile bourgeoisie, and on the other by the introduction of the new repertory into noble libraries of northern Italy. Thus, by the second half of the Quattrocento the humanistic book assumed practically throughout Italy the double function of private deluxe book for cultivated nonprofessionals and of courtly book for and in princely libraries.

The collapse of organized production, which in any case had been left in the past to the initiative of individual scribes and tiny shops, was probably immediate. Already in 1429 Ambrogio Traversari complained to Leonardo Giustinian, who had asked him to find codices of vernacular texts in Florence, that he could do so only at very high prices.[45] It seems apparent that commerce in such texts, neglected by the larger entrepreneurs, had been left to modest shops such as that of the Florentine *cartolaio* Giovanni di Michele Baldini, whose inventory following his death in 1425 included a Marco Polo, books of legends and songs, Boccaccio's *Filostrato,* and similar volumes, along with small scholastic works.[46] Yet such texts must still have had a public, which the ever broader diffusion of literacy would have made progressively wider, especially in the larger cities. And it was a public with an almost exclusively vernacular culture, constrained in practice by the crisis of organized book production to copy for themselves the texts they wanted to read and preserve, and which they wrote especially in the mercantile cursive that, for those excluded from the schools of *grammatica,* had become their customary and only script.

In effect, there was a graphic bipolarism of literate Italy that manifested itself in the most obvious and crude way in the course of the fifteenth century, in that those who studied and knew Latin adopted the new humanistic script or its cursive typifications, while others, restricted by knowing only the vernacular, wrote *mercantesca.* Some contemporaries were well aware of this bipolarism, for in 1454 Enea Silvio Piccolomini reproached one of his correspondents who was guilty of having written him an incomprehensible script by reminding him that he had learned "latinas litteras, non uncinos mercatorios" (Latin letters, not mercantile *uncini*)."[47] The *uncini* of the merchants, that is mercantile cursive, was thus taking on not only a graphic-cultural connotation but—as a visible sign of a literate but monolingual culture—also a social connotation of difference and marginalization. And yet the production of vernacular books—entrusted to humble writers of paper books in mercantesca, to monks and nuns writing in dying and deformed gothic,[48] and to individual scribes of more elegant "half-gothic" cursive-like

45. The episode is noted by B. Migliorini, *Storia della lingua italiana,* p. 250.

46. A. de la Mare, "The Shop of a Florentine 'Cartolaio' in 1426," in B. Maracchi Biagiarelli and D. E. Rhodes, eds., *Studi offerti a Roberto Ridolfi* (Florence, 1973), pp. 237–48.

47. Cited in S. Rizzo, *Il lessico filologico degli umanisti* (Rome, 1973), p. 143.

48. Such as those working at the end of the century in the Perugia monastery of Monteluce,

"bastarde"—continued and, in precisely this period, spread numerically and geographically into every region of Italy. Writing in 1963 of the survival of texts in Franco-Venetian in fifteenth-century copies, Gianfranco Folena commented that "these copies bear the mark of a degradation or a cultural decline, but often also of a social broadening in addition to the tenacious love of vernacular literature: the new gold money of humanistic coinage, both Latin and vernacular, devalued older money but also created new markets and a widespread retail commerce."[49]

Let us look more closely at those who fed such a commerce and spread the new markets for vernacular books in a century dominated by the humanistic model book in Latin. A summary census of the scribes of vernacular in the fifteenth century, conducted in the same way as that already used for the fourteenth century, reveals the existence of about 230 individuals writing books with Italian texts. Of these, there were only seventeen who were or seemed to be professionals, including two notaries and one master; some, including famous humanist amanuenses such as Cinico, Veterano, and Lunense, also or even mainly wrote in Latin; twelve of these professionals worked in the second half of the century. Among the rest—"copyists from passion"[50] and taste—one can identify eighteen religious (ten regular clergy, one nun, and seven secular clergy) and thirteen notaries. The rest—an overwhelming majority—were literate but not professionals of the pen; many of them wrote for themselves and for their little family libraries, stating that they did so for "amusement," for "pleasure," for "consolation," or to "spend their leisure." A typical situation is that of the Benci brothers who, around the middle of the century, formed a rich private library in Florence of vernacular codices by buying and copying them, taking turns in the work of writing;[51] alternatively, there was already in 1416 Giuliano Bardi, who, in copying a vernacularized Ovid, remarked of the book: "Se tu piacessi a 'lchuno, chopisene uno" (If someone likes your book, he should copy it).[52]

Copying to read was thus more than a pleasure; it was a necessity. And one cannot but notice the external appearance of the product, whose errors and carelessness the copyists themselves sometimes lamented ("schrito stra-

---

on whom see U. Nicolini, "I minori osservanti di Monteripido e la 'scriptorium' delle clarisse di Monteluce," *Picenum seraphicum* 8 (1971): 100–130.

49. G. Folena, "La cultura volgare e l'Umanesimo cavalleresco' nel Veneto," in V. Branca, ed., *Umanesimo europeo e umanesimo veneziano* (Florence, 1963), p. 156.

50. So termed by V. Branca, "Copisti per passione, tradizione caratterizzante, tradizione di memoria," in *Studi e problemi di critica testuale. Convegno di studi di filologia italiana nel centenario della Commissione per i testi di lingua (7–9 aprile 1960)* (Bologna, 1961), pp. 69–83.

51. G. Tanturli, "I Benci copisti," *Studi di filologia italiana* 36 (1978): 197–313.

52. Bénédictins de Bouveret, *Colophons de manuscrits occidentaux*, no. 12,066.

pazadamente" is how a Dalla Corgna described one of his books [53]). But they never complained of their own physical labors, as had been done for centuries by worker-scribes whose lamentations or expressions of relief at having finished the work characterizes so many subscriptions. And this too seems an aspect we should emphasize about that "freedom to write" of the nonprofessional literates mentioned above—a freedom conquered by ever more extensive categories of laity since the thirteenth century, and in the fifteenth still not threatened in its graphic and book creativity by the arrival of printing with movable characters and by a more rigid organization of scholastic instruction at the elementary levels. [54]

Writing and Print

During the last thirty years of the fifteenth century, Italian book production was dominated by an event of enormous cultural and social importance: the introduction and initial diffusion in the peninsula's larger and smaller centers of printing with movable characters. But this event, which certainly enlarged the reading public enormously and turned books into a product whose cost was relatively accessible to many, did not, at least in the fifteenth century, provoke any fundamental modifications in the typology of book production. The first printers, indeed, restricted themselves to transferring into the new books the sizes, dispositions of text, characters, and ornament found in manuscript. They thus kept alive in new forms the same types of books that were in commerce in the peninsula during the middle of the century, even though this involved a process that was neither direct nor linear but rather contradictory, sometimes uncertain, and often traumatic.

As had already been the case in Germany, the first type of book to be transposed into print was that solemn desk-book of ecclesiastical or university nature, in gothic or half-gothic characters. Next was the "humanistic" reading-book, of medium format and with different graphic and typographic characteristics. Only then, at the end, does the vernacular book, the book *da bisaccia*, receive consecration in print, with production that from the seventh decade of the century onward gradually became broader and more widely diffused. [55]

53. Francesco Dalla Corgna in 1464; ibid., no. 4280

54. On this series of problems, see some comments in P. Lucchi, "La Santacroce, il Salterio e il Babuino. Libri per imparare a leggere nel primo secolo della stampa," *Quaderni storici* 13 (1978): 593–630; and in A. Petrucci, "Scrittura, alfabetismo ed educazione grafica nella Roma del primo Cinquecento: Da un libretto di conti di Maddelena pizzicarola in Trastevere," *Scrittura e civiltà* 2 (1978): 163–207, esp. 186–97.

55. Here and earlier I summarize views already expressed in A. Petrucci, "Alle origini del libro moderno. Libri da banco, libri da bisaccia, libretti da mano," *Italia medioevale e umanistica* 12 (1969): 295–313.

In 1479 Vespasiano da Bisticci, the Florentine stationer and bookseller who for decades had been the greatest provider of deluxe humanistic books for noble libraries, ended his entrepreneurial activity.[56] The next year Antonio Sinibaldi, the most skilled Florentine scribe of the time, explicitly accused the new typographical art of having destroyed the art of writing by hand and of having ruined him personally: "Et lo exercitio mio è solo di scriverer a prezo, quale è riducto per mezo della stampa, in modo che apena ne tragho il vestito, et è exercitio infermissimo" (And my business is only to write for pay, which is reduced by printing, so that I can barely buy clothes to wear, and business is so poor).[57] Nonetheless, manuscript books continued to be made for the rest of the fifteenth century and beyond; but although they were of every kind and type, two categories at extreme opposite ends of the typological scale stand out with special prominence. On the one hand there were "courtly" books on parchment, of an increasingly refined level (and high cost), and on the other private vernacular books on paper, of a steadily lower textual and material level—these last almost concluding that process of degradation singled out by Folena as typical of the later Franco-Venetian codices.

In the last quarter of the century it became increasingly common for deluxe "courtly" codices to assume a rather small format. These generally are parchment books executed with complete accuracy, ably written in humanistic bookhand or cursive, and generously decorated or illuminated. For the most part these codices contain texts of classical authors without commentaries or notes, and were produced in the larger centers of culture and of Italian book production of the time: at Florence or Milan, in the Veneto, at Rome or Naples. These are obviously deluxe exemplars, meant for use in private reading by personages who were socially and culturally eminent, or for conservation in private or noble libraries. Sometimes these little codices, so precious and luxurious, and so richly illuminated, contained poetic vernacular texts. But when this occurred, it was always a particular, even unique kind of text: the *Rime* or the *Trionfi* of Petrarca.

From this point of view, the production of two of the greatest Italian calligraphers of the late fifteenth century seems exemplary: the Florentine Antonio Sinibaldi already mentioned, and the Venetian Bartolomeo Sanvito. Both wrote many codices containing classical texts, of which several are of rather small format (height less than 20 cm). Sanvito, in particular, copied even delicious epigraphic collections. Both also wrote little books of hours,

---

56. See G. M. Cagni, *Vespasiano da Bisticci e il suo Epistolario* (Rome, 1969), pp. 34–37.
57. In T. De Marinis, *La biblioteca napoletana dei re d'Aragona* II (Florence, 1947), pp. 311–12, doc. no. 965 (passage cited is on p. 312.)

a fact that seems important because throughout late medieval and Renaissance Europe the book of hours represented the first and only example of a
small-format manuscript book. Finally, both scribes wrote only one kind of
vernacular text: Petrarca's poetic works in Italian, and always in codices of
small format.[58] If one extends the investigation into other deluxe Petrarca
codices produced in late fifteenth-century Italy, one sees that this phenomenon was not restricted to the two copyists just cited. Indeed, there exist
numerous deluxe *petrarchini* produced by anonymous scribes in the larger
Italian centers between 1460 and the fatal year 1500, all of which share the
same characteristics of format, impagination, care in manufacture, and rich
ornament and illustrations.[59]

What is behind this phenomenon? There are certainly many factors, of
different origin; perhaps there is even the suggestion—distant, but alive in
the venerable manuscripts—of *libretti* written by hand by the poet himself
(even if only of works in Latin). Certainly there is the influence of the daily
reading books most diffused among the laity, the little books of hours; but
there is also the emergence of a new mode of reading, favored by the diffusion of printed books that transferred the operation of reading from the
formerly few, solemn, and specially equipped places (the study, library, or
cell) to places and means more commonly encountered in daily life. This
was the mode of reading appropriate to "a cultured society that was not
literary by profession, and that would have quickly learned to love the elegance of the characters, the texts free of comments, and the manageable
formats suitable not to desks or shelves but to writing tables or hands":[60] of
a society both bourgeois and bilingual.

Thus was born, by the work of scribes and handicrafters of books who
were among the most ingenious and refined that Italy had ever known, the
"libretto da mano" or hand-book: a type of book that was new in format,
impagination, and use of text (to read rather than study) and thus also new
in function, but was limited to a "courtly," elite circulation as long as it
remained confined to manuscripts—until, to be precise, at the opening of
the new century (1501) Aldo Manuzio, with an intuition of its potential value
as a commodity for the masses, transformed this model into a product of
broad diffusion (his "libelli portatiles in formam enchiridi"), even while

58. For Sinibaldi, see B. L. Ullmann, *The Origin and Development of Humanistic Script*
(Rome, 1960), pp. 118–23; for Sanvito, see J. Wardrop, *The Script of Humanism. Some Aspects
of Humanistic Script, 1460–1560* (Oxford, 1963), pp. 19–35.
59. See G. Guerrini, "Il sistema di comunicazione di un 'corpus' di manoscritti quattrocen-
teschi: I 'Trionfi' del Petrarca," *Scrittura e civiltà* 10 (1986): 121–97.
60. As I wrote in *Alle origini del libro moderno*, p. 308.

maintaining unaltered the external characteristics of great refinement.[61] The series of hand-books inaugurated by Aldo in 1501 under the guidance of Pietro Bembo contained Latin, Greek, and Italian books; by July 1501 there was a *volgare* Petrarca edited by Bembo. It is thus appropriate to say, in closing this discussion, that the manuscript book, at the very moment when it began to yield the field to printing, still showed itself able to renew types, modes, and functions of book production, and to maintain and transmit to the industrial process a fruitful rapport with the reading public.

ANCIENT LIBRARIES

Religious and Scholastic Libraries

During the eleventh and twelfth centuries, in the crucial period when Italy knew the first real experiments in written vernacular, the library as an institution constituted a physical and conceptual element that belonged exclusively to religious culture as a place designated for the conservation-reproduction of written texts in Latin.[62] In reality, from the earlier Middle Ages to our point of departure at the turn of the eleventh and twelfth centuries, libraries had not been only libraries, at least as they are understood in our culture. Indeed, in addition to being a place of conservation, libraries were also places of writing books and thus scriptoria; very often they were also archives where, alongside the books, the documents of the institution to which the library belonged—its *munimina*, cartularies, and so forth—were also preserved.

Usually linked to an ecclesiastical community, which might be of regular or secular clergy and situated in a town or isolated on a mountain, the early medieval library constituted a property of notable value for that community and thus made up part of its treasury; at the same time, it was a necessary complement to carrying out the religious functions of the church to which it was joined; finally, it was an indispensable instrument for the cultural preparation of literate ecclesiastical personnel and for the functioning of the school (whether internal or open to the outside) usually joined to the insti-

---

61. See *ibid.*, and also L. Balsamo and A. Tinto, *Origini del corsivo nella tipografia italiana del Cinquecento* (Milan, 1967), pp. 25–41.

62. One must refer generally to E. Lesne, *Histoire de la propriété ecclésiastique en France,* vol. 4: *Les livres. Scriptoria et bibliothèques du commencement du VIIIe à la fin du IXe siècle* (Lille, 1938); to J. W. Thompson, *The Medieval Library* (New York, 1957); and to J. de Ghellinck, "Les bibliothèques médiévales," *Nouvelle revue théologique* 65 (1938): 36–55. Still useful is A. Vernet, "Etudes et travaux sur les bibliothèques médiévales, 1937–1947," *Revue d'histoire de l'église de France* 34 (1948): 63–94.

tute. But we should understand that, in speaking of libraries of this period, we mean a more or less ordered collection of books rather than an autonomously functioning institution. In general, what was involved was only a room of rather reduced dimensions, located alongside the church, connected to or identical with the scriptorium; it was used only for keeping books in one or more special armoires and not for reading or consulting them. Reading, indeed, took place in the cells when it was understood as an individual event, in the refectory or church when it was understood as an event both communitarian and devotional, and in the school when it was understood as an event both communitarian and didactic.

The connection of the library with the scriptorium on one hand and the archive on the other was symptomatic of a overall conception of the written culture typical of the early medieval ecclesiastical intellectual. This conception derived from a cultural model and behavior of late antique origin, in which reading and writing were regarded as closely connected activities and in which books and documents belonged to the same overall sphere of writing; in addition to Latin-speaking Western Europe, the same model was shared by Byzantine Greek culture and even by written Arabic culture in the same period. The complementarity between the activity of reading and the activity of writing, which at least in Saint Jerome and afterward[63] characterized the late antique and early medieval ecclesiastical cultural model, was not limited to the obvious physical contiguity between the place of depositing books and copying them—between, in short, the library and the scriptorium—that one finds in so many great monasteries of Western Europe. It also, especially from the Carolingians on, determined the very process by which ecclesiastical intellectuals were educated and which conditioned their relationships with sources and with creative activities according to specific schemes. Indeed, the scholar read to write: that is, he read to compose a text of his own that was largely made up of the citations of others; he read by writing, because he continuously annotated books in the margins and between the lines; and then he wrote in practice while reading or soon after having read. Thus Guibert de Nogent, at the beginning of the twelfth century, could rightly juxtapose "perpetuitas legendi" and "continuatio scribendi" as the essential and complementary phases of intellectual activity.[64]

On what kinds of texts did this sustained operation of reading-writing come to be continuously exercised? At the opening of the twelfth century,

---

63. Still essential for this subject is E. Arns, *La technique du livre d'après saint Jérome* (Paris, 1953).

64. Cited by M.-C. Garand, "Le scriptorium de Guibert de Nogent," *Scriptorium* 31 (1977): 3.

the repertory of the ecclesiastical libraries was substantially homogenous throughout Western Europe and essentially monolingual, being constituted almost exclusively of texts written in Latin. Apart from those liturgical texts that were useful for Divine Office and biblical texts with related commentary, a predominant place had long been held by texts of the Church Fathers, especially Augustine and Jerome. As Haskins observed, "a library of *ca.* 1100 would have little beyond the Bible and the Latin Fathers, with their Carolingian commentators, the service books of the church and various lives of saints, the textbooks of Boethius and some others, bits of local history, and perhaps certain of the Latin classics, too often covered with dust."[65] This substantially accurate picture is confirmed for Italy by the famous partial catalogue of the library of Pomposa, drafted in 1093, which contains references to 240 works gathered in about 70 codices, composing an essentially Augustinian collection to which were added some historical works and a certain number of classical authors.[66] Pomposa had a great library and the number of books preserved was notable for the time; ordinarily a middle-sized ecclesiastical institution had fewer, around twenty or thirty pieces which could easily fit in an armoire: hence the famous adage according to which "claustrum sine armario est quasi castrum sine armamentario" (the cloister without an armoire is like a castle without an armory).

With the twelfth century, the material conditions of book production changed decisively because of higher cultural requirements, the development of the great university schools, and the formation of a broader public of educated and literate people. Thus the number of books produced increased notably, and ecclesiastical libraries had not only to broaden their repertory but also, over time, to modify their very physical structure and to open themselves to a broader consultation. At the same time, there gradually grew up models of library institutions different from those of the past, such as the libraries of university colleges and private libraries for lay teachers, that were also distinguished by legal character and by function. Also contributing to this profound modification in the field of the conservation of books and letters were both the structuring of the universities, with their didactic demands based entirely on books, and—especially—the organization of the new mendicant religious orders (the Carmelites and Augustinians as well as the Dominicans and Franciscans) as great bearers of scholastic culture.

For it was in the environment of the mendicant orders, during the last

65. *Renaissance of the Twelfth Century* (Cambridge, Mass., 1927), p. 7.
66. The text of the catalogue is in G. Becker, *Catalogi bibliothecarum antiqui* (Bonn, 1885), n. 70, pp. 157–71; see J. Leclercq, "Cultura spirituale e ideali riformatori dell'abbazia di Pomposa nel secolo XI," *Analecta pomposiana* 1 (1965): 73–88; G. Billanovich, ed., *La biblioteca di Pomposa. Pomposa monasterium modo in Italia primum* (Padova, 1994).

quarter of the thirteenth century, that there was born a new model of a religious library which was destined to achieve a broad popularity for several centuries: the consultation library with the books chained to the reading desks.[67] This model differed from preceding ones in several important respects. In the first place, the library did not retain any connection with the collections of documents belonging to the community to which it belonged; indeed, with the scholastic mentality now having broken the ties between book culture and document culture, sharing of activities between the library and archive was no longer possible. Further, with a good part of the collection of books preserved coming from the outside by commission, purchase, gift, or bequest, the ancient autarchical circularity of the link between scriptorium and library was broken (even if not completely) at the same time as that between library and archive. Finally, one must notice the fact—which is of great importance at the level of the techniques of acculturation—that the library returned to being the place not only where books were kept but also (at least in part) where they were read and consulted. Specifically, there was a new spatial model consisting of an oblong hall in which two series of desks in several parallel files filled two lateral aisles leaving an empty corridor at the center. This model was naturally inspired by that of the church itself, with its single nave. It also may have been influenced, more subtly and unconsciously, by the visual model of the page of the scholarly codex constructed out of two dense columns of text with lines separated by a narrow intercolumnar space and surrounded by margins: as spaces were left empty in the book for the interventions of the reader, so the lateral and central spaces in the library were left empty to allow for the movements of the public of scholars.

In fact, the books of European libraries not only increased in number during the thirteenth century; they also changed in quality, as the repertory of texts underwent substantial renovation. In and around 1200, as Haskins affirmed, to the works previously in use there had already been added "the *Corpus Juris Civilis* and the classics partially rescued from neglect; the canonical collections of Gratian and the recent popes; the theology of Anselm and Peter Lombard and the early scholastics; the writings of Bernard and other monastic leaders; a mass of new history, poetry, and correspondence; the philosophy, mathematics, and astronomy unknown to the earlier medieval tradition and recovered from the Greeks and Arabs in the course of the twelfth century." This picture can be made more precise by observing that,

67. See, in general, the still useful treatment of J. W. Clark, *The Care of Books* (Cambridge, 1901); and in particular K. W. Humphreys, *The Book Provisions of the Medieval Friars, 1215–1400* (Amsterdam, 1964).

under the influence of the more advanced sectors of university culture, the repertory of new European libraries became steadily more specialized in a professional sense, that is, to the end of preparing friars and clerks and doctors fully expert in their respective professions but with a common foundation of philosophical culture with an Aristotelian-scholastic imprint.

This tendency, readily apparent in some catalogues of the thirteenth century and obvious in the Trecento, inevitably meant a progressive numerical restriction of the previously dominant area reserved to the works of the Church Fathers. At the beginning of the Duecento, fully thirty of the ninety pieces that can be identified in the private library of Cardinal Guala Bicchieri (d. 1227) belonged to patristic literature, twenty-seven to biblical literature, and fifteen to canon and civil law;[68] the survival of this old model into the new age can be seen in the fact that the book collection of the cathedral of San Martino in Lucca was not greatly different in 1297.[69] But the contemporary library of the papal collector Cristoforo Tolomei (d. 1298), which then passed to Cardinal Pietro Colonna, contained more biblical commentaries, philosophical texts, and legal texts than patristic works,[70] and the incredible library of the Pisan canon Giacomo, originally from Benevento, contained many classics but few Fathers among its 162 codices.[71] Similarly, in the course of the fourteenth century some great libraries of the mendicant orders had drastically reduced the total percentage of works of patristic literature to barely 10 percent of all works possessed: this was the case at San Francesco of Pisa in 1355,[72] with the Franciscans at Gubbio about five years later,[73] and with the Dominicans at Bologna in 1386;[74] in the great Franciscan library of Assisi in 1381 the presence of Church Fathers was derisory.[75] On the other hand, the number of biblical commentaries and sermon collections in such libraries increased steadily, because in addition to texts of scholastic theology, this type of literature represented the backbone of the professional preparation of the new ecclesiastical intellectual.

Also steadily increasing were the absolute numbers of the books preserved

68. A. Hessel and W. Bulst, "Kardinal Bicchieri und seine Bibliothek," *Historische Vierteljahrschrift* 27 (1932): 772–94.

69. Edited by T. Gottlieb in *Centralblatt für Bibliothekswesen* 5 (1888): 487–90.

70. See R. Mather, "The Codicil of Cardinal Comes of Casate and the Libraries of Thirteenth-century Cardinals," *Traditio* 20 (1964): 319–50; A. Paravicini-Bagliani, "Le biblioteche dei cardinali Pietro Peregrosso (d. 1295) e Pietro Colonna (d. 1326)," *Revue d'histoire ecclésiastique suisse* 64 (1970): 104–39.

71. The catalogue was edited and published in N. Caturegli, "Due biblioteche private in Pisa alla fine del secolo XIII," *Bollettino storico pisano* 3d ser. 24–25 (1955–56): 22–90.

72. Humphreys, *Book Provisions*, pp. 102–03.

73. Ibid.

74. Ibid., pp. 94–95.

75. Ibid., pp. 107–08.

in each collection. It is true that in Italy one does not see the numbers found in large fourteenth-century French and English libraries, some of which contained more than 1,000 volumes, much less the 2,059 pieces of the papal library of Avignon in 1369, when it was probably the largest in Europe. But Italian libraries did participate in the general movement toward a conspicuous and progressive growth of book resources that characterized all European collections between the thirteenth and fifteenth centuries. Thus, one sees the 718 pieces at Assisi in 1381,[76] the 472 of San Domenico of Bologna in 1386,[77] the 731 of the Florentine Carmelites before the end of the fourteenth century,[78] the 426 pieces of Sant'Antonio of Padua in 1396 that by 1449 would be 1,025—an average increase of 14 pieces per year.[79]

The high number of books that each community possessed posed grave problems of both conservation and use that could not, over the long term, be managed within the framework of a consultation library that was organized by desks with books literally and figuratively chained to fixed positions. The solution was found in the practice of physically relocating the book patrimony into various collections and in various locations according to the function that each group of books had to perform. Thus the rule in the larger religious libraries of the fourteenth century was to have a consultation or public collection, ordered by desks; a collection enclosed in armoires with shelves, known as the secret collection, that was mostly intended for loan and was generally larger than the consultation collection; a group of liturgical books in the sacristy; another group of books for devotional reading in the refectory; and possibly also special collections on long-term deposit in the cells of brothers of special importance or in other places in the religious house. The best example of such multiple physical and functional dislocations was the papal library at Avignon, which in 1369 seems to have been spread over a total of eleven different locations within the papal palace, ranging from the library in a proper sense next to the chapel, to the chapel itself, the treasury tower, the chamberlain's study, and so forth.[80]

Although one notices that there was a Marco Polo in the library of the Franciscans of Gubbio in 1360,[81] and that there were five texts described as

76. Ibid.

77. Ibid., pp. 94–95.

78. K. W. Humphreys, *The Library of the Carmelites at Florence at the End of the Fourteenth Century* (Amsterdam, 1964).

79. K. W. Humphreys, *The Library of the Franciscans of the Convent of St. Anthony, Padua, at the Beginning of the Fifteenth Century* (Amsterdam, 1966), esp. p. 7.

80. See F. Ehrle, *Historia bibliothecae romanorum pontificum tum Bonifatianae, tum Avenionensis*, vol. 1 (Rome, 1890), pp. 274–450; for places where books were kept, see p. 438.

81. Humphreys, *Book Provisions*, pp. 105–06.

"romances" (none of them in Italian) in the papal library in 1369,[82] the canon of ecclesiastical book culture was nevertheless too rigidly tied to both didactic and professional needs, and too specialized despite its subdivision into various branches, to be open to literature in vernacular languages and especially to that in Italian. For this to happen, the canon itself had to become less rigid as a result of the rise of new needs and by the creation of new functions.

Other Models

Whether one considers the canon, the physical structure, or even the ideology of its functioning, the dominant model for educated Europe until the beginning of the Quattrocento was constituted by the religious library articulated in several collections around a central consultation node and characterized by a strictly monolingual religious and philosophical repertory. But other models did exist or, rather, could have existed. During the thirteenth century, the library of Frederick II and Manfred, located probably at Palermo, could have constituted such an alternative pole. About it we know only that it possessed books in Latin, Greek, Arabic, Hebrew, Provençal, French, "italiano," and perhaps German, in every subject, of every possible appearance and manufacture, coming from every region of Europe and the Byzantine and Arabic east. These books were bought, received as gifts, sought or commissioned in the court and without; and they were kept, divided according to language and subject matter, in closed wooden armoires analogous to the crown treasures, in a single place where the emperor used to visit to read or meditate.[83] It was, therefore, an aristocratic library developed to the highest possible level and characterized by some singular features that made it different from the model of religious library so far discussed.

In the first place, the library of Frederick II was multilingual like no other in medieval Europe. Moreover, because it was independent of any didactic or professional purpose, it was a library apparently lacking any fixed canon. It was a library for *reading*, not *consultation* or *writing*. It was a library whose tendencies were universal and diachronic rather than specialist and synchronic, like religious or scholastic libraries. It was an "open" library, both for its infinite possibilities of additional accessions and for the absence of any hierarchy of genres, subjects, or languages. After the death of Manfred and the disappearance of the Swabians from southern Italy, one would have

82. Ehrle, *Historia bibliothecae romanorum pontificum*, p. 447; for a sixth doubtful case, see A. Pelzer, *Addenda et emendanda* (Città del Vaticano, 1947), p. 146.

83. This description is culled from an encyclical letter of Frederick II or Manfred published in J.-L.-A. Huillard-Bréholles, *Historia diplomatica Frederici II*, 6 vols. (Paris, 1852–61), vol. 4, pt. 1 (1854), pp. 383–85.

to wait for late humanism and the era of printing for such tendencies again to animate the book collections of Western Europe.[84]

Adherence to the canon and to the dependence on professional functions was thus rigid in the great public libraries of the thirteenth and fourteenth centuries. The structure and repertory of private collections could certainly be less rigid, but only as a result of adaptations reflecting the demands of individual social status that inescapably affected each possessor as he exercised his function as a collector and reader of books. Thus, one searches in vain in the (very few) Duecento and Trecento inventories of books possessed by great ecclesiastics, jurists, physicians, and philosophers for appreciable deviations from the norm, significant escapes from the professional canon, or even indirect glimpses of interests not organically linked to the scholastic/ university culture that each person absorbed within didactic structures. Henri Bresc has noted the substantial homogeneity of the libraries of medical doctors in different regions of Italy, which all show a strong presence of works of natural philosophy, astrology, Greek and Arabic classics translated into Latin, and scant rhetorical-literary interests;[85] the personal libraries of members of the upper clergy were similarly homogeneous in being predominantly given over to works of logic and moral philosophy, canon law, and sermons. The libraries of jurists were generally numerically and qualitatively broader, being the only ones studied by Bresc in thirteenth- and fourteenth-century Sicily to exceed 100 volumes[86] and in a few cases reaching 200 or 300 pieces, probably because of the broader financial possibilities that characterized doctors of law compared to other professionals, including others with doctorates, in late medieval Italy. While in 1273 the library of the late Accursius (or what remained of it) counted only 73 volumes, all in law except for a lonely Vegetius;[87] in about 1350 the library of Giovanni Calderini, another jurist and professor at Bologna, comprised 294 books. These were ordered by subject in twelve sections, showing that alongside the crushing presence of juristic texts (more than 90) and of works of philosophy and theology (81) there was also a broad representation of classics (27) and biblical and patristic literature (more than 50 works). Yet the classics were the traditional ones of the medieval schools, from Vergil to Seneca, Horace to Terence, Macrobius to Pliny

84. For a recent, encompassing appraisal of Swabian culture, see R. Antonelli, "Politica e volgare: Guglielmo IX, Enrico II, Federico II," in *Seminario romanzo* (Rome, 1979), pp. 58–59.

85. *Livre et société en Sicile (1299–1499)* (Palermo, 1971), p. 91.

86. Ibid., p. 85.

87. H. Kantorowicz, "Accursio e la sua biblioteca," *Rivista di storia del diritto italiano* 2 (1929): 193–212.

the Younger, Josephus Flavius to Cassiodorus; the newer authors, rediscovered by Venetian humanists and by Petrarca, were entirely lacking.[88]

In truth, the library of the scholar—the master or doctor of theology or law or medicine—was nothing other than the projection in a private dimension of the great religious consultation libraries discussed above: both kinds of library were and continued to be defined by the needs of scholastic/university culture not only in repertory but also in arrangement, daily functioning, and the manner by which they were provisioned. Thus the private library, with its fixed scheme of the desk and armoire situated in one room made familiar by so many figural representations of the Trecento and Quattrocento, repeated either the model of the consultation library with desks on a reduced scale or, more directly, the model of the monastic cell of the religious scholar enriched by borrowed books. The process of acquiring books, which was done mainly through purchase or by outside commissions from specialized artisans, confirmed the links with the structures producing university books that similarly characterized the larger Italian libraries of the time and placed them among the protagonists of the activities of the contemporary Italian book industry. To all these elements, finally, one can add another important characteristic shared by almost all book collections of the time: they consisted almost entirely of modern books, executed and produced not much earlier than they were acquired and used. In short, at the physical level of the repertory these collections were simply the product of the contemporary book industry that they in turn mirrored and for which they constituted the most prestigious clientele.

An alternative to the scholastic library canon is not, therefore, to be sought in the environments linked to university culture and to the book industry that issued from it. That alternative had other sources, in the progressively less marginal presence in thirteenth- and fourteenth-century Italy of a curial culture that, although not entirely foreign to the university, was largely formed outside of it—a culture created by laymen, notaries, judges, and chancellors from the so-called Venetian prehumanists to Giovanni Del Virgilio, from Geri d'Arezzo to Convenevole da Prato, and so forth, following a branch of interpersonal connections and transmigrations of people and books that we have only recently begun to understand. The protagonists of this movement were all technicians of written language and tended, by means of a more refined rhetoric, to renew the expressive code of contemporary oratorical and chancery Latin. They sought the models for such renewal in

88. M. Cochetti, "La biblioteca di Giovanni Calderini," *Studi medievali* 3d ser. 19 (1978): 951–1032.

ancient authorities—known, less known, and unknown—whose texts they consequently desired and whose codices they discovered, read, and copied. In the process, they renewed their private libraries and created—unconsciously, one might say—a new model of book collection that would find its culmination and its definitive model in the library of the greatest of them all: Francesco Petrarca.

The adventure of Italian humanism (as Guido and Giuseppe Billanovich have taught us)[89] began already in the Duecento at Padua, where the first book collections of the new type, such as that of Lovato Lovati, were born from the encounter with the large, illustrious library of Pomposa. It was at Pomposa around 1290 that Lovato completed the arduous and pious labor that later would become typical of so many book hunters: uncovering and copying ancient authors. Unsuspected riches came to the Paduans from Pomposa: Propertius, Martial, Tibullus, Lucretius, Statius. The encounter with the venerable remains preserved in the old monastic library in practice meant the birth of the new model humanistic library that soon would be multiplied in many exemplars, feverishly formed in the course of the Trecento in various regions and localities of north-central Italy and in Avignon.

The years of Lovato were the years of Dante; but of the latter's library we do not yet have a trace. We cannot, however, disguise the fact that at the base of his Latin and vernacular production there is a fundamental problem of reading and thus of library, or rather of libraries—private, courtly, or religious as they may have been. It is not possible today to resolve this problem, behind which is hidden a turning point, a key moment in the process of the modifications that were occurring in fourteenth-century Italian culture. Dante certainly read (but where? how?) Latin texts of scholastic authors and classical texts, collections of Provençal poets and of vernacular Italian poets, French romances and medieval authors, Church Fathers, rhetorical treatises and encyclopedias, crossing various strands of book tradition and written culture and forcefully joining them as no one had been able to do before and few would be able to do after.

But the new model of library was not complete until Petrarca arrived to set upon it the seal of his own strong personality, of his prestige as a master

89. As revealed in Guido Billanovich, "*Veterum vestigia vatum* nei carmi dei preumanisti padovani," *Italia medioevale e umanistica* 1 (1958): 155–243; and affirmed in Giuseppe Billanovich, "Les bibliothèques des humanistes italiens au XIVᵉ siècle," in A. Fourrier, ed., *L'humanisme médiéval dans les littératures romanes du XIIᵉ au XIVᵉ siècle. Actes du Colloque organisés par le Centre de philologie et de littératures romanes de l'Université de Strasbourg, du 29 janvier au 2 février 1962* (Paris, 1964), pp. 195–203, esp. pp. 196–97; see also, more generally, Giuseppe Billanovich, "Biblioteche di dotti e letteratura italiana tra il Trecento e il Quattrocentro," in *Studi e problemi di critica testuale. Convegno di studi di filologia italiana nel centenario della Commissione per i testi di lingua (Bologna, 7–9 aprile 1960)* (Bologna, 1961), pp. 335–48.

independent of the universities, and of his genius in creating cultural models. The Paduan humanists had, first of all, renewed the mode by which codices were supplied, preferring the personal copy to an artisanal one and in this way opening the road to a new mode of book production; and they had modified the structure (and nature) of collecting by bringing new books copied from old ones together with old books that they used as if they were new. But it was only with Petrarca that new books began to imitate old ones even in their appearance,[90] and, especially, it was only with him that the repertory of canonical authors was radically refurbished compared with contemporary scholastic libraries: as Giuseppe Billanovich remarked, Petrarca "placed the old texts and the old school under a strict ban; he made use of classical authors almost exclusively and, in general, cited only them"[91] together with the Church Fathers, and most especially Augustine.

In truth, the new library was not constituted only of these two elements, typical of noble romanesque models: it was more than, to use Billanovich's expression again, "the richest library—public or private—of rare literary texts that had been formed in the course of the near millennium since the last Romans, Boethius and Cassiodorus."[92] It was, first of all, a structure that was perennially open, intended to be enriched continually without an interruption in new discoveries. It was a multilingual structure, with Greek and vernacular authors who, even if outside the official canon, had their place on the shelves and coexisted side-by-side in reading. And it was, especially, a structure based on a diachronic vision of the history of culture that took as its point of departure the physical juxtaposition between the *old* book written in caroline and the *modern* book written in gothic, both being placed next to each other on the shelves. This new library drew sustenance from Petrarca's own new vision of historical process as seen in his second redaction of the *De viris*, which was stretched to "in unum contrahere" events and dates taken "ex omnibus seculis": it was a vision that, although based on an essentially scholastic and thus traditional combinatory method, was based as well on a universal conception of written culture—and thus of the very book patrimony that was possible and necessary for a renewal of contemporary culture—that transcended both chronological and geographical frontiers.[93]

90. On the graphic characteristics of this renewal, still useful is A. Petrucci, *La scrittura di Francesco Petrarca* (Città del Vaticano, 1967), although its list of autograph and annotated codices could be broadly updated.

91. "Bibliothèques des humanistes italiens," p. 201.

92. "Da Dante al Petrarca. Il Virgilio Ambrosiano e l'Orazio Morgan," *Accademia Nazionale dei Lincei. Adunanze straordinarie per il conferimento dei premi della Fondazione A. Feltrinelli*, vol. 1 (1966), pt. 3, p. 65.

93. G. Martellotti, "Linee di sviluppo dell'umanesimo petrarchesco," *Studi petrarcheschi* 2 (1949): 51–80 (citations come from pp. 69, 70–71).

From what we know of Petrarca's library, more than half of the books were two or three centuries old and thus written in caroline. Latin classics made up the largest category of texts (almost a third), while the Fathers (especially the beloved Augustine) and medieval authors trailed far behind; there were few books of the Bible or biblical commentaries; and rare texts of philosophy and theology: in short, as has been said, there was both a disruption of the customary canon and an obvious tendency toward an all-inclusive universality of cultural interests. Petrarca, indeed, did not simply replace one repertory with another. Rather, he replaced an ideology of a library instrumental for teaching and professional acculturation for laity and cultivated clerics with another ideology, of ancient derivation, of the universal library that would be a thesaurus of written culture of every time and country and thus open and diachronic. There was even a precise moment in his life, in 1362, when he projected its realization to the smallest detail, offering his private collection to the Republic of Venice, which would make of it a "bibliotheca publica" meant "ad ingeniosorum et nobilium . . . consolationem . . . et commodum" (for the consolation and use of the capable and noble) and enrich it subsequently with opportune accessions in order to arrive at the formation of a "magnam et famosam bibliothecam . . . parem veteribus" (great and renowned library equal to the old ones).[94] As we know, Petrarca's project was not realized, and he ended up leaving his books to his beloved Carraresi. As a result, what should have been a public library, administered by a public authority, ended up becoming part of an aristocratic library that was private in both use and juridical nature.

The Books of the Humanists

Only one vernacular text figured in the library of Petrarca as it is known so far: Dante's *Commedia*, in a contemporary Florentine exemplar (Vat. lat. 1399) given to him by Boccaccio, presumably in 1351, and barely touched by the pen of the great humanist.[95] But there certainly were, and had to be, other vernacular texts in verse and prose in addition to Petrarca's own *Rerum vulgarium fragmenta*, from Provençal to Italian poetry to the *Decameron* of his friend and disciple Boccaccio. But it is doubtful that Petrarca considered such books as belonging to the canon of the new library. They probably remained with his heirs and closest disciples, as did the autographs of the poet, and thus experienced a different fate from what was considered the main and most worthy nucleus of the Petrarchan book patrimony.[96] This,

94. For details of this episode, see E. H. Wilkins, *Life of Petrarch* (Chicago, 1961).
95. Petrucci, *Scrittura di Francesco Petrarca*, pp. 48, 118.
96. P. Sambin, "Libri del Petrarca presso suoi discendenti," *Italia medioevale e umanistica* 1 (1958): 359–69.

indeed, as is well known, was the fate of almost all the book patrimonies in vernacular languages possessed by the humanists. When they had to make final dispositions of their personal library, they separated out the vernacular books that they had acquired, copied, used, and read, considering them to be outside the canon and unworthy of public preservation or of utilization for study, and left them privately to relatives and friends.[97] In this way, the scholastic/university canon came gradually to be replaced by another as part of the process by which the new cultural life was slowly organized into didactic practices and a process of acculturation, took on rules and schemes, and provided itself with its own tools.

This process occurred parallel to and within another process whereby individuals sought to transform private libraries into public ones by willing legacies of books to a religious community. The supporters and adherents of the new culture in the Trecento and Quattrocento had, indeed, clearly announced the substantial foreignness of their method and cultural patrimony with respect to existing institutions: universities and religious libraries. Consequently, there was an effort, initiated in the wake of Petrarca's example, to impede the physical dispersion of the patrimony of books they had collected—which represented a substantial portion of their own work—and to constitute fixed places for study, at least in theory open to all, within institutions such as the convents of the mendicant orders that were already to some extent predisposed to playing such a role. This was a library politics (if one can use such a term) that foresaw the occupation of strategic places, already consecrated to the diffusion of the old culture, and replacing both the cultural message transmitted there and the book patrimony with a sign that was different if not actually opposed. Even Boccaccio, in making dispositions so that after his death his library would be incorporated, at Santo Spirito, into that of his friend and heir Martino da Signa, effected a traumatic linguistic purge of its contents; he removed all books written in vernacular, including even his own, while he left in place medieval as well as classical and patristic texts, as if to indicate that the canon for him was first of all a canon in Latin.[98]

Although it is still difficult to discern exactly the overall features of Boccaccio's library, one can grasp more easily the characteristics and overall cultural value of the rather large book collection of Coluccio Salutati, chancellor of the Florentine Republic from 1374 to his death in 1406, who after Petrarca was the greatest master outside the universities of Tuscan and Italian hu-

97. See Giuseppe Billanovich, "Biblioteche di dotti," pp. 335–36.
98. A. Mazza, "L'inventario della 'parva libraria' di Santo Spirito e la biblioteca del Boccaccio," *Italia medioevale e umanistica* 9 (1966): 1–74, esp. 4–5.

manism.[99] Coluccio possessed about eight hundred books, a rather large number for the time that was equaled only by the total reached by Niccoli more or less in the same period and city. Slightly more than a hundred of these books remain; of these, about half contain classics and another fourth contain texts of patristic literature, but there are also works of medieval authors, of philosophy and theology, and finally two books in vernacular: a Petrarca canzoniere and a collection of poets in the Dolce Stil Nuovo. Coluccio, too, had his mind set on the model of the public library, ancient and modern, which he intended specifically as guarantor of a correct textual tradition of the works conserved there;[100] he even to some extent revived the role of the university library to which, in 1377 after the death of Petrarca, he wished to entrust the text of the *Africa*.[101] Good *borghese* that he was, however, he left his books together with the rest of his property as an inheritance to his children, in this way dooming the library to dispersion.

Part of Salutati's books were acquired by another well-known Florentine humanist, Niccolò Niccoli, merchant and bibliophile, who died in 1437; his testament provided for the protection of his great book collection, which in numbers equaled that of the Florentine chancellor, by committing it to a committee of testamentary executors for the purpose of placing it at the disposition of the public—naturally, after having excluded texts in the vernacular. From the point of view of the new humanistic culture, Niccoli's library was rather well stocked and very specialized. It was, to begin with, bilingual, because there are 61 Greek codices of the 242 known to have been his; it was made up in large part of ancient codices, so that only 8 of the Greek codices were of contemporary origin and 126 of the Latin ones were early medieval (ninth to twelfth centuries).[102] As for the repertory, beyond the predominance of classical texts, many of which came from Poggio's discoveries, there were a notable number of works of Church Fathers, both Latin and Greek, and of biblical texts; in practice, it was a repertory along Petrarchan and thus romanesque lines, although extended to the Greek literary tradition and colored with a certain antiquarian flavor by the predominance of books two or three hundred years older than contemporary ones. One further recognizes the decisive contribution made by the Florentine

99. For Salutati and his library, see B. L. Ullman, *The Humanism of Coluccio Salutati* (Padua, 1963); and, for a general overview, A. Petrucci, *Coluccio Salutati* (Rome, 1972) and Ronald G. Witt, *Hercules at the Crossroads: The Life, Works, and Thought of Coluccio Salutati* (Durham, N.C., 1983).

100. Ullman, *Humanism of Salutati*, p. 101.

101. Petrucci, *Salutati*, pp. 116–17.

102. See B. L. Ullman and P. A. Stadter, *The Public Library of Renaissance Florence. Niccolò Niccoli, Cosimo de' Medici and the Library of S. Marco* (Padua, 1972), esp. pp. 60–73.

merchant-bibliophile to the formation of a model of the humanistic library
when one considers that even the modern books possessed by Niccoli were
commissioned by him to imitate precisely those of the eleventh and twelfth
centuries: from such taste were born a book style and industry planned in a
manner entirely different from those in the past. And his role was probably
just as important on levels that are more specific and difficult to evaluate:
the ideology of public use and the definition of modes of reading that were
new compared to the past.

In his solemn commemoration of his dead master and friend, Poggio
Bracciolini remembered how Niccoli's house already seemed a "publica quaedam biblioteca" and that his books were "communes . . . omnibus etiam ig-
notis" (available to all, even those he did not know); and he contrasted the
desire of the dead merchant-bibliophile to that of other illustrious *literati*
and humanists such as Petrarca, Boccaccio, Luigi Marsili, and Salutati, who,
by poorly providing for the future of their own libraries, caused their dispersion and segregation in private houses or in nonpublic libraries, thus reducing their value to scholars and to all humanity. But this was not the case
with Niccoli, who did not want to have his own books "sold or transferred
into a private house, or left to the arbitrary use of an individual, or closed
into someone else's library," but rather had provided for them to remain "in
communem utilitatem, in publicum munus, in locum omnibus patentem":
in a place open to everyone, and thus in a library that was "public" in the
strict sense of the word, intended for the use of all scholarly citizens and
administered in a new way by that committee of literate executors whom
Niccoli himself was at pains to designate in his double testament.[103] As we
know, things went otherwise, and Niccoli's library ended up in San Marco,
to which, even though reduced in number, it constituted the largest enrichment. But in Niccoli's determined will to constitute a book collection that
would be new in its legal nature, administration, and public use, one can
perhaps glimpse a manner of behaving that differed from current practices
of studying and reading. For Niccoli was not a professional of the pen as
either a teacher or as a member of the ecclesiastical hierarchy; he was a
merchant and layman. Rather than writing (in the sense of composing texts:
for he was a skilled scribe), he read; and he read freely, not as a function of
composing a text, and thus without writing. He read, therefore, without
professional or ideological concerns.

In assuming this attitude, Niccoli—who had eliminated from the canon
of his own library the texts in Italian—was adopting a manner of reading

---

103. The passages of the oration are found in P. Bracciolini, *Opera* (Basel, 1538; repr. Turin,
1964, ed. R. Fubini), pp. 271, 276–77.

that was typical not of the humanists, who were still professors and professionals even if only unofficially, but of nobles and the cultured and reading bourgeoisie: the attitudes, in short, of the environment from which he came personally and whose habits and tendencies he continued to share. It was not by chance that, although Niccoli was a refined writer of "littera antiqua," when he wrote in the vernacular he reverted to using the "mercantesca" cursive of the bank and shop.

The Aristocratic Library

Niccoli was and remained an exception, because the places for reading without writing continued to be separated in the thirteenth and fourteenth centuries from those where, in contrast, reading and writing constituted two sides of the same intellectual activity. And it was precisely from the practice of free reading that the process first developed of using libraries to preserve the first vernacular literature written in books.

The practice itself had distant roots: in the moment when the European aristocracy, having become literate, ceased having prose or poetic texts recited by others for amusement during their hours of relaxation or eating or rest and instead began to read alone on their own the books out of which their knightly and courtly culture was woven. In general, these were literary texts in vernacular languages, like the romance that Paolo and Francesca were reading together before the kiss immortalized by Dante;[104] or they were texts of love poetry, or chronicles or translations from Latin of historical or even devotional texts. And the texts were not only in the mother tongue, but in many languages, at minimum French and Provençal in addition to Italian, because aristocratic education, at least at the highest levels, provided for learning and understanding the languages of "courtly" European literature through reading and usage.[105]

From what we know of these aristocratic and courtly libraries (and it is too little compared to what must have been their numbers and geographic distribution throughout the peninsula), they were rather different from the other libraries with which we are acquainted, religious and professional, of the thirteenth to fifteenth centuries. In the first place, the repertory was made up mainly of vernacular works of narrative, devotion, more or less fantastic histories and chronicles, and translations; Latin texts consisted mostly of those for private devotions (books of hours) and of biblical texts and Gospels; finally, there might be some Latin and vernacular works on military arts,

---

104. *Inferno*, canto 5, ll. 127–38.

105. For proof, one can observe that many Italian *trovatori* of the late twelfth and thirteenth centuries were noble; see G. Bertoni, *I trovatori d'Italia* (Modena, 1915; repr. Rome, 1967).

farriery, medicine, and astrology. But these collections of books were also different from others in the means of preservation, for they were kept in particular locations situated in safe places of the palace or castle (for example, a tower) close to the archive and treasury of the lord: evidently, they were seen mostly as part of the lord's patrimony. Following a practice more suitable for private collections of individuals than for institutions that would last over time, they were stored in chests rather than armoires; and care of the collection was generally entrusted to generic officials and dependents of the court rather than to specialized personnel. These features could not fail to influence the modes of use, which were those appropriate to leisure reading rather than study, and which took place in the residential and sleeping spaces of the house rather than in specially reserved places such as the study or library. It was a reading that, lacking precise reference to physical points, was therefore itinerant, not only within the aristocratic habitation but even outside; thus the books often changed locations by being transferred, with the lord and his household, from one of his residences to another.

We have somewhat more information for some of the larger aristocratic libraries of fourteenth- and fifteenth-century Italy: the library of the Savoy,[106] of the Gonzaga,[107] of the Visconti,[108] and finally of the Este.[109] The collection of the Savoy at the beginning of the Quattrocento had a rich assortment of books in French but none in Italian; it had only a few Italian books in 1434, and at the end of the century, in 1498, it contained 91 codices in French, 12 in Italian, and 3 in Spanish: these figures can be compared with the 150 manuscripts in Latin. Much greater, for both the number and importance of the pieces, was the library of the Gonzaga that in 1407 numbered 292 volumes, of which 67 were in French and 32 in Italian; among the Latin volumes, ordered by subject, was an obvious predominance of religious literature (86 pieces), law (30 pieces), and astrology (28 pieces). The 1426 inventory of the Visconti library, which was kept in the castle of Pavia, reveals the existence of almost 1,000 volumes, about 90 of which were in French and 52 in Italian vernacular, only 2 in Greek, and one in Hebrew,[110] with the remaining 844 in Latin of various origin, provenance, and nature. In fact, this was a great collection of patrimonial character, formed in the second

106. See S. Edmunds, "The Medieval Library of Savoy," *Scriptorium* 24 (1970): 318–27; 25 (1971): 253–84; 26 (1972): 269–93.

107. See P. Girolla, "La biblioteca di Francesco Gonzaga secondo l'inventario del 1407," *Atti e memorie della Reale Accademia Virgiliana di Mantova* 14–16 (1923): 30–72.

108. E. Pellegrin, *La bibliothèque des Visconti et des Sforza ducs de Milan au XVᵉ siècle* (Paris, 1955).

109. A. Cappelli, "La biblioteca Estense nella prima metà del secolo XIV," *Giornale storico della letteratura italiana* 14 (1889): 1–30.

110. Pellegrin, *Bibliothèque des Visconti*, p. 16.

half of the fourteenth century more as fruit of the rapine and conquests of the Visconti, especially Gian Galeazzo, than of natural development; the complex stratification that distinguishes this collection makes it difficult to recognize any autonomous or organic character. The library of the Este was rather more limited in 1436, before its transformation into a humanistic collection: of 279 volumes, 58 were in French (romances, Bibles, translations); 20 in Italian, including Dante and Boccaccio; among the Latin codices, there were many classics (73), but the usual ones, and some humanistic authors, with Petrarca foremost; also notable was the presence of military and musical works, chronicles, and one Greek codex.

In truth, aristocratic libraries (especially the smaller ones, but also the largest) had a character that was rather precisely defined by the needs of the courtly culture of which it was the mirror and instrument. But these were also fragile institutions, subject to continuing dangers of dispersion due to the physical mobility to which they were subjected and the frequent division of goods on occasions of hereditary succession; they were institutions usually lacking organization and with the barest capacity to grow and develop; they were, especially, cultural instruments that were little and poorly used, frequented by a very limited and occasional public, and thus lacking any capacity for broader influence. Precisely for this reason, within the cultural map of Italy the splendid book collections of the late medieval Italian aristocracy wound up constituting a weak and discontinuous strand lacking internal links and continually subject to the risks of dispersion and physical destruction. Their public certainly loved to read and often included, in contrast with other environments, numerous women among the readers; but their love was confined to only a few books, although ones varied in subject matter and language, and they did not receive from them the stimulus to other, wider reading or, in short, to an institutionalized and critical acculturation. It was on this point that Francesco Petrarca, in composing the second, longer redaction of the *De viris,* reproved a noble whom some have tried to identify with the young Brizio Visconti: "There are some, especially soldiers, who, occupied in their business, to pass a little time at rest choose only one book, to which pleasant text they have recourse day and night, when they are tired from their affairs; and they remain so tied to that reading that they consider anything not contained in it to be not only new but even false."[III]

Yet it was precisely in the ambiguous and little cultivated terrain of these libraries that one can sometimes catch glimpses from their owners and users of difference and novelty with respect to the rigid reality of official cultural structures. Not by chance, in the research already mentioned on the libraries

III. Cited in G. Martellotti, "Linee di sviluppo," p. 74.

of Sicily, Henri Bresc encountered a multiplicity of interests and significant cultural openness only among the patrician book collections.[112] On the other hand, it was also through the mediation of the aristocratic libraries that the humanistic libraries would succeed in institutionalizing themselves in a fixed and definitive way during the second half of the Quattrocento, first in Italy and then in the rest of Europe, and in transforming themselves into one of the dominant models of reading and study.

Vernacular Books

Already in the Duecento, ecclesiastical authorities had been constrained to address the problem of the free and uncontrolled reading that was being done by some lay individuals. According to the Council of Toulouse of 1229, the laity could possess only a Psalter, a breviary, or a book of hours—not the Bible or Gospels. And they were "arctissime" prohibited to possess religious books translated in vernacular; the same prohibitions (with the second extended even to clerks) were reissued by the Council of Béziers of 1246.[113] In the same period, Roger Bacon addressed the problem of the knowledge, and of the science, of laymen, even though they lacked Latin, the technical language of learning.[114]

Free reading, done elsewhere than the places set aside for study and outside the schemes appropriate to the professions, was thus born first as the reading (in Latin) of individual clerks, that is, official intellectuals who were reading outside the official discipline of reading. It was then extended generally to the reading of the laity, that is, of nonclerks, of those who were not professionals of the pen and book, necessarily becoming reading in vernacular of the vernacular. Thus it was also, in parallel fashion, the heretical reading of heretical texts[115] which provoked the intervention of the ecclesiastical hierarchy and the deliberation of councils already mentioned.

But what most interests us for the purpose of research on the manuscript libraries of late medieval Italy is the moment when the push toward free reading was transformed into a generalized push for the organic conservation of book patrimonies intended and collected for such purposes, as well as the physical characteristics and repertory of the collections themselves. In the absence of general research on this issue, especially as regards Italy, one can

112. *Livre et société en Sicile*, pp. 95–104; C. de Frede, "Biblioteche e cultura di signori napoletani del '400," *Bibliothèque d'humanisme et renaissance* 25 (1963): 187–97.

113. See M. Richter, "Kommunikationsprobleme im lateinischen Mittelalter," *Historische Zeitschrift* 222 (1976): 43–80, esp. p. 51.

114. Ibid., p. 71.

115. For the emblematic case of Montaillou, see E. Le Roy Ladurie, *Montaillou. Village Occitan de 1294 à 1324* (Paris, 1975), pp. 345–76.

answer such inquiries only in a summary and hypothetical way. But it is probable that the beginning of a process of nonprofessional acculturation using books and affecting substantial quantities of lay urban dwellers can be located between the end of the thirteenth century and the beginning of the fourteenth; certainly, it is not by chance that the oldest evidence of laymen writing books in vernacular is found precisely in this period. And it is also probable that the phenomenon was manifested especially in the communes of north-central Italy and was linked directly to the economic, social, and political advances of merchants and artisans. In short, not only were books with vernacular texts copied and sold in the larger Italian cities of the Trecento and Quattrocento, but they were also preserved in private houses and constituted collections intended to be perpetuated over time. Such collections had particular characteristics that were rather different from those of the libraries discussed so far, public and private, to the extent of constituting an entirely new phenomenon both in standing apart from current practices of book conservation and in some particular elements whose archaisms seem to echo experiences reaching back before the ecclesiastical environment.

These were, to begin with, almost always small collections, from two or three pieces to, at most, twenty.[116] In Sicily the average number of books possessed by merchants was three;[117] the Florentine Filippo Quattrucci owned seven in 1387;[118] a certain Ugo Vecchietti had fourteen;[119] Giovanni Sercambi himself had twenty works in all;[120] twelve pieces formed the collection of Bardo de' Bardi, a Florentine merchant who died in Padua in 1441;[121] and the list could be continued.

But what were the texts that came to be read and preserved? On 3 June 1395 the great merchant and banker of Prato, Francesco Datini, wrote his confidant and friend, the notary ser Lapo Mazzei: "Chompero molti libri in volghare, per legierli quando mi rincrescierà i fatti della merchantantia, e per fare quello debo inverso Dio. Sono tutti libri che parlano di chose vertudiose, cioè sono tutti Vangeli, Epistole, il Detto e la Vita di tutt'i Santi e molte altre chose e buone" (I buy many books in *volgare*, to read them when

116. See. C. Bec, "I libri dei Fiorentini (1413–1608). Ipotesi e proposte," *Lettere italiane* 31 (1979): 4, 502–16 (esp. table II, p. 513); repr. in *Il Rinascimento, aspetti e problemi attuali. Atti del X Congresso dell'Associazione internazionale per gli studi di lingua e letteratura italians (Belgrado, 17–21 aprile 1979)* (Florence, 1982), pp. 215–30, esp. p. 225.

117. Bresc, *Livre et société en Sicile*, p. 85.

118. Bec, *Les marchands écrivains* (Paris and The Hague, 1967), p. 407.

119. Ibid., p. 412.

120. Ibid., pp. 412–13.

121. P. Sambin, "Libri in volgare posseduti da Bardo de' Bardi e custoditi da Palla Strozzi," *Italia medioevale e umanistica* 1 (1958): 371–73.

business affairs burden me, and to do what I owe to God. They are all book that speak of virtuous things, that is, they are all Gospels, epistles, the sayings and lives of all the saints, and many other good things).[122] In effect, the percentage of works of religious and devotional literature in the book collections based exclusively or predominantly on the vernacular was very high; often it represented half of the entire collection and might be nearly the entirety of numerically very limited collections.[123] Following such texts in interest and number were those belonging to narrative literature: romances, tales, and chronicles; among these, naturally, from the last quarter of the Trecento on there often appeared the *Decameron*.[124] Next were school texts, on the abacus, and technical texts; and translations of classical authors (Cicero, Boethius, Ovid, Livy, and so forth), the *Commedia* of Dante (whole or in part), lesser works by Boccaccio in the vernacular, works on medicine, rhetoric, and law, and texts in French.[125] One should be aware that this picture is mostly if not entirely based on Florentine and Tuscan evidence. Wider and deeper investigations of book collections of urban merchants and artisans of other zones of the peninsula might produce results that are at least partially different. Indeed, even though the data relative to fourteenth- and fifteenth-century Sicily apparently seem to confirm the data just summarized, this is probably due to the fact that the categories of case histories examined concern persons who immigrated there from other regions of Italy.[126]

Rather special means were used to keep such small book collections. Often they were found scattered in various places in the house; when the inventory was made of Sercambi's possessions, for example, books were found in the main room, the bedroom, the writing desk, and in a chest.[127] In this regard, the merchants could not but copy practices found in the noble aristocracy whose book collections were just as private and thus just as "domestic." But merchants, especially those of rank and importance, did have a writing desk in the house, and it was there that books mostly came to be kept, along with registers and documents relating to economic activities and to the real property of the master of the house. There was thus a physical mix between book

122. Cited by Bec, *Marchands écrivains*, pp. 393–94.

123. Ibid., p. 394.

124. See V. Branca, "Per il testo del *Decameron*, I. La prima diffusione del 'Decameron,'" *Studi di filologia italiana* 8 (1950): pp. 29–143; and Aldo Rossi's *Nota testuale* appended to his edition of the *Decameron* (Bologna, 1977), pp. 581–637.

125. Bec, *Marchands écrivains*, pp. 394–415; "I libri dei Fiorentini," p. 514 [1982 ed., p. 227].

126. Bresc, *Livre et société en Sicile*, table 2 (pp. 86–87) and p. 75.

127. Bec, *Marchands écrivains*, pp. 412–13.

and archival materials such as had been found in the ecclesiastical libraries of the early Middle Ages and the romanesque period, although it had since disappeared.

Vernacular books possessed by private readers were mostly made of paper rather than parchment, and poorly bound.[128] Such circumstances, together with the disorder and precariousness of their preservation, condemned them to rapid destruction, and owners in their annotations vainly recommended that they be kept far from lamps and children, those great enemies of books. The perishability of private *borghesi* collections was thus inherent in their physical nature, their disorganization, their numerically small size, and in the close ties linking volumes and persons that made them equivalent to simple domestic objects in both their use and ultimate fate.

Vernacular books did not enter the public libraries. Only with difficulty did they enter the normal market for books and they were not easily found at booksellers,[129] so they came to be copied and, especially, lent out by their owners. The circulation of books by loans between private individuals, for reading or copying, was not, indeed, a practice confined to humanists. For there is abundant evidence of circulation of vernacular books by interpersonal loans, and it documents the effort that *borghese* readers made to compensate by private means for the absence of public structures for study and reading open to book production in their language and to establish channels for communications and circulation of the works which they had an interest in reading.

The book collections of the monolingual townspeople of thirteenth- and fourteenth-century Italy were thus characterized by special modes of preserving and acquiring books. But there were also, certainly, special modes of using books and thus of reading. The readers of these collections were, indeed, readers of a few books, like the aristocrats against whom Petrarca directed his own critiques; and their reading was not for study but for leisure or devotion, so although it was attentive, it was not conditioned by the necessity for profound comprehension and critical understanding. Nevertheless, given the small number of texts that each reader had at his disposal, and the obvious difficulty of procuring others, this was necessarily a reading that was repeated many times, as is always the case with reading in social environments characterized by having few books. Consequently, it was a reading that was to some extent mnemonic, that permitted or could permit

---

128. Thus Lapo Mazzei in 1395: "Tutto dì vedete che si vergognano le genti di tenere loro libri, eziandio mondani, con triste coverte in casa" (letter to Margherita Datini, 13 Nov. 1395, in *Lettere di un notaro a un mercante del secolo XIV con altre lettere e documenti*, ed. C. Guasti [Florence, 1880], vol. 2, p. 181).

129. See above, at n. 52.

the acquisition of the text read at the structural and verbal level, and thus, by extension, a possibility of autonomous repetition of these texts in writing or orally: thus we see the frequent citation of vernacular authors from memory (especially, but not only, Dante) in spontaneous texts of Italian merchants and businessmen of the fourteenth and fifteenth centuries. Still more relevant is the singular phenomenon of the interpolations and transformations to which vernacular texts were subjected during the work of copying, in which the mnemonic library of the writer naturally intervened, that library including texts that were analogous or similar and therefore easily assimilable to the ones which they were copying.

The "State" Libraries

Around 1440, when Cosimo de' Medici wanted to "ordinare la libreria di Santo Marco," he turned to Tommaso Parentucelli (the future Pope Nicholas V) so that "gli piacessi fargli una nota come aveva a stare una libreria," that is, a real canon of the subjects, authors, and works that the library being established should contain.[130] And when, in 1456, Cosimo wanted to found the new library of the Badia of Fiesole, he turned to the most capable Florentine bookseller of the time, the famous Vespasiano da Bisticci, commissioning him to make two hundred books containing the very texts of that canon; in twenty-two months, thanks to the efforts of forty-five copyists, the library was in place.[131]

Bracketing the middle of the fifteenth century, therefore, two libraries came into being in Florence at Cosimo de' Medici's initiative that in several ways were prototypes of an institutional model that would become common and dominant in Italy during the last half of the century. We can call this institution the "state library," not in the strict legal (and modern) sense but rather in a symbolic and representative sense, for there is no doubt that the library institutions of humanist stamp in many cases ended up constituting a distinctive and characterizing element, even if a minor one, of the new signorial state then taking shape. This new form of library was rooted in a composite terrain, with more than one model influencing its process of formation. On one side, certainly, was the revolutionary novelty of the classicist repertory of triumphant humanism; on the other was the prestigious heritage of the domestic book collections of the signorial aristocracy. But the decisive elements for its definitive establishment as an instrument of the new state

---

130. Vespasiano da Bisticci, *Le vite,* ed. A. Greco (Florence, 1970–76), vol. 1, pp. 46–47; the text of the "canon" is in G. Sforza, *La patria, la famiglia a la giovinezza di papa Niccolò V. Ricerche storiche* (Lucca, 1884), pp. 359–81.

131. Bisticci, *Vite,* vol. 2, pp. 183–89.

formations were both the influence exercised by the tradition of religious libraries typical of official culture, and the indispensable and determining presence of the new book industry.

In the mid-Quattrocento, the libraries of the great religious institutions continued to play a primary role in the preservation and diffusion of the official cultural patrimony in Italy and in Europe, functioning as great store-houses of knowledge that were conveniently open to a varied public and sufficiently flexible in the various articulations of the repertory. In 1481, the library of San Francesco at Siena, with its nearly 1,340 volumes and its substantially traditional structure, was still the richest and probably most frequented in the city;[132] at Genoa, between 1386 and the end of the Quat-trocento, the library of the cathedral of San Lorenzo, although modest in its book patrimony, substantially modified its repertory by adding a notable number of classics that had been lacking before and the works of fourteenth- and fifteenth-century humanists.[133] And it was precisely in Quattrocento Italy that the libraries of the reformed religious orders, recently founded in some of the larger cities of the peninsula according to the the old double scheme of the consultation and "secret" library, naturally seemed to be the physical-ideological model of the library. The Dominican library of San Marco of Florence, which Michelozzo had designed and Cosimo stocked with books, recast the traditional structure of an oblong hall in modern architectonic forms by dividing it into three aisles according to the model of the basilica, thus offering a model to the new libraries of the century.[134]

Looking at this from another angle, Pearl Kibre has already stressed the substantial continuity between the book patrimony of the larger fifteenth-century libraries and those of religious collections of the preceding centuries.[135] Parentucelli's canon serves both to confirm this continuity at the level of the repertory and to mark its definitive restoration, arrived at by overcoming the doubts that had seen two different contrasting schemes at the ideological-cultural level: one mostly or entirely religious and monolingual, the other mostly or entirely classicist and bilingual. His canon, indeed, was explicitly constituted of authors and works of medieval culture—from the Bible

132. K. W. Humphreys, *The Library of the Franciscans of Siena in the Late Fifteenth Century* (Amsterdam, 1978).

133. G. Pistarino, "Libri e cultura nella cattedrale di Genova tra Medioevo e Rinascimento," *Archivio della Società Ligure di Storia Patria*, n.s. 2 (1961): 1–117, esp. 27–28.

134. See J. F. O'Gorman, *The Architecture of the Monastic Library in Italy, 1300–1600* (New York, 1972), pp. 19–29.

135. P. Kibre, "The Intellectual Interests Reflected in Libraries of the Fourteenth and Fifteenth Centuries," *Journal of the History of Ideas* 7 (1946): 257–97.

to patristic literature, from scholastic literature (present to an overwhelming extent) to a few basic classics. But he concluded with the warning: "De studiis autem humanitatis, quantum ad grammaticam, rhetoricam, historiam et poeticam spectat, ac moralem, quae auctoritate digna sunt, vobis credo esse notissima. Ego tamen, si bibliothecam conditurus essem, cum omnia a me haberi non posset, vellem ista praecipue non deesse." (Of humanistic studies, as regards grammar, rhetoric, history, poetry, and morals, I think that you know quite well everything worthy of authority; for if I am to found a library, even if I cannot have everything, I would wish that these principal works not be missing.)[136] There was thus, at least in Parentucelli's intentions, some expression of a desire to integrate and combine canons rather than to insist on an absolute one. In practice, however, by the very arrangement of the presentation and by the detailed listing of traditional knowledge, he ended up constituting an implicit program of ideological dominance in and of itself favoring the scholastic/university book repertory—and by extension the culture—that belonged to the two preceding centuries.

In expressing such a precise arrangement of selections and exclusions, Parentucelli's canon naturally took into account the demands and real limits of contemporary book production, and also the market concerns and cultural orientation of his greater protagonists, whether they were entrepreneurs or patrons. When Vespasiano da Bisticci, the great dealer of books for the largest libraries of the century, described the reading attitudes of rulers and aristocrats in his *Vite,* he emphasized first of all their attachment to the Bible and its commentaries, and to religious and patristic literature;[137] he thus provides both an implicit confirmation of the canon adopted by Cosimo and precise testimony about the literary tastes of the patrons of the richest (and humanistically oriented) libraries of the time. On the other hand, a book industry such as that in Florence could not subsist by producing only works of the new culture. A canon such as Parentucelli's permitted book producers a broader selection, less taxing executions, secure and continuous supplies of exemplars, conspicuous orders—in short, a broad and ample market. It was certainly not by chance that it fell to Vespasiano da Bisticci, who himself was a man of vernacular and mercantile culture, and to the Florentine book industry generally to furnish volumes according to Parentucelli's scheme for the libraries desired by Cosimo and for a good part of the other libraries, in and outside Italy, that were founded in the second half of the century. Among these, the Malatestiana Library of Cesena, completed in 1452, stands

136. See Sforza, *Patria,* p. 380.

137. For Cosimo de' Medici, *Vite,* vol. 2, p. 195; for Alfonse of Aragon, vol. 1, pp. 84–85, 110–11; for Federico da Montefeltro, vol. 1, pp. 380–82.

36. Malatestiana Library of Cesena (photo: Alinari)

out for having the good fortune to survive intact to our time (fig. 36); it was incorporated by the principal lord of the local monastery of Friars Minor and built in basilical form according to the architectonic scheme of San Marco. It was a "state library" in the assiduous attention given it by the lord, in the public use for which it was intended, and in the entrusting of its supervision to municipal authorities, although the direct care remained in the hands of the friars of the convent; it was a library that was entirely local, because it was furnished with an endowment of newly made books almost exclusively executed on the spot by a chosen group of scribes and illuminators.[138] Belonging to the same type, apparently, were Alessandro Sforza's library at Pesaro, arranged according to Parentucelli's canon with "both sacred and courtly books," which was later destroyed in 1512,[139] and what remains of the library of the Malatesta "Temple" in Rimini, founded in 1440

138. A. Campana, "Origine, formazione e vicende della Malatestiana," *Accademie e biblioteche d'Italia* 21 (1953): 3–16.
139. Bisticci, *Vite*, vol. 1, pp. 422–23.

and similarly dispersed, but which in the Cinquecento still numbered almost 300 pieces following its enrichment by the legacy of Roberto Valturio in 1475.[140]

According to Vespasiano da Bisticci, however, only Federico da Montefeltro "had the spirit to do what no one is known to have done for more than a thousand years, to have had made the most worthy library that had been made since that time."[141] The Urbino library of the Montefeltro was probably the princely library of the Quattrocento that most completely developed the characteristics of the "state library," so much as to be the only one in Vespasiano's opinion to deserve the comparison with antiquity. To begin with, it was based on Parentucelli's canon; it was entirely new, that is, made of books produced for it (and for the most part provided by Florentine shops); it was supervised in the least detail and preserved only magnificently bound books of splendid appearance; it was open to public use by scholars, eminent men, and courtiers; it was managed by specialized personnel; and there existed alongside it, in the same location of the ducal palace, another collection of less valuable books, printed or in paper, that remedied the faults of the first collection, which comprised only books for display.[142]

Also to some extent following the model of state library were the great Sforza library of Pavia, which was the heir of the Visconti library and later emigrated to Blois,[143] and the Aragonese library of Naples, created by Alfonso V of Aragon and then developed by his son Ferdinand.[144] Both libraries were essentially courtly, with varying riches due to acquisition over a long period of time; both were formed essentially of new books executed on commission and provided by specialized personnel; and both were instruments of culture for the circle of scholars around the lord, or ruler, for his glory and that of his dynasty.

But at the beginning of the last quarter of the century, the best model of a collection of books that was organically both the ideological mirror and symbolic portrait of a power supreme in both temporal and spiritual cases

140. G. Mazzatinti, "La biblioteca di S. Francesco (Tempio Malatestiano) in Rimini," in *Scritti vari di filologia [dedicati a Ernesto Monaci]* (Rome, 1901), pp. 345–52.

141. Bisticci, *Vite*, vol. 1, pp. 386–99 (the cited passage is on p. 386).

142. See L. Michelini Tocci, "Agapito, bibliotecario 'docto, acorto et diligente' della biblioteca urbinate alla fine del Quattrocento," in *Collectanea Vaticana in honorem Anselmi M. Card. Albareda . . .* , vol. 2 (Città del Vaticano, 1962), pp. 245–80.

143. See Pellegrin, *Bibliothèque des Visconti et des Sforza*.

144. See the monumental work of T. de Marinis, *La biblioteca napoletana dei re d'Aragona*, vols. 1–4 (Milan, 1952–57); *Supplemento* (Verona, 1969); and A. Petrucci, "Biblioteche, libri, scritture nella Napoli aragonese," in G. Cavallo, ed., *Le biblioteche nel mondo antico e medievale* (Bari, 1988), pp. 187–202.

was the library that Sixtus IV founded on 15 June 1475 and that by 1481 Platina had arranged in four large rooms of the Vatican palace.[145] The initial collection of the new library consisted of almost a thousand codices collected previously by Nicholas V, who himself had intended, as Vespasiano da Bisticci affirmed, "to make a library in Saint Peter's for common use of all the court of Rome."[146] The project of Parentucelli was not realized. But that of Della Rovere did succeed in giving life to a solidly stable institution, with its own location, personnel, and collection. The pontiff in his bull of foundation, in addition to enumerating the provisions he had made, both established the public character of the new institution—which would be open to the "sectatores liberalium artium" and directed toward the "commodum et honorem" of the scholars and men of letters—and specified what José Ruysschaert has happily termed an "ecclesiastical purpose" inserted in "a broadly humanist context":[147] the fact that the library was constituted for the dignity of the Church militant and for the increase of the Catholic faith. The ecclesiastical character of the initiative was made more evident by the book patrimony housed in the library, which in large part followed after Parentucelli's repertory and, in a bilingual scheme, gave predominant weight to religious literature and to the ecclesiastical tradition.

Despite this fact (or even because of it?), the library of Sixtus IV succeeded in establishing itself as the greatest model of public book institutions of the time. Rich in works (it numbered 3,500 pieces in 1481), grandiose in its disposition in multiple places (the Latin library, Greek library, secret library, pontifical library), decorated with frescoes that extolled papal munificence or the *auctoritates* of the Church, managed in every detail of equipment and financing, the Sistine library was also governed with enlightened liberality, as is shown by the registers of its loans from the first year.[148] The ideological and cultural orientation exemplified in the repertory, the mechanisms of organization for reading and study, and the modes by which the public was linked with the ancient and modern book patrimony on which the collection was based, all appeared as unsurpassable models not only of ecclesiastical libraries but also of all public libraries. At the close of the century of hu-

145. See E. Müntz, *Les arts à la cour des Papes pendant le XVe et le XVIe siècle*, vol. 3 (Paris, 1882), pp. 117–35; J. W. Clark, "On the Vatican Library of Sixtus IV," extract from *Proceedings of the Cambridge Antiquarian Society* 1898–99; idem, "Care of Books," pp. 202–27; J. Ruysschaert, "Sixte IV, fondateur de la Bibliothèque Vaticane. 15 juin 1475," *Archivum historiae pontificiae* 7 (1969): 513–24 (text of the foundation bull is edited on pp. 523–24); and J. Bignami-Odier, *La bibliothèque Vaticane de Sixte IV à Pie XI* (Città del Vaticano, 1973), pp. 20–25.

146. *Vite*, vol. 1, p. 65.

147. "Sixte IV," p. 518.

148. M. Bertola, ed., *I due primi registri di prestito della Biblioteca Apostolica Vaticana* (Città del Vaticano, 1942).

manism, they set forth in an exemplary way the unchallengeable hegemony the Church held over the instruments for the formation and diffusion of written culture.

From the Library to the Text

In 1494, in the space of little more than a month and a half (specifically, between 29 September and 17 November), Agnolo Poliziano and Giovanni Pico della Mirandola died at Florence, thus beginning the dispersion of two book collections that, for opposite reasons, wonderfully represent the phase when the private library underwent its transition from the medieval to the modern model, from the treasury of manuscript codices to the collection of printed books.

The library of Giovanni Pico was one of the largest private libraries of his time, numbering 1,190 volumes, of which 489 were printed.[149] But its uniqueness did not consist so much in the quantity of pieces as in the overall variety of interests represented in the repertory and reflected in the multiplicity of languages and cultures represented. Although the volumes of Latin texts obviously constituted an absolute majority of the total, there was also a notable representation of Greek texts (157), a significant presence of 70 Hebrew texts, 7 Arabic codices, and some Aramaic manuscripts; in comparison, there were few volumes in vernacular Italian (among which were Dante, Cecco d'Ascoli, Jacopo da Varazze) or in French. In addition to the owner's particular interests in philosophy and occult and natural sciences, Pearl Kibre has already noted that the collection of Latin texts represented a fairly complete picture of the classical literary and humanistic repertory, and also of the great late medieval scholastic tradition.[150]

Pico's aspiration was evidently to possess a total library, a complete thesaurus of written culture within the wide range for which he is known. And it was certainly not by chance that inventories of the library of Sixtus IV and the Montefeltro library of Urbino—two of the larger "state libraries" of contemporary Italy—were found among his books. According to an anecdote told by Pietro Crinito, one day when Pico was being praised by Poliziano and others for his brilliance and his learning, he maintained that his natural endowments were not exalted so much as intense study and what he called "nostram supellectilem," the treasures of books collected; and Crinito described the library as rich, exceptionally equipped, and provided with an abundance of books of every kind.[151]

---

149. Pearl Kibre, *The Library of Pico della Mirandola* (New York, 1936).
150. Ibid., p. 112.
151. P. Crinito, *De honesta disciplina*, ed. C. Angeleri (Rome, 1955), p. 84.

It seems, therefore, that for Pico acquiring knowledge could and should occur by only one means—the book—and by only one method—reading; thus his vision of the formative process eliminated in practice both oral elements, which had constituted such an important part of cultured medieval education, and also the writing which had integrated orality and reading within the sphere of that education. Pico's overall vision of written culture, formed in the obsessive connection with his library, thus ended up advancing new terms for the modes of reading themselves and for the connection between reader and book; moreover, these modes and connections were rather freer and more complex than those hypothesized by the old scheme that was still alive in the contemporary reality of the public library with chained books. Pico's modes and connections were those of a new cultural reality that had changed rapidly and profoundly as a result of the bursting out of the printed book, its rapid diffusion at the private level, and its quantitatively invasive reality.

Agnolo Poliziano was not only an admirer and faithful friend of Giovanni Pico but also an assiduous user of his library. The connections between the two friends were close and frequent, although Pico felt keenly Poliziano's literary professionalism, which he contrasted, in an outburst not to be taken as false modesty, to his own supposed dilettantism.[152] But while Pico's rich library, in its imposing organicity, could seem like the library of a professional of culture, Poliziano's private library had a consistency and outward appearance that was entirely different. Thus, as Augusto Campana wrote twenty years ago: "Poliziano's library, if we mean the books he actually owned, could seem rather small and miserable in comparison to the great aristocratic and monastic collections of his time and even in comparison with those of some colleagues who were better provided or who lived lives not as short and as burnt out as his. And it certainly was limited in the number of volumes, in an age that as a result of the book revolution produced by printing began to see rich private collections; and it was a library that was also poor in its exterior appearance." It was, in short, a "small and poor library,"[153] of which, in the wake of the dispersion it experienced, fewer than 60 pieces survive today, including codices, incunabula, autographs of his own works, and *zibaldoni* for study.[154]

Much more marked, to modern eyes, is the disparity between the small

152. G. Pico della Mirandola, letter to Agnolo Poliziano, in Poliziano, *Opera omnia* (Venice, 1498), fol. a6v.

153. A. Campana, "Contributi alla biblioteca del Poliziano," in *Il Poliziano e il suo tempo. Atti del IV Congresso internazionale di studi sul Rinascimento (Firenze, 23–26 settembre 1954)* (Florence, 1957), pp. 174–75.

154. Thus according to I. Maier, *Les manuscrits d'Ange Politien. Catalogue descriptif* (Geneva, 1965).

book collection of the literary genius and the massive quantity of his reading, out of which, by assiduous discipline, he gave substance to his "eruditio interior atque politior" (interior and polished learning), in the expression of Filippo Beroaldo.[155] This was a disparity filled in by work habits undertaken no longer in the closed space of a professionally equipped study but in the Florentine public libraries, in the private libraries of the Medici and of his friend Pico, in the libraries of Rome and elsewhere in Italy,[156] and by means of loans conceded generously and amply. The disparity and habits find a point of contact, as well as their very functionality, in the formal philology of Poliziano, which led him naturally to privilege the verbal connection with the text rather than with the physical book, and to consider the use of a codex or a printed book on the same level in part because he was one of the few in his time who were able to collate manuscript evidence, even if with some approximation (fig. 37). The disparity and habits were typical of the way poor scholars work in any age, but in the experiences of Poliziano they must also take on the appearance of a personal refusal to adopt some of the ritual elements of the humanistic and professional role, for which the possession of many books was (and is) an essentially symbolic component; and he must have also felt again that sense of tragic precariousness that burdened every moment of his brief life and that evidently conditioned even his modes of study and reading.[157]

For these were certainly understood by the Medicean philologist in an entirely hedonistic perspective on the facts of his life, in which reading was located alongside and almost as a consequence or premise of other and different attitudes of body and mind: thus he himself explained, in a letter in vernacular written to Clarice de' Medici on 8 April 1476: "Iersera giunti a San Miniato, cominciamo a leggere un poco di santo Agostino. E questa lezione risolvessi infine nel musicare e in iscorgere e dirozare un certo modello di ballerino che è qua." (Yesterday evening we began to read a little Saint Augustine. And at the end this reading turned into playing music and jumping up and polishing a certain model of dancing practiced here.)[158] Comparing citations such as these with data and impressions drawn from Poli-

---

155. Letter in Poliziano, *Opera omnia*, fol. b5v.

156. See V. Branca and M. Pastore Stocchi, "La Biblioteca Vaticana nella seconda Centuria dei Miscellanea di Angelo Poliziano," in *Mélanges Eugène Tisserant*, vol. 6, pt. 1: *Bibliothèque Vaticane* (Città del Vaticano, 1964), pp. 141–59 (repr. in V. Branca, *Poliziano* [Turin, 1983], pp. 91–107); and A. Poliziano, *Miscellanea centuria secunda*, ed. V. Branca and M. Pastore Stocchi (Florence, 1972), pp. 12–16.

157. The most persuasive reconstruction of the figure of Poliziano in this perspective is by C. Mutini, *Interpretazione del Poliziano* (Rome, 1972).

158. Letter in A. Poliziano, *Prose volgari inedite e poesie latine e greche edite e inedite*, ed. I. Del Lungo (Florence, 1867), p. 47; and in C. Mutini, *La cultura a Firenze al tempo di Lorenzo il Magnifico* (Bologna, 1970), p. 75.

37. An example of Poliziano's notes. Misc. Centuria II, cap. 7. Venezia, Bib. della Fondazione Giorgio Cini, MS 1, fol. 9v

ziano's activities as a scholar and man, which are still vivid in his autographs, letters, and works, one can affirm that through his experience of global reading, beyond any limits of ideology, ritual constrictions, and fixed rules, he found new and freer connections with the written text as well as a new constitution for the operation of reading, going beyond the old modes of book acculturation to deny by his actions the symbolic value of possessing books.

It would certainly be excessive to draw conclusions of a general character from two personal situations such as those of Pico and Poliziano, both of whom, moreover, belonged to the same period and the same cultural environment. But there is no doubt that, in Italy of that time, these were two extreme situations that, parallel to the rise of printing, had the merit of advancing entirely new kinds of relationships between books and readers, and of refuting, and surpassing, fixed ideological or linguistic canons of knowledge such as the dominant canon of Parentucelli—a canon, one can say here in passing, that no longer corresponded to the developmental potentials of the new means of production.

In reality, toward the end of the Quattrocento, more general factors of renewal converged to make vernacular texts eligible for the right to long-term preservation and consecration in libraries, a right that until now had been denied. In addition to the exemplarity of the experiences of a Pico or a Poliziano, which anticipated future developments and progress, there was also and especially the pressure of a nascent publishing industry in search of new markets and the beginning of an unstoppable process of canonization of the written Italian language. The effect of such tendencies on the practice and theory of book conservation is noticeable only later; but it cannot be denied that the beginning of the modification that made the libraries of the Cinquecento profoundly different from those of the century before is to be located in the few years comprising the experiences of Pico and Poliziano, and of Manuzio and Bembo—years that saw the book itself change even before the places where books were preserved.

10

THE ILLUSION OF
AUTHENTIC HISTORY:
DOCUMENTARY EVIDENCE

A FULL DISCUSSION OF THE THEME entrusted to me by the organizers of this conference would require more than my fair allotment of time and a competence wider than I possess; thus I have decided to limit my discourse to a series of arguments mainly relating to written documentation in the early and later Middle Ages, which I will address essentially by examples and citation. It is my hope that this approach does not result in a discourse that is too loose or inconsequential. But my personal experience is that of a historian of writing and documents; and I will try to confront the problems that lie at the base of the theme I am addressing, using the methodology and formal-analytical instruments that belong to diplomatists: an attentiveness to the mechanisms by which documents were produced and to the modes and moments when documents were written that promises in some way to help us understand, at least partially, the real nature of some of these sources and their real value as a potential source of information.

In my opinion, it is useful to begin by quickly examining, through examples, some of the ways in which the historiography of this century and the last has addressed and resolved the problem of its relationship with written documents that are properly diplomatic in nature. These are ways that have often reflected, and still do, some of the different attitudes that historians arrived at in their colloquies with documentary sources, which

Originally published as "L'illusione della storia autentica: Le testimonianze documentarie," in *L'insegnamento della storia e i materiali del lavoro storiografico*, Società degli Storici Italiani, *Atti* 3 (Messina, 1984), pp. 73–88.

from being at first almost worshipped as absolute truth, then had their nature dissected and investigated and eventually saw their function as privileged bearers of data actually denied.

I would begin with one of the first masters of Italian diplomatics: archivist, diplomatist, and paleographer Cesare Paoli. In 1899, during the twenty-year period that, according to Ernesto Sestan, "included the most prestigious accomplishments in Italian historical erudition,"[1] Paoli defined the document as "written evidence of a deed of juridical nature, compiled observing certain specific forms which were intended to establish its trustworthiness and status as legal proof."[2] This is a rigorous and essential definition that is still authoritative today,[3] but one that makes the mistake of reducing the always projecting and variegated density of documentary sources to the pure and simple connection with the juridical event. It is not therefore surprising that in Paoli's wake, a diplomatist as informed as Luigi Schiaparelli could declare in 1909 that documents "are direct evidence of the social-economic life of an age, coming to us in their original garb. They are based on law, in which they originate. They are living fragments of the history of that law. . . . Documents do not narrate historical facts, they are themselves the written, historical-juridical deed . . . ; they are primary historical sources."[4] This definition, in which are reflected not only the historical methodology of an age that was entirely bent on the conquest of "positive truth" but also its most authentic cultural ideology, has left a profound and enduring mark on how the historiography of this century has dealt with its relationship with written documentation.

It might seem unfair to this definition, which is so touching in its disarmingly organic ingenuousness, to juxtapose it by a leap of many decades with the "ambiguous praise of the contract" (meant in a rather encompassing sense that passes over written expression) which a great semiologist of our age, Roland Barthes, offers in speaking of himself: "The first images that he had of the contract (agreement) is, all things considered, objective: the sign, the language, the narration, and the society all function by contract; but since this contract is often masked, the critical operation consists of deciphering the embarrassment of reasons, alibis, and appearances—in short, of

---

1. E. Sestan, "L'erudizione storica in Italia," in *Cinquant'anni di vita intellettuale italiana, 1896–1946*, vol. 2 (Naples, 1950), p. 445.

2. C. Paoli, *Programma scolastico di paleografia latina e di diplomatica*, vol. 3 (Florence, 1899), p. 18.

3. It is quoted by A. Pratesi as "the most exact definition of the document in a diplomatic sense" in *Genesi e forme del documento medievale* (Rome, 1979), p. 8.

4. L. Schiaparelli, *Diplomatica e storia* (Florence, 1909), p. 7; repr. in his *Note di diplomatica (1896–1934)*, ed. A. Pratesi (Turin, 1972), p. 101.

everything that is socially *natural,* to render manifest the regulated exchange on which the semantic path and collective life is based. . . ."[5]

What has changed? Everything, or nearly: in the first place, the perspective of the observer with respect to the object; and then the object itself in its manifestations, and the questions that we ask as we deal with it and the context in which it is situated and from which it issued. From the discourse on the univocal connection between written evidence and juridical event, one thus arrives through a natural evolution of mentality and taste at the point of preferring a connection with the sources that is both more tangential and deeper, placing emphasis on the linguistic masquerade, the semantic shell, appearance, sign, and interpretative voice that is the natural attribute of any text. Hence, in this same perspective, a historian of collective mentalities like Jacques Le Goff, writing in the prestigious Einaudi *Enciclopedia* (at the entry "Documento/monumento"), ends up announcing: "The document is a monument. It is the result of a complete effort of historical societies to impose on the future . . . a given image of themselves. As an extreme position, there does not exist a document-truth, for every document is a lie. It is incumbent on the historian not to be naive."[6] These remarks thus completely destroy the position exemplified by the quotations from Paoli and Schiaparelli: from the document-as-truth, one thus comes to prefigure the document-as-lie.

On an entirely different historiographical field, a rather finely articulated position in regard to the correct connection with documentary sources is represented today by the perceptive contributions of Mario Liverani, an Italian historian of the ancient Near East. His attentive examination of authentic, written documentation of the earliest civilizations has led him to state: "The 'true thing,' for now, is undoubtedly the text (or the refiguration, or in any case the documentary datum); next comes the ideological system of which this text is an expression; and finally, across these filters, one can get to the factual support that in itself one must realistically consider to be lost forever. We do not study physical acts . . . but documents that are *word* acts of an ideological *language* whose reconstruction should be our preliminary and preeminent task, if not perhaps our only one."[7] This is a conclusion that every diplomatist should claim as a program for his or her own discipline, and that every historian who regularly studies documentary sources can only feel to be profoundly just.

Indeed, it is not by chance that the most recent approaches within the

5. *Barthes di Roland Barthes* (Turin, 1980), pp. 69–70.

6. *Enciclopedia Einaudi* (Turin, 1978), vol. 5, pp. 38–48.

7. These are the closing words of an article entitled "Dono, tributo, commercio: Ideologia dello scambio nella tarda età del bronzo," *Annali dell'Istituto Italiano di Numismatica* 26 (1979): 9–28.

discipline of diplomatics—which is institutionally the discipline closest to the problematic we have been discussing—have not been directed at investigating the external and internal appearance of the document, understood as a unitary and univocal evidence-text that thus would be directly linkable to the event. Rather, they have addressed what might be called the process of documentation, that is, a reality that can be broken down into several temporal and textual phases, only at the end of which does the documentary text as we mean it come to be constituted. This is a complex reality, always influenced by varying moments, to whose achievement different persons and environments make contributions: it is a reality made of obligatory formalities, of more or less long times of execution, and "administrative" and "propagandistic" deformations that are more or less conscious and vast.[8] In short, rather than being evidence of a preceding or contemporary juridical-historical event, which is to some extent external to it, the document is first and foremost evidence of a process entirely internal to its own making. And only the reconstruction of the process of documentation, of its articulations and reasons, can permit us again to consider, with both greater insight and greater humility than before, the complex relationship between written document and the event that from time to time gave (or should have given) impulse to the process of documentation: what we call, in the language of diplomatics, the connection between action and documentation.

In truth, this was a problem, and a relationship, recognized even by those in the Middle Ages who made documents and who participated in the process of documentation: the drafters, the chancery dictators and writers, and the notaries. Their preoccupation with affirming the validity of written evidence in comparison with the transience of oral evidence emerges especially in the numerous preambles of Italian private and semipublic documents from the tenth to eleventh centuries and later. With regard to the value and importance of this practice, Francesco Calasso wrote in 1959 that "it would be an error to look with indifference on this formulaic aspect of the legal document, given the lamentable scarcity of instructional sources from that epoch [the early Middle Ages] . . . ; it is in those lines, where the notary displays his own learning and, sometimes, even his literary fancies . . . that many times he uses words or expressions that reveal movements or directions of juridical awareness for which one searches in vain in the parts describing the legal structures."[9]

Early medieval juridical awareness, for the period before such formulas appear, had already expressed itself on the problem of the value of written

8. Ibid., pp. 18, 19.
9. F. Calasso, *Il negozio giuridico* (Milan, 1959), p. 176.

documentary evidence. Its usefulness was asserted in some of the most important formularies of the period—Marculf's formulary, [10] the formulary of Tours, [11] and a visigothic formulary[12]—and it appears in full relief in Lombard legislation from Rothari onward.[13] This theme also echoes (to offer a first example) in a Sabine document of May 747, where, with some rhetorical embellishment, it was declared that when the parties come together "bono ordine," it was necessary to confirm the fact "scripture testimonio" so that disputes would not arise in the future, when the length of days and space of years had caused forgetfulness.[14] But in none of these sources does there appear a full articulation of a motive that particularly characterizes some Italian *arenghe* from the tenth to eleventh centuries and later: the reference to the memory of human events that live only in writing and that are contrasted with the *oblivio* inexorably induced by the passing of time. This is a broadly diffused motif, whose evolution and modifications in time permit us to identify an important change in the collective mentality regarding the relationship between documentation and juridical action, or between authenticated text and event, that occurred concomitantly with other, deeper changes in contemporary documentary practices and juridical culture.[15]

A quick survey, made without any pretense of completeness on a limited number of early medieval document collections of central and southern Italy, reveals a situation that can be schematically summarized in the following terms:

1. In territories under Roman law—specifically at Ravenna, beginning in 967 and lasting at least until around 1030—a recurrent formula appears in the prologues of *placita* in which the drafter, after having revealed that "ea que gesta esse videntur" cannot be retained in human memory because of the inexorable passing of time, affirms the usefulness ("cautum" or "equum est") of fixing events by the "vincolo scripture";[16] in 1015, a *tabellio* of Ferrara provided a rhetorical variant that was rather rich in new elements, most notably a

10. See *Marculfi Formulae*, in *MGH*, *Legum sectio V, Formulae merowingici et karolini aevi* (Hannover, 1886), pp. 84, 89.

11. Ibid., p. 144, n. 17.

12. Ibid., p. 581, n. 12.

13. See Calasso, *Negozio*, pp. 72–73.

14. *Il Regesto di Farfa di Gregorio di Catino*, ed. I. Giorgi and U. Balzani, vol. 2 (Rome, 1879), n. XXXII, pp. 38–39.

15. A hint in A. Bartoli Langeli, "A proposito di storia del notariato italiano," in *Il pensiero politico* 10 (1977): 103.

16. C. Manaresi, ed., *I placiti del Regnum Italiae*, 3 vols. (Rome, 1957–60), nn. 155, 204, 227, 260, 263, 264, 279, 286, 313, 331.

reference to an unspecified "lex" requiring that land transactions be recorded.[17]

2. Analogous concepts were expressed by *scriniarii* from 1002 until around 1030 in documents drafted in Sabine and Roman territories and in Rome itself; these were ample formulas, in which the running of time and the fallacies of mind and human memory were always contrasted with the firmness of writing, which guarantees that new conflicts and litigation would not arise in the future;[18] there is also one case (from 1013) where reference is made to a "lex" that is not otherwise specified[19]; at Fondi, in 1028, a "sacer scriba" recalled ecclesiastical authority and the "lex romana" as the basis for choosing written documentation.[20]

3. Still in Lazio in the first half of the eleventh century, notaries and *tabellioni* used rather simpler and more schematic formulations to express the analogous concepts.[21]

4. Later, at the beginning of the twelfth century, lay notaries in Tuscan territories adopted analogous formulas that underlined the necessity of written documentation without adding further elements.[22]

5. Calasso believed that such preambles, based on a specific emphasis of the role of writing, were also intended to exalt the function of the drafters;[23] but it is likely that in the rhetorical contrast between "memoria" and "oblivio" and in the stress on the materiality of graphic evidence ("exarate littere"; "paginarum series scripturarum") these preambles actually show traces of cultural motives derived from the Church and from a generically sacral and symbolic conception of writing.

6. With the mid- and, especially, the late twelfth century, preambles exalting the function of writing were again adopted by the local *scriniarii* in Rome and in Roman territories, with the addition of

17. Ibid., n. 290: "Omne igitur litis negotium, quod coram presentia aliquo magistratu vel preside sive iudicum legaliter inter utrasque partes fuerit de rebus immobilibus diffinitum, iubet lex illud tabularium litterarum industria adnotari, ne propter vergentia tempororum oblivioni tradatur et ad novam iurgiam devolvatur, sed ratum et firmum et stabile permaneat in perpetuum."

18. There are frequent appearances of this formula in the *Regesto di Farfa*; for example (but not exhaustively), nn. 446, 470, 502, 504, 628, 647, 650; see also L. M. Hartmann and M. Merores, *Ecclesiae S. Mariae in Via Lata tabularium*, vol. 1 (Vienna, 1895), n. LIV.

19. *Regesto di Farfa*, n. 637.

20. *Regii Neapolitani Archivi monumenta*, vol. 4 (Naples, 1854), n. 338.

21. *Regesto di Farfa*, nn. 476, 477, 609; Hartmann and Merores, *Ecclesiae*, vol. 1, n. XLVIII.

22. See L. Mosiici, "Le arenghe nei documenti privati pistoiesi (secoli VIII–XII)," *Bullettino storico pistoiese* 78 (1976): 26–28.

23. *Negozio*, pp. 94–96, 174–80.

eminently juridical concepts of the public act and of writing executed in public;[24] such concepts also appear elsewhere, as at Pistoia in 1186.[25]

7. In the same Roman environment, the concept of memory comes to be flanked in 1188 by that of "veritas";[26] in the same period, it also appears in the eloquent subscription of a notary in the Marches: "cartulas indago—verumque medullitus ago."[27]

8. The Latin charters of Calabrian abbeys published by Pratesi in 1958 rather interestingly summarize the evolution just traced as reflected by an eccentric and thus backward environment; there, indeed, an ecclesiastical writer in 1218 could still exhume the contrast between "oblivio" and "memoria" in an ample, rhetorically involuted preamble;[28] but a little later, from 1228 and after, lay notaries of Petilia Policastro, Belcastro, and Mesoraca acquired the concept of "instrumentum publicum," to which they joined that of "veritas."[29]

This change from preambles emphasizing *oblivio-memoria* to those stressing *publicitas-veritas* (reducing to its essentials the terms of the evolution that I believe that we have been able to identify) cannot be explained simply as a different stance adopted by documentary rhetoric or by making a generic reference to the dominant influence of the juridical renaissance, which in itself would have produced meaningful expressions and lucid formulations. To grasp the real sense of the shift, it is helpful to ask what happened to documentary practices and to the status of their principal practitioners in Italy between the mid-tenth century and the first half of the thirteenth. In fact, the period from the second half of the eleventh to the early thirteenth century was one that saw a decisive, progressive growth in the production of both private and public written documentation, in Europe generally as well as in Italy. According to a suggestive recent hypothesis by English historian and diplomatist M. T. Clanchy, who has studied the phenomenon in Norman England, the number of surviving written documents is directly correlated with, and thus provides a measure of, the overall number of documents produced; for this period, moreover, that number is incomparably

24. Hartmann and Memores, *Ecclesiae*, vol. 3 (Vienna, 1913), nn. CLXXII and CC; *Codice diplomatico del Senato romano dal MCXLIV al MCCXLVII*, ed. F. Bartoloni, vol. 1 (Rome, 1948), n. 37; but see also the more recent evidence of nn. 57, 85, 105, 116.

25. Mosiici, "Arenghe," pp. 29–30.

26. *Codice diplomatico*, n. 42.

27. E. Ovidi, ed., *Le carte dell'abbazia di Chiaravalle di Fiastra* (Ancona, 1908[?]), n. 372, pp. 315–16.

28. A. Pratesi, *Carte latine di abbazie calabresi provenienti dall'Archivio Aldobrandini* (Città del Vaticano, 1958), n. 112.

29. Ibid., nn. 152, 165, 186.

higher than for the preceding periods. In addition, still according to Clanchy, the number of private or public documents produced in a specific period is directly correlated with the diffusion within a society of the capacity to write; thus, the decisive growth of documentary production in England (and in Europe) in the eleventh to thirteenth centuries would constitute an obvious—and sufficient—proof of a parallel broadening of the diffusion of the use of writing in the same region.[30]

Historians of documentation in medieval Italy, however, must adopt a perspective somewhat different from that of students of the same problems for other regions in Europe. This is because a notariate organized as a professional category exercised incomparably more weight and influence in Italy, not only directly determining the quantity and quality of the social use of written documentation but also influencing the general process of diffusion of writing in the social body. Moreover, as is well known, it was precisely in the eleventh and twelfth centuries that the private document drafted by a notary underwent a profound transformation from the *charta,* whose credibility as legal proof rested on the subscriptions to the text, to the *instrumentum,* which had the force of legal proof because it was drafted by a professional invested with the *publica fides.*[31] This fundamental transformation was further accompanied by a parallel process that broke up the procedure of documentation into several successive phases, all of which were prepared by the notary, consisting of various written drafts that were physically distinct and sometimes separated by significant periods of time.

Standing behind such complications of the process of documentation were the simple memoranda containing only the essential terms of the contract that early medieval notaries wrote out on the verso of documents, sometimes using a tachigraphic script incomprehensible to nonexperts. Between the tenth and eleventh century, these memoranda grew, became more precise, and came to contain more detailed data, with the result that they took on the nature of an actual minute with some probative value of their own, despite being still normally drafted on the verso of the document. All this documentation was normally in the hand of the notary and could not—or should not—be otherwise, in part because all operations of writing linked with manufacturing documents tended to be concentrated in the notary's sphere of competence by the steadily increasing complication of the process of documentation itself and by the parallel growth of the notary's professional

30. M. T. Clanchy, *From Memory to Written Record: England, 1066–1307* (London, 1979), esp. pp. 13–14, 34–35; see also the expanded second edition of this work (Oxford, 1993).

31. For this process, see esp. G. Costamagna, *La triplice redazione dell'"instrumentum" genovese* (Genoa, 1961); M. Amelotti and G. Costamagna, *Alle origini del notariato italiano* (Rome, 1975), pp. 205–82.

prestige. Not by chance, the same period sees a diminished participation in writing by persons other than the notary such as authors and witnesses, a trend that applies both to the preparatory phases of the document and to the final version, which we call the *originale*. Already in the eleventh and twelfth centuries, the *originale* especially lost almost everywhere the autograph subscriptions that, by attesting the physical presence of the participants, had, or should have, represented a direct and immediate link between the phases of juridical act (the event) and documentation (written and authenticated evidence).

The professionalization of the notariate was consecrated by the acquisition of a definite weight in the civic and institutional life of the communes, and by a notable increase in the prestige of notaries as public figures. It was symptomatic that, according to a process that Girolamo Arnaldi clearly reconstructed some years ago,[32] notaries were entrusted with the task of drafting the civic chronicles that had to have the publicity, truth, and authenticity characteristically guaranteed by the notarial function. Parallel to this growth in the prestige of the notariate in its professional activity and public life, there occurred—also by the efforts of the notaries themselves and during the twelfth and thirteenth centuries—a vast theoretical elaboration of notarial doctrine, including its introduction into official university teaching, that further clarified the concept of publicity and thus of the truth of authenticated acts drafted by notaries.

The proemium of the *Ars notarie* of Salatiele, drafted in 1242 and revised around the middle of the century, affirmed that "est autem notarius quedam publica persona publicum officium gerens ad cuius fidem hodie publice decurritur ut scribat et ad perhemnem memoriam in publicam formam reducat ea que ab hominibus fiunt";[33] later, among the responsibilities of the notary it is specified that he should write "fideliter et caute."[34] In the work of this Bolognese master, the modern motifs of publicity and veracity in these and other passages existed side by side with echoes of the ancient motif of *memoria* that was recurrent even in the opening of the work.[35] In Rolandino de' Passaggeri, the awareness of the difference between "antiqui tempores" and the "iunior eo perspicacior etas nostra" is crystal clear;[36] and accompanying the proud claims for the professionalism of the notary—to whom

32. I refer to G. Arnaldi, *Studi sui cronisti della Marca trevigiana nell'età di Ezzelino da Romano* (Rome, 1963).

33. Salatiele, *Ars notarie,* ed. G. Orlandelli, vol. 2 (Milan, 1961), p. 7.

34. Ibid. p. 13.

35. Ibid., p. 7, passage already cited.

36. Rolandino, *Summa totius artis notariae* (Venice, 1546), fols. 1r–2r.

Rolandino attributes prudence, ability, and culture[37]—is a precise knowledge of the connection between publicity, authenticity, and veracity of the *instrumentum* that would remain classic and be would taken up by Rolandino's commentators.[38]

The entire process that I just summarized schematically had notable consequences for the connection between action and documentation, but not in the sense of the greater connection and reciprocal correspondence that seem to be indicated by its exterior manifestations. Indeed, the consequences that seem to me most evident are these:

1. As has already been mentioned, the elimination of the direct participation of the parties and witnesses from the final phase of writing the document—the *originale*—also eliminated one of the elements linking the phase of action and the phase of documentation that had been implicit in the early medieval *charta*.

2. Breaking up the documentary routine into several successive phases, sometimes at great distance from one another, had the effect of temporally distancing the phase of action from the phase of documentation.

3. The compilation of successive, more or less abridged redactions of the documentary text sometimes resulted in miscarriages, omission, and errors in the transmission of data; the classic cases include poorly drafted minutes that lead to an error in the *originali*,[39] and arbitrary additions introduced by the notary in the number of witnesses registered in the written minute at the moment of the action.[40]

Not by chance, Gian Giacomo Fissore, in revealing obvious discrepancies between minutes drafted after an event and the more elaborated *originali* that are formally much more detailed, stressed the importance of the formal element in the drafting of originals: "The definitive drafting in fact turns out to be constituted not only by juridical formulas essential to the contract, but also by that complex ceremonial that politically more than juridically designates the parties with names, qualifications, and hierarchical ranks: all

37. Ibid., fol. 238r.
38. Ibid., fol. 406v.: "Et est notarius persona privilegiata ad negocia hominum publica et auctentice conscribenda"; see on fol. 406r the comment of Pietro de Unzola, "Tabellionatus scientia . . . consistit in illuminatione intellectus et cognitione veritatis."
39. For example, *Le carte dell'abbazia di S. Croce di Sassovivo*, vol. 1: *1023–1115*, ed. G. Cencetti (Florence, 1973), n. 107, pp. 165–66.
40. An example of this phenomenon is in G. G. Fissore, *Autonomia notarile e organizzazione cancelleresca nel Comune di Asti* (Spoleto, 1977), p. 68, n. 98.

these data, which were certainly also the data that were most conspicuously influenced by ideological positions, were omitted from the first draft. It is easy to suppose that, in analogous cases, the notes of the notaries served simply as a foundation for structuring a literary composition that, although it certainly could not greatly distance itself from the facts, just as certainly had to introduce substantial elements of order to obtain, for example, the limpid hierarchies present in the document of Asti."[41]

These, then, are some of the consequences of the process that led to the notariate's conquest of the *publica fides,* understood as the exclusive right to authenticate, and to the introduction of formal complexities in the documentary routine that carried it progressively further from the juridical action for which it continued to constitute the written evidence. But next to these consequences one must also consider the singular coincidence that, in precisely the period when everything I have listed occurred, Italy and Europe as a whole saw a vast and diffused production of documents that were forged, or counterfeited or fraudulently interpolated—a production concentrated in the very period in the twelfth and thirteenth centuries[42] when the authenticated *instrumentum publicum* was created and diffused.

How can one explain this undeniable coincidence? Brooke would relate it to the fact that this was the period of passage between oral and written evidence, and that in such a period "the occasions, temptations, and urgent summons to duty must have been almost exceptional."[43] Clanchy, in contrast, would investigate more deeply the connection, which he regards as undeniable, between the production of false documents and the growth of literacy.[44] But one must consider that very often the authors of forgeries were religious archivists and chroniclers of religious institutions who habitually proclaimed the truthfulness of what they were writing in their works of historical compilation; moreover, it is undeniable that they themselves possessed extensive and precise understanding of diplomatics and, in particular, that they must have known the process of contemporary documentation rather well in all its complex characteristics. This kind of consideration, which remains to be verified but which seems plausible, suggests the con-

41. Ibid., p. 68.
42. See some recent contributions: H. Fuhrmann, "Die Fälschungen im Mittelalter," *Historische Zeitschrift* 197 (1963): 529–54, repr. in *Einfluss und Verbreitung des pseudoisidorischen Fälschungen von ihrem Auftauchem bis in die neuere Zeit,* vol. 1 (Stuttgart, 1972), pp. 64–136; C. Brooke, "Approaches to Medieval Forgery," in *Medieval Church and Society* (London, 1971), pp. 100–120; Clanchy, *From Memory,* pp. 248–57; and the relevant articles in *Fälschungen im Mittelalter: Internationaler Kongress der Monumenta Germaniae Historica, München, 16.–19. September 1986,* MGH Schriften 33 (Hannover, 1988).
43. "Approaches," p. 115.
44. *From Memory,* p. 248.

clusion that, in Europe and in Italy of the twelfth and thirteenth centuries, there was probably a connection between a proclaimed tendency toward the truthfulness of written documentation and a parallel push toward the fabrication of documentary forgeries; at the same time, there was probably also a connection between the progressive complexity of authenticated documentation and a developed capacity to produce falsified documents.

A parallel kind of paradoxical coincidence between the maximum of authenticity and the maximum of nontruthfulness comes to light by examining not just private documents, on which we have lingered until now, but rather public documents that inherently differ from private ones in having the highest degree of authenticity as a result of being issued directly by public authority using their own administrative apparatuses. Almost always, the public document concerns (and reflects) links between public entities (one thinks of treaties or diplomatic correspondence), or between persons unequal in dignity, importance, or political weight. By virtue of its formal structure, such a document of necessity ends up expressing above all the entire hierarchical relationship that existed between the two parties—author and recipient—involved in the action of which it constitutes the written evidence; it is thus always essentially a political document.

By its very nature, the underlying message contained in any public document is essentially ideological and consists of a representation of the power of the issuing authority as defined by the hierarchical connection of superiority, equality, or inferiority in force with its recipient,[45] who might in turn be a public person or entity, or a private person. These characteristics of public documentation explain the extreme formalization of its structure and of the process by which it was produced—a process that also reflects the nature, which in this case is rather particular, of the connection between action and documentation on which it is based and that it sometimes configures. It is particularly in public documents that the rhetorical procedure of emphasis, prolixity, and repetition of formulas acquires a high value for the way that the formulas underline specific aspects of the ideological message that constitute its deep structure. Such purely formal procedures can result in undue broadening of the formulas of *narratio* beyond any correspondence with the real course of events; alternatively, they can result in inserting among the participants of the action intercessors or interveners who were absent in reality or who were dead at the moment claimed in the dating of the documents, or titleholders who had offices or dignities different from those stated in the document. In effect, for almost any medieval chancery beginning at least in the twelfth century (and especially for those two greatest

45. See Liverani, "Dono, tributo," pp. 9–11.

chanceries of the pope and emperor), the extreme formalization of the public documentary text involved a steadily more complex routine of written elaboration, accomplished by means of multiple phases of composition and drafting, that even produced some cases of an *originale* itself being declassified into a minute by a further addition or corrective intervention executed *in extremis*.

Exaggerated and extreme cases of multiple elaboration over a prolonged time are particularly frequent, and still reconstructable, in the fourteenth- and fifteenth-century diplomatic documentation concerning relations between different states. I have in mind examples produced by the chancery of republican Florence at the time of the chancellorship of Coluccio Salutati and of Sforzesca Milan under the chancellorship of Cicco Simonetta, whose documents, in the different phases of elaboration to which they were subjected, underwent modifications of great importance in both form and substance; sometimes (one thinks of cases when the dating was changed) these modifications directly affected the relationship between action (here taking the shape of a manifestation of the will of the issuing authority) and documentation.

A particular although extremely diffuse category of public documents, that of documents granting concessions, lends itself to another kind of consideration that also directly concerns the degree to which written documentation adheres to the juridical action, that is, to the fact or event which is or ought to be at its origin. My interest is in the role played by the recipient or recipients during the phase of elaboration of the text of the document, a role that may have been more or less active but was always present. Often the recipients' activities consisted of their solicitation of the provision, that is, the action; but sometimes they went so far as to include drafting the very text of the document of benefit, which was then subjected to the approval of the issuing authority. In a case like this, one can say that, paradoxically, the documentation ends up preceding the action, thus undercutting in the eyes of contemporaries (and in our own) every usual parameter of valuing the document as a source with respect to the course of the events as they actually happened. But there is more: in cases of requests for the renewal of old concessions, the participation of the recipient in the issuing of a public document of beneficial character often took the shape simply of exhibiting and presenting to the relevant chancery some preceding documentation whose renewal was requested. At times, however, this documentation was forged, or partially counterfeit, or more or less seriously interpolated by and to the advantage of the recipient who presented it for renewal; and the chancery of the authority asked to renew it simply proceeded to repeat literally the text it received without subjecting the document to any control (which in any case it would not have had the technical ability to do). The result was a document that was at once substantially false and completely authentic: a singular phenomenon that diplomatists, who are quite familiar with such cases, call "chancery forgeries."[46]

In this way, one arrives at the configuration of that paradoxical coincidence, mentioned above, between the maximum degree of nonveracity and the maximum degree of authenticity that constitutes the extreme exemplification of a situation in which the divide between written documentation and event might be accentuated to a greater or lesser extent but was never entirely avoided. There are multiple reasons for this divide, of which I have mentioned some (but only some!) that were inherent to the process by which authenticated documents were produced in the medieval period. But as I now near the end of this problematic contribution, it seems appropriate to try to sketch an interpretative discourse of the phenomenon that moves on a more general level.

From what has already been said, and by studies of a formal and structural character that can be applied to any type of authentic document, it becomes absolutely clear that written documentation, precisely to the extent that it is produced by a textual formulation accomplished solely by specialized technicians, always takes shape, with respect to the event, through a complex process of manipulation that is directed toward achieving multiple purposes. As a rule, this process appears to be articulated into several strongly interconnected formal subsystems that we can define as moments of generalization (introductory formulas), moments of exposition, moments of disposition and moments of certification; these always assume the external characteristics of a system for remembering an event, or several events, all dated and identifiable, whose more or less verifiable reality appears in fact to be entirely irrelevant to the ends of the functionality of the textual system in which the document operates; this reality, moreover, must have interested only indirectly the public to whom the documentary message is addressed. Seen independently from the presumed or real event of which it constitutes the memory or evidence, authenticated documentation therefore appears as an organic and compact system of writing in itself, with the individual documentary products correspondingly appearing mainly as maps indicating paths of reading and comprehension whose rules could then and can still be decoded and comprehended within themselves (rather than in an impossible comparison with a presumed factual reality).

In such a situation, what can be the position of the historian in relationship to authentic written sources? Freed from any laziness to interpret sim-

---

46. A case in Fuhrmann, "Fälschungen," p. 532 *(Einfluss, p. 69)*.

plistically, he or she must try to reconstruct the writing system of the documentary text, to reveal the mechanisms by which it was elaborated, and to identify the process of production in order to arrive at being able to explicate the reading paths of the textual map and decode the deep message etched within. But even beyond this, the historian must also try to understand fully the function that written documentation, with its hard thickness of words and its burden of ambiguity and formalisms, performed (and performs? an investigation in this sense might show many surprises) within the sphere of the society that produced and received it. This function varied substantially according to whether one deals with public or private documents: for while the former, with their high degree of formality and authenticity, served mainly to "represent" power by means of a complex symbolic message turned outward, the latter had the role of giving certainty to juridical relations in force between private individuals for the present and future. But neither public nor private documentation was put into place with the primary purpose of constituting evidence or memory of one or more events, whose factual reality outside the tight formal structure of written discourse was and remains almost always impossible to determine.

To cite again the judgment of Mario Liverani: "Texts equivocally called historical . . . were not conceived and written to provide data to future historians, but to obtain political consensus in their present; they thus are strongly interwoven with ideological and propagandistic elements. If these elements are ignorantly or incorrectly understood, they result in a complete misunderstanding of the text, a misunderstanding that involves even the identification of what is and is not a 'datum,' and of what is and is not 'news.' "[47] It goes without saying that, in citing this statement, I agree with Liverani in rejecting any explicit or implicit accusation of pessimism or ideologism.[48] In reality, the very identification of the function that a piece of written evidence from the past must have played according to status and structure in the environment in which it was produced indicates the parallel, and different, function that it can play today in the consciousness of the historian and in the writing of history. But this is true only for a historiography that is not vitiated by easy indolence, that is ready to discuss candidly its own status and its own uncertainties, and especially that is fully aware of its own limits and interpretative duties with respect to the written products of the past.

47. "Dono, tributo," p. 10.
48. Ibid., p. 28.

INDEX

INDEX